George Barton Ide

Battle Echoes

Or, Lessons From the War

George Barton Ide

Battle Echoes
Or, Lessons From the War

ISBN/EAN: 9783337010027

Printed in Europe, USA, Canada, Australia, Japan

Cover: Foto ©ninafisch / pixelio.de

More available books at **www.hansebooks.com**

BATTLE ECHOES,

OR,

LESSONS FROM THE WAR.

BY

GEORGE B. IDE, D.D.

"God is great; His name is mighty!
He is victor in the strife!
For He bringeth Good from Evil,
And from Death commandeth Life."

WHITTIER.

BOSTON:
GOULD AND LINCOLN,
59 WASHINGTON STREET.
NEW YORK: SHELDON AND COMPANY.
CINCINNATI: GEO. S. BLANCHARD AND CO.
1866.

Entered according to Act of Congress, in the year 1866, by
GOULD AND LINCOLN,
In the Clerk's office of the District Court for the District of Massachusetts.

ROCKWELL AND ROLLINS, Printers,
122 Washington Street, Boston.

PREFACE.

DURING the dread struggle through which the nation has passed, no conviction was stronger or more universal, than that of God's interference in human affairs. So clear were the revealings of His hand, that even the undevout were compelled to bow before them with awe and reverence. There is ground for the fear, that this impression is becoming weaker with the return of Peace; and that unbelief and indifference are creeping back to their old seats in the public conscience. Sad, indeed, will it be, if the great teachings, which the Almighty has inscribed, in letters of blood and fire, on the most pregnant page of our history, shall fade away, and leave us as unwise and as unregardful as in the former days. In the hope of contributing, however slightly, to the prevention of such a result, the writer has been induced to send forth the present volume. The thoughts which it contains were pondered, and, for the most part, written out, while the startling events of the war were still in progress; or while every heart was yet thrilling with the wonders of its end. Change of circumstances may have lessened their interest, but not their importance; for the truths to which they relate, are eternal, and, therefore, never inopportune. And, perhaps, at this calmer hour, the momentous questions which the conflict has decided, may be more intelligently and effectively considered, than when that conflict was at its height. To Him, who has so signally come forth for the vindication of His own honor, this feeble attempt to trace the way of His outgoing is humbly committed.

CONTENTS.

CHAPTER I.

THE WAR FOR THE UNION A RIGHTEOUS WAR . . 9

CHAPTER II.

REASONS FOR GRATEFUL CONFIDENCE 35

CHAPTER III.

GREAT ERAS MARKED BY GREAT JUDGMENTS . . . 60

CHAPTER IV.

PIOUS MEN THE NATION'S HOPE 104

CHAPTER V.

THE MOVING PILLAR 135

CHAPTER VI.

THE FREEDMEN OF THE WAR . . .

CHAPTER VII.

THE LAND CARING FOR ITS DEFENDERS

CHAPTER VIII.

THE DEEP PLEADING FOR ITS HEROES

CHAPTER IX.

MEMORIES AND LESSONS . . . .

CHAPTER X.

GOD'S METHOD OF RECONSTRUCTION .

CHAPTER XI.

OUR DAY AND ITS WORK . . . .

BATTLE ECHOES.

CHAPTER I.

THE WAR FOR THE UNION A RIGHTEOUS WAR.

"AND THE CHILDREN OF ISRAEL WENT UP AND WEPT BEFORE THE LORD UNTIL EVEN, AND ASKED COUNSEL OF THE LORD, SAYING, SHALL I GO UP AGAIN TO BATTLE AGAINST THE CHILDREN OF BENJAMIN MY BROTHER? AND THE LORD SAID, GO UP AGAINST HIM." — *Judges* xx. 23.

THE geologist, in exploring the earth's crust, finds numerous petrified remains of animals and plants, which are supposed to have lived and perished ages before the creation of man, or of any of the present forms of organized life. These fossilized bodies, though belonging to races long since extinct, have yet so many points of analogy with races now existing on the earth, as to furnish abundant evidence that they were produced by the same Divine Hand, and are included in the same general system. Hence they have for the student of natural science a living interest, and shed an important light on the field of his inquiries.

Very similar is the relation which the narratives of the Bible sustain to the facts of to-day. The men and the events to which they referred have passed away; but the great principles which they embodied still remain, and are as fresh, as full of meaning, as fruitful in instruction, at the present hour, as in the periods when they were first unfolded to the world.

From the historic treasures of the Old Testament we have extracted a very interesting fragment, relating to an ancient civil war which occurred among the tribes of Israel, soon after their establishment in the inheritance of Canaan. The particular occasion out of which it grew, is to us of little practical moment. Nevertheless, the general features of the transaction are marked with characteristics in which we have a vital concern. The motives which governed it, the spirit in which it was conducted, the recognition of Jehovah's agency, the feeling of dependence upon him, by which every movement was pervaded and inspired, are fraught with lessons ever timely, ever emphatic; and which reaching down, in their deathless significance, through all the centuries, are as pertinent to our own circumstances as to those of the hosts of Israel, three thousand years ago.

The inhabitants of Gibeah, one of the principal cities of Benjamin, had committed a fearful crime.

A Levite, journeying with his wife from Bethlehem to his home in Mount Ephraim, was compelled to sojourn among them for a night. A band of ruffians assaulted the house in which he lodged, subjected the man to gross abuse, and murdered the woman under circumstances of most revolting atrocity. Intelligence of this shocking act was sent by the husband to all the tribes, accompanied by an appeal for help and vengeance. From city to city, from hamlet to hamlet, from the wooded slopes of Lebanon to the burning plains of Kadesh, from the fountains of the Jordan to "the way of the sea," sped the summons, telling of the outrage which had polluted the land, and calling for its punishment. The whole nation was stirred by the tidings as by an electric shock. All sprung to arms. The crime was so utterly without provocation; it struck so vitally at the foundations of public order and of public safety, that every heart felt that it must be wiped out in blood, and every hand grasped its weapon to aid in the work of retribution. The conviction was universal, that thus only could the national character be vindicated, and even the national existence maintained.

With this view, the forces of Israel assembled at Mizpeh, four hundred thousand footmen that drew sword — all binding themselves, by a solemn vow, that they would not look upon their homes again until they had meted out to the offenders the just penalty of their wickedness. That the innocent, however, might not be involved in the same doom with the guilty, they despatched messengers to all the towns of Benjamin, rehearsing the iniquity which had been committed, and demanding the surrender of the criminals. Instead of complying with this reasonable requirement, the entire people of the tribe arrayed themselves on the side of the murderers, and determined to resist the collected might of the land. Thus, by indorsing the infamy, they made it their own, and inaugurated rebellion in its defence.

In this terrible emergency, the army of Israel presented itself before the Lord, and, with many prayers and bitter weeping, asked counsel from Him, saying, "Shall I go up to battle against the children of Benjamin my brother?" This it was in the impending conflict that made them pause — the fact that it was to be waged, not against a foreign enemy, but against one of the Chosen Tribes, against men of the same blood with themselves, united in the same national bond, and sharers in the same heritage of Divine care and bounty. And well might they pause, and seek guidance from a Wisdom higher than their own; for civil war is in itself a calamity so dreadful; there is something so unnatural and shocking in the deadly strife of brother with brother, that nothing short of God's command, either communicated by express revelation, or clearly inferred from His providence, could justify its inception. So they felt — and therefore supplicated the Almighty One, who had led them in the difficulties and perils of former years, to make known to them His will in the new and doubtful crisis that was now upon them. The answer to their petition came back from the Throne of Infinite Power, in the brief but decisive words, "Go up against him." Deplorable as was the shedding of kindred blood; frightful as would be the struggle between warring legions of the same race; it were better than that crimes subversive of all law and government should pass unrebuked; better, aye, a thousand fold better, intestine war with all its horrors, than that profligacy and treason should trample down decency and purity and justice, and render the very name of Israel an abomination in the earth.

The striking similarity between the position occupied by the men of Israel, and that in which the loyal States of America are now placed, must be apparent to all. They stood on the bloody edge of battle with their brethren and fellow-countrymen; and so do we. They were summoned to disregard fraternal ties in the upholding of constituted authority; and so are we. A portion of the commonwealths composing this great Confederacy, have cast off their allegiance to the General Government; have risen up in rebellion against it; and are plotting the overthrow of everything which, as a nation, we hold dear and sacred. The loyal States are sending forth their thousands and hundreds of thousands of brave, patriotic men, to put down this rebellion, and defend from the attack of traitors the glorious institutions which our fathers founded in suffering and blood. Those whom I now address are among the number.[1] You have relinquished the joys of home, and the peaceful pursuits of civil life, that you may go to the rescue of your country in this the hour of its sternest need. You go to meet, not the invading legions of a foreign power, but your kindred and late compatriots, transformed by treason into ruthless and implacable foes. It is an awful mission — an exigency in its greatness and in its solemnity unparalleled in the annals of the world. Every just-minded and God-fearing man amongst you cannot but ask, "Is it right? Is it in harmony with the holy purposes of Him who is sovereign over all?" This thought is, doubtless, agitating many a heart now present; and from many a lip the question is ready to break forth, "Shall I go up against the children of Benjamin my brother?"

To this inquiry we cannot expect an answer as direct as that which was given to the men of Israel.

---

[1] 10th Regiment, Mass. Vols.

They lived in the days when Heaven held miraculous converse with earth. To those that feared and sought Him, God then spoke, in audible accents, as a man with his friend. He made known His will to His ancient people in distinct announcements suited to each separate occasion. Such announcements were given, sometimes in voice-like responses, sometimes in dreams and visions, but more commonly by the symbolic utterances of the Urim and Thummim. This consisted of the twelve precious stones set in the breastplate of the high priest; and the ordinance of Jehovah was, that when in momentous emergencies His will was consulted, an affirmative reply should be known by the increased brilliancy of the jewels, and a negative by their fading into dimness. It was probably by this method that the answer of God was received in the instance before us.

No such supernatural medium of ascertaining the Divine pleasure is intrusted to our hands. But we are in possession of other means, by which the same end may be secured in a manner not less convincing. Our Urim and Thummim is the Providence of God. His will is declared to us by the out-flashing of events on the bosom of Time, which is God's priest. If, then, we would be assured that, in going forth to battle against our rebellious brethren, we go in accordance with God's designs, and at

God's bidding, we must look on the breast of the stupendous movement which is passing before us, note the features that are prominent in it, and study well their indications. In these we shall find the clearest proofs of the righteousness of our cause, and ample grounds for confidence in the Divine approval.

One feature which stands out conspicuously in this Rebellion, is its utter want of any just pretext. We deny not the right of a people, in certain circumstances, to sever the bonds of constituted rule, and modify or change their political relations. Though governments are ordained by God, and as such are entitled to obedience, yet when, through corruption or tyranny, they become dangerous to the welfare of the subject, they no longer fulfil the end of their appointment, and may lawfully be subverted. But no such justification can be set up on the part of the States which have seceded from the Union, and are now levelling war against it. The Federal Government has never oppressed them. It has never favored other sections to their disadvantage. It has not robbed them of a single immunity, or imposed on them, in one solitary instance, unequal burdens. It has fulfilled to them faithfully, and even jealously, all the provisions and compromises of the Constitution. And not only have they enjoyed every guaranty secured to them by the national compact, but they have been, from the very beginning of the Government, the object of its special patronage and protection. In the revolutionary period, the chains of colonial vassalage were riven from the older of these States by Northern troops. A majority of their people were tories then, as their descendants are traitors now; and left to their own resources, not one of them, with the exception perhaps of Virginia, would ever have achieved independence. The territory occupied by the newer of these States was purchased from foreign powers by the General Government, and donated to them. Their very homes were the gift of the Union. In their feebleness and infancy, they were fostered by its care, and defended by its armies; and in the case of some of them, it has expended for their benefit an amount exceeding a million of dollars for each white inhabitant they now contain. During three fourths of the period since the Government was organized, the administration of public affairs has been in the hands of the South. Her's have been the chief commands in the army and navy; her's the richest posts in the civil service; her's the most potential voice in the Senate and on the Bench. To her interests, whether real or imagined, all other interests have been compelled to bow. Though more and more in a minority at each decade, she has managed by insolence and threats always to dominate, and to have her own way in everything. No, no! the Government has not wronged the South. At no point, and in no relation, has she suffered damage from its control. On the contrary, the Union has been to its Southern members the source of all their social and political blessings. It has given them respectability abroad, peace and security at home. Instead of assailing, it has upheld even their "peculiar institution," — abhorrent as it is to the heart and conscience of the free North, — guarding them from the dangers with which it teems, and interposing the shield of a great nation's influence between them and the moral execration of the world. Thus has the Union been to its rebel children a fond and indulgent mother, lenient to their faults, yielding to their caprices, watchful for their happiness, doing them good — good in their infancy, good in their manhood, good ever — nothing but good.

Why, then, do these children rise up against their mother, trample her authority under their feet, and plot to expel her from the estate which she has superintended so well — aye, to wound her to the death? Why? Because, and only because, their Northern brethren, believing slavery to be a sin and a curse, will say so, and will not consent to its extension over the whole domain. Because, and only because, these same Northern brethren, living in the atmosphere of freedom, work, delve the soil, ply manufactures, foster commerce, build cities, grow rich and powerful; while the Southern branches of the family, nurtured by slavery in idleness and pride, are constantly sinking into greater relative inferiority. This, the consequence of their own vicious system of labor, they ascribe to the Union, and on that account seek its destruction. Insane with envy and ambition, they have conspired to overturn the Government, because they see that the days of their ascendency in it are passing away.

Suppose that on the green bank of some crystal lake a community of beavers have established themselves, and on a barren crag near by a colony of rattlesnakes. The sunshine falls alike upon both, without partiality, and without regard to their different natures and habits. The beavers, intelligent, industrious, construct houses, provide food, lay up stores for future needs, rejoice in warm furs, and are happy. The snakes, coiled up in their den, or basking lazily at its mouth, filling their poison bags, and sharpening their poison teeth, live in holes, go naked, and eat dirt. Suppose, further, that the snakes, becoming conscious that the beavers were outstripping them in enterprise, and wealth, and comfort, should attribute the fact to the sun, and accuse it of pouring its beams more profusely on their rivals than on themselves; and, for that reason, should make war on the blessed luminary, and attempt to tear it from the sky? Would you not say that the wisdom of the serpent had forsaken them?

So false, so fatuous, are the charges of the disaffected States against the justice and good faith of the Union. The annals of human wickedness can show no instance of crime more black, more unprovoked, more utterly without the shadow of excuse, than this attempt of the Southern oligarchs to destroy the freest and most beneficent government which the world ever saw. And see we not in this fact a manifest token that God is with us in the struggle? When, in lowly prostration before his throne, we ask, Shall we go up to battle against the conspirators, do we not read, in the very atrociousness of their purpose, the clear and emphatic answer, "Go up against them"? To believe otherwise, would involve the monstrous supposition that the All-Holy could be indifferent to the Right, and sanction and sustain the Wrong.

Another feature of this conflict, giving forth the same reply, may be seen in the great results which it involves. It is not a war based on any of the ordinary questions which disturb the peace of nations — not a war for increase of territory, for political supremacy, for carrying out some diplomatic punctilio — not a war of ambition or of aggrandizement. It is strictly, on the part of the North, a war of self-defence — a grapple for existence. All the momentous interests of Nationality, Freedom, Christianity, and human progress are committed to it. We must roll back these swelling waves of treason, or see the grand old ship of the Government, which heroes launched and sages have piloted, go down, with all its precious freight, into the depths forever.

It has often been asked, Why not recognize the independence of the revolted States, and allow them to try their experiment of a Slave-Confederacy? To this it is a sufficient answer to say, that, were the lawfulness of secession once acknowledged, the pillars of the Constitution would be undermined, and the whole fabric of the Government must, sooner or later, topple to the ground. With such a right expressly conceded, or constructively established by precedent, the Constitution would not be worth the parchment on which it is written. The claim that a State may withdraw from the Union at pleasure involves a solecism so monstrous, that only a brain drunk with the maddening cup of slavery, could have given birth to it. It was not by the States that the Union was formed, but by the people themselves, acting in their sovereign capacity. And they made, not a Confederation, but a Union — not a League of Independent Sovereignties, but a Nation.

The General Government, as they established it, was not merely the organ of the States, but the central and controlling Power, invested with eminent domain, and crowned with paramount authority. And not only is this supremacy of the Union provided for in the Constitution—it arises necessarily from the very nature of representative government. Without it, such a government would be impossible. On any other basis, we might have an Alliance of States, but no national Oneness, no recognized Sovereignty, that could insure us stability and repose at home, or command the respect of the world.

In the contest, therefore, to which we are summoned, our very life as a nation is at stake. The continuance of whatever is valuable to us—of everything that has made us what we are—depends on the preservation of the Union, and the vindication of its sacredness. Our civil institutions, our political importance, our material prosperity, our religious privileges, the glorious memories of the past, the more glorious hopes of the future—all, all are embarked in the issue. Let the champions of secession succeed in their destructive project, and our coming history will present the spectacle of a once mighty people arrested in its noble career, disintegrated, and split into separate communities, each pursuing its dark way alone, or all rushing and clashing together in wild anarchy, like those nebulous bodies that roam aimlessly over the sky, and which astronomers suppose to be the fragments of shivered planets. Or we shall exhibit the yet sadder spectacle of a universal Slave-Despotism—its throne a cotton bale, its ensigns whips and chains, its trophies a muzzled press, a dumb pulpit, and the groans of chattelized humanity. Where now shines, high up in mid-heaven, the broad, bright sun of American Nationality, the light and the joy of the world, countless meteors will shoot, and glare, and go out in darkness; or a vast, bloody comet, sweeping them all from the firmament, will blaze along its baleful track, scattering astonishment and affright among the constellations, and dropping mildew over the earth. Woe! woe! to the day in which that sun shall set! Woe! woe! to us and to our children— woe! to Civilization—woe! woe! to the fettered and struggling nations—if sacrilegious hands shall tear down the pillar of our greatness, put out its beacon-fires, and trail its banner in the dust. When Babylon and Rome fell, the world shook with the concussion. Yet its face retains now no scar to mark where they struck. They were despotisms; and their overthrow could inflict no permanent evil on mankind. But if the American Union falls, the last hope of self-government for our race will fall with it. The grave of this Republic will be the grave of Freedom for the world.

When such issues are depending, can we doubt on which side the help of the Omnipotent stands pledged? Can we fear that He will permit this noble country, the favored child of His Providence, whose planting was superintended by His agency, whose onward course has been directed by His hand, and with whose future weal the highest interests of His Kingdom are identified, to be rent in pieces by rebellion, and trodden under foot by the most foul and ruthless oligarchy that ever cursed the earth—an oligarchy whose Gospel is human bondage, and whose mission is to spread barbarism and chains over the fairest regions of the globe? It were blasphemy to think so. There is not an attribute of God that can ally itself with the propagandists of slavery, or rejoice in their success. And here again, in the stupendous consequences involved, we read the answer, "Go up against them."

The glorious uprising of the North in defence of the Union is another indication eloquent with a like response. Scarcely four months have passed since the gloom of doubt and indecision hung, like a deathpall, over all the Free States. The new Administration, which had then just entered upon office, found every channel of Governmental action deranged and obstructed by the weakness or the treachery of its predecessor. Treason battened in all the Departments—raved in the halls of Congress—pervaded the Army and Navy—corrupted every branch of the Public Service. Treason had plundered the nation's treasury, stolen its munitions of war, seized its forts and arsenals, and rendered unavailable its scanty forces on land and sea, by scattering them to remote and widely separated points. State after State was declaring its connection with the Union dissolved. Fortress after fortress was passing into the power of the insurgents. And all this while, a dead torpor, a hideous enchantment, benumbed and stupefied the loyal States. The North was thought to be divided; the Government seemed paralyzed; its friends confounded; its enemies alone awake and jubilant.

At length, the spell was broken. As the first roll of the thunder lays open the cloud and sets free the pent-up shower; so the first gun at Sumter dissolved the deathlike trance of Northern patriotism. Then outgushed the Northern heart. Then uprose the Northern might, to avenge the dishonored flag. Strife and dissension were abashed into silence. Parties, long hostile, vied with each other in their zeal to sustain the Government. All voices were merged in the one cry, "The Union must and shall be preserved." As the fiery cross sped over the hills of Scotland, summoning the clans to battle; so from mountain to mountain, from valley to valley, from sea-coast and river, and lake and prairie, over all the vast North, went that cry, growing sterner and louder as it went, till it swelled into the shout of twenty millions rallying for the Union. Treasure flowed forth like water. Men volunteered in myriads. An army was extemporized in a day. On, on to the rescue of the Capitol — on, on to the succor of the Government — on, on, to hurl back the traitorous assailants — rushed the shouting legions. And on still they go, regiment after regiment, with steady tramp, and in quick succession, burning to meet the rebels, and drive treason from our shores. The North, which yesterday was palsied by apathy and rent by faction, is erect, energetic, united to-day. The Government, that appeared imbecile, tottering, forsaken, is now firm, strong, buttressed by unnumbered hearts and hands. And the flag, "the dear old flag," that a little while ago was torn by rebel cannon and insulted by rebel scoffs, now waves over three hundred thousand men in arms for their country; while behind them stand countless thousands more, eager to engage in the same glorious service.

It is a marvellous transformation — the most magnificent outburst of patriotism which human history has ever seen. What has done it? Not politics, not the Press, not the Pulpit, not eloquent harangues stirring up the passions of the masses. It is the power of God. His finger has touched the hearts of the people, as the rod of Moses struck the rock in the desert. The same energy, which at the creation woke the dead universe into life, has breathed over the stagnant, slumberous depths of popular feeling, and the nation has been born again. It is a resurrection. Love of country, love of liberty, self-sacrificing devotion to the public safety, have come up from the graves in which Mammon and political partisanship had buried them; and the redeemed land, shaking off the sluggish dreams of a long peace, confronts the rebellion to-day with more than the heroism of Revolutionary times. In view of such a fact — in view of this wonderful upspringing of patriotic unanimity and zeal, which only God's interposition could have produced — can we fail to discern His will? The regeneration of the North is the great central jewel which Jehovah has set on the bosom of the age; and in its lustre, which now fills the earth, inspiring the nations with admiration, carrying hope to the oppressed, and flashing dismay on the bandit hordes leagued to stay the march of Freedom, how legibly, how impressively, may we read the command, "Go up against them!"

That God's hand is in this war, and that His voice calls us to it, is evident from its harmony with the general movements of His providence throughout the world. The scene so sublimely pictured by prophecy — the great Battle of Armageddon — is now enacting on our globe. It is a conflict of principles, in which the antagonistic powers of Light and Darkness have met in final encounter to decide the destiny of our race. On one side are ranged Tyranny, Barbarism, Irreligion — on the other, Civilization, Liberty, Christianity. Wherever and however the combat may be waged, it is the same — the struggle of the Many to break from the domination of the Few, and assert the dignity of their being; and the effort of the Few to retain their hold upon the victims who have so long worn their fetters. We may call it the war for Independence in Italy, the war for Nationality in Hungary, and the war with Slavery in America. But the battle is one, the cause one, the impulse one. There are volcanic currents underlying the seas, and producing eruptions and earthquakes at the same moment in continents separated by a thousand leagues of ocean. So there are moral currents that reach and influence, at the same time, populations widely distant from each other. We failed in our Atlantic telegraph. But God has not failed in His; and along its wires He sends the electric spark of His power to all the nations. It is that spark which has kindled the holy flame now burning within us and around us. The contest with Slavery is a part of the grand warfare which He is carrying on for the moral redemption of the world. It is His purpose that men of all ranks and climes shall finally be free, enlightened, and happy. To the fulfilment of this benevolent design Slavery is one of the chief hindrances. In its nature and in its tendencies, it stands in direct opposition to the humanizing spirit and precepts of the Gospel. Its overthrow is, therefore, essential to the ultimate triumphs of Truth and Salvation. Hence, the connection of our present struggle with the unfoldings of Providence, and the cause of Humanity in all lands, is readily seen. That struggle, though nominally carried on against rebellion, is really against the Slave-power itself, in whose behalf the rebellion has been undertaken. Slavery is our true antagonist. And when we marshal our forces to resist its aggressions, and cripple the despots who would extend its evils over the whole continent, and perpetuate them through all time, do we not see that we work in perfect concert with that Divine Agency, which is everywhere active, "overturning, overturning, till He shall come whose right it is"? Here, then, we again have the answer, "Go up against them."

So clear, so numerous are the proofs that the Almighty is with us in this war for the Government and the Union. It is under His sanction, and by His command, that we have taken up arms against the foul treason that has struck at the heart of Freedom, and against the fouler institution which incited the deed. If the armies of the Crusaders could march to the recovery of the Holy Sepulchre, shouting, "It is the will of God! it is the will of God!" much more may we march with that battle-cry, to save from pollution the Ark of our liberties and the altars of true religion.

Let us, then, prosecute the war with confidence and energy. It must necessarily involve great cost and sacrifice. We shall suffer in our pecuniary interests. The business of the country may be widely deranged, and even prostrated. We may be required to send forth to battle, perhaps to death, our sons, our husbands, our brothers. But the result when achieved, will bring ample compensation for all the toil and loss incurred in its attainment. Righteous wars are means of grace; and the last few months of unselfish solicitude for the country's weal, and of active preparation for its defence, have done more to elevate the North, to give manliness to its people, and raise them above the walks of mere money-getting, to the high plane of conscience and duty, than could have been effected by a hundred years of peace. We have every reason to go into this war with our whole hearts, and with all our means. Let us strike hard, and strike home, assured that God strikes with us, and that under His leading victory is certain.

We should carry on this war in a deeply religious spirit. It is a holy war, embracing in its issues all that is dear to us, not only as patriots, but as christians. Never ought we to forget, in the petitions of the Closet and of the Sanctuary, to beseech Him in whom all wisdom dwells, and in whose ordering are all events, to guide the nation's leaders by His counsels, and to go forth with our armies in the day of battle. And, above all, let us take heed that the outward stir and excitement inseparable, perhaps, from the present condition of public affairs, do not overpower our interest in the duties of personal religion, and thus provoke Jehovah to withhold from our churches and from our country the blessing which alone can insure success and triumph.

The circumstances in which we are placed, call upon us to cherish a feeling of entire dependence on that Omnipotent One, who holds the destinies of nations in His hands; who doeth according to His will in the army of heaven, and among the inhabitants of the earth. Without His aid, we cannot hope to achieve the tremendous undertaking which lies before us. However ample may be our resources in men and means, however large our armies, however sagacious and skilful our commanders, if we trust in these, and put God out of sight, we may well fear that He will humble our self-confidence by repulses and disasters. Such was His dealing with the men of Israel. Relying on their vastly superior numbers, they did not, at first, supplicate the aid of the Almighty in putting down the rebellion of Benjamin, but merely asked which of the Tribes should begin the attack. In this spirit, thrice they essayed the battle, and were thrice defeated with great slaughter. And it was not till they prostrated themselves before the Lord in despair of their own sufficiency, and penitently implored His intervention, that victory rested on their banners. Similar may be our experience, if we confide in mortal strength alone. Let us, then, keep our eye fixed on the Eternal Throne from which our help must come. So shall the end be glorious, bringing peace to the country, perpetuity to the Union, and health and succor to the world.

Soldiers of the Tenth! Brave sons of Western Massachusetts! You see the sacredness of your vocation. You have enlisted in a high and holy cause — the cause of Freedom against Despotism — of Order against Anarchy — of Civilization against Barbarism — of Righteousness against the most flagrant system of Wrong that ever polluted the earth. You are God's soldiers. His behest sends you forth. His honor, and the welfare, not only of your native land, but of the human race, are interested in the manner in which you bear yourselves. Be true; be valiant; be worthy of the blood from which you sprung — worthy of your New England home, the nurse of free thoughts and of free men, where the love of Liberty is drawn in with the first breath of infancy, and where every wind that rocks her mountain pines, and sweeps her wild blue lakes, sounds out its glorious anthem.

And if you are God's soldiers, see that the character be not dishonored in your keeping. Avoid the temptations of the camp. Flee from intemperance, profanity, licentiousness. Let your conduct be as bright in illustrating the goodness of your cause, as your swords are sharp in defending it. By faith in the atonement of Christ, seek to be in heart, as well as in body, soldiers of the Lord. Thus combining religion with courage, the fear of God and prayer with military ardor, you will so act your part as to insure the approval of your country and of Heaven.

In this spirit, gallant men, give yourselves to the work you have chosen. Our prayers and blessings shall follow you to the tented field, and to the bloody conflict. We trust that, under the protection of a merciful Providence, you may all be permitted to return to us in safety when your task is done, and to enjoy for long years the love and gratitude of your fellow-citizens, as the reward of noble deeds achieved in this Second War of Independence. But should it be the pleasure of Him who sees not as we see, that any of you should fall, tenderly shall your companions send back to us the bodies slain in Freedom's fight. Tenderly will we receive them. Tenderly will we strew them with garlands and bedew them with tears. Tenderly will we carry them to their rest among the green hills and valleys you love so well, and tenderly lay them there, in spots hallowed evermore, in the hope, the cheering hope, that you will each have so lived and died, as to receive, not merely the crown of honor below, but the crown of Immortality above.

CHAPTER II.

REASONS FOR GRATEFUL CONFIDENCE.

"Though war should rise against me, in this will I be confident." — *Psalm* xxvii. 3.

NEVER since the first planting of our Commonwealth has the summons to public thanksgiving gone forth under circumstances so peculiar, and apparently so inopportune, as those in which we are now assembled. War has risen against us — a war of the direst and deadliest kind — civil war — a war of treason and rebellion. The whole slaveholding section of our country, insane with its hatred of freedom, urged on by ambition and a mad lust for power, has thrown of its allegiance to the General Government, conspired to break up the Union cemented by the toil and blood of our fathers, and inaugurated for the carrying out of their fell scheme, an intestine conflict the most ruthless and gigantic which the world has ever seen. An earthquake rocks the nation. The songs of peace, the cheerful hum of industry and traffic, have given place to the din of martial preparation, the clash of arms, and the shout of battle. Over large portions of our once happy land, the fields of the husbandman are trampled down by the hoofs of marching squadrons, and the fruits of his labor swept away by rapine. Social order is annihilated. Schools are dispersed. Churches are converted into barracks or hospitals. Public works are destroyed. Towns and villages are laid waste. Families are broken up and scattered. The heavens are red with the light of burning homes; and the ground is wet with blood shed by kindred hands. A million of men, lately clasped in the bonds of amity and brotherhood, now stand with hostile weapons levelled at each other. The struggle is terrible, vast, all-embracing. From the Eastern to the Western Ocean, from the frozen Lakes of the North to the fervid waters of the Gulf, the Demon of Slaughter unfurls his gory flag, cries "Havoc, and lets slip the dogs of war."

And is it at such a time — is it amidst calamities like these — that we are called to the exercise of thanksgiving? Shall we celebrate our harvest-home, and exult in the bounties that have crowned the year, while War's sharp sickle is strewing the earth with its bloody sheaves? Shall we be required to keep the Feast of Joy, while our hearts tremble for the Ark of Freedom, and the gloom of doubt and peril hangs thick over the future of our country? Shall we, can we lift up the voice of praise in the Sanctuary, and then gather with wonted cheer around our richly furnished boards, with children and friends by our side, when we think how many New England homes are desolate to-day, mourning for the loved ones who lie buried in the soil of Virginia, or sleep beneath the waves of the Potomac? Oh! the accustomed observances of Thanksgiving do seem incongruous and unseasonable at such an hour; and the Proclamation of the Executive sounds like the mocking command of the Assyrian conquerors, asking of the Jews the festive songs of Zion in the land of their captivity. Whose harp, if struck now, must not send forth a dirge? The present condition of public affairs would appear, on a cursory survey, to afford far more cause for tears than for laughter; far more occasion for anxiety than for confidence; far more reason to humble ourselves under impending judgments, than to rejoice and be glad in the review of our blessings.

And yet the Proclamation is right. Even amidst the tremendous crisis in which we stand, the eye that is illumined from above can discover abundant grounds for assurance and gratitude. The royal bard of Israel, while environed by difficulty and danger, — looking to a help mightier than man's — could say, "Though a host should encamp against me, my heart shall not fear; though war should rise against me, in this will I be confident." And we, if, guided by a similar faith, we study more closely the aspects of the storm that is sweeping over the land, and mark the bow of promise which God has set on its front, shall perceive, mingling with its fierce and destructive elements, much that is adapted to inspire trust and thankfulness.

It will, therefore, be my endeavor to trace some of those bright spots in the cloud that hangs over us, which beam with hope, and call for grateful confidence.

One of these may be seen in the striking alleviations of the hardships incident to a state of war, with which Divine Providence is favoring us. War, especially civil war, is the most fearful disaster which can befall a people. From whatever cause it may originate, and for whatever objects it may be carried on, it is, in itself, and during its continuance, an unspeakable calamity, spreading, like the tornado, ruin and devastation wherever it goes. The arrest which it puts on national development; the shock and dislocation which it produces in the moral sentiments and habits of society; the blood which it pours out like water; the hecatombs of valuable lives which it immolates — render it the fellest scourge that ever came from the abyss to ravage and pollute the earth; a thing of woe and horror, to be shrunk from and averted by every sacrifice save that of right and justice.

Among the evils of war, not the least afflictive, perhaps, is the prostration of material interests which it usually occasions. War is a great waster. Lavish expenditure, interruption of commerce, paralysis of industry, the blocking up of all the customary channels of business, financial derangement, panic and bankruptcy, are the dire followers that stalk in its train. The bustle of trade, the whirr of the spindle, the whistle of the ploughman as he drives his team afield, soon cease amid the braying of trumpets and the roaring of cannon. And the suffering and misery inflicted, when the whole industrial machinery of a people is thus brought to a pause, are not less in severity, and far greater in extent, than those which are caused directly by the wounds and bloodshed of battle.

Now, these monetary disturbances, so inseparable from war, were the very evils to which, at the commencement of the Rebellion, we looked forward with the liveliest dread. We feared that, in the loss of Southern trade, our manufactures would languish, the music of our looms and anvils die away, and our ships lie rotting at their wharves. We feared that a general stagnation of business, and consequent lack of employment, would bring starvation to the doors of our toiling millions. We feared that the products of our soil would be absorbed in feeding the vast armies that must be maintained; and that, in the cessation of the export of cotton, an immense foreign debt would accumulate, whose liquidation would drain our specie, crush our banks, and spread financial ruin, from the crowded marts of the seaboard to the farthest hamlets of the Western wilds. This we feared. This the rebels hoped. They hoped that their foul conspiracy would create throughout the Free States, and especially in New England, a depth of pecuniary distress, such as human experience had never before fathomed. And we feared that their fiendish hope might, in a large degree, be realized.

But how little of these wishes on the one side and these forebodings on the other has actually come to pass. It is true that we have been shut out from the markets of the South. It is true that uncounted millions due the North have been shamefully repudiated by the traitors. And equally true is it that from these causes our merchants and artisans have suffered for a time much loss and inconvenience. But the embarrassment has been only temporary. No fluctuations of business, no infelicity of events, can permanently cripple the energies of a free people, dwelling in a free land, where labor is honorable, and success open to all. The vigorous North, strong to do and to bear, rose up elastic from the blow. Enterprise, dammed up in its old channels, soon found for itself new ones. The mechanical skill, formerly employed in ministering to the wants or the luxuries of the Southern oligarchs, now busies itself in furnishing supplies and fabricating arms for the mighty hosts, by which the rebellion of those oligarchs is to be put down and punished. The innumerable rills of industry, which spring forth all over this land of working men, welling from every hill-side, and sending their refreshing waters through every valley, though obstructed and thrown back for awhile, have broken through the barrier, or made other ways for their passage; and the great river of public wealth, swelled by their united contributions, flows on again with banks as full, and a current as broad and swift as ever. We cannot now, indeed, pay for foreign fabrics by the export of Southern products. But we can do better, as we have already begun to do. We can cease, as we have ceased, importing, and depend on our own resources. The grain of our broad Western fields has more than supplied the place of the lost staples of the South. King Cotton, imprisoned in his own dominions by his own subjects, has torn off his crown, and kicked over his throne in disgust. But King Corn, marching from the Prairies, with bristling spears, and tassels waving, and countless legions at his back, puts on the fallen crown, and mounts the abdicated throne.

How signal has been the interposition of Providence in our behalf! At the very point of time when the wants of the Government required extraordinary revenues, and the sources were closed from which treasure had been wont to flow in from abroad, the almighty Disposer of events ordained short crops and scarcity for Europe, and ample harvests and overflowing plenty for ourselves; thus creating a demand for bread there, and a supply here, which have caused the tide of wealth to set strongly upon our shores. This immense exportation of food comes back to us in gold and silver. The inflowing stream of the precious metals goes into the vaults of our moneyed institutions, thence into the Treasury of the Government, thence out again, by channels endlessly ramified, into all the departments of trade and occupation, till there is not a workshop in our villages, nor a cabin in the wilderness, where the yellow drops send not their tribute. By this remarkable chain of circumstances, England and France, though their rulers may look coldly on our cause, and their haughty aristocracies exult in our expected fall, and their merchants rave at the blockade, and their financiers cry down our national loan, are nevertheless compelled to be our bankers. We feed their starving millions; and they, in turn, are forced to send us the sinews of war, by which the Government will overwhelm the Rebellion, and confound the enemies of Liberty throughout the world.

As a consequence of this state of things, thus brought about by Divine interference, the entire

North, with only here and there an exception, is enjoying a high degree of prosperity. Enterprise is active. Business thrives. Labor is in demand, and well rewarded. Our railways and canals are gorged with freight. In all branches of employment, in all classes of production, there beats the pulse of a vigorous life. And these benefits are showered on us in a time of war. We are struggling to subdue the most formidable insurrection which human wickedness ever fomented. For this purpose, we have furnished hundreds of millions of treasure, and half a million of men. But we miss them not. Not a rood of ground lies idle for want of hands to till it. Not a bench or a tool is silent, because the fingers that gave them voice are now pulling the trigger against the cruel and insolent foe. Amidst the uproar of a great civil conflict, and the distracting anxieties which it awakens, all the common avocations of life go on as quietly, and with as little disturbance, as if the whole land were at rest under the sheltering wing of peace.

And while this is in a measure true of all parts of the loyal States, it is pre-eminently true of the favored spot in which our lot is cast. Never was our city so prosperous as now. Never were our streets so thronged, and all classes of our people so busy and so successful. What know we of the privations and sacrifices of war? Who, in looking at the smiling faces of our citizens, or watching the steady flow of our industrial pursuits, would dream that the country was staggering under the blows of a mighty Rebellion? The scene of combat is far removed from us. We hear not the noise of the battle, the shouts of the victors, the groans of the dying. We see not the rush, the collision, the smoke, the carnage. These are to us distant things, of which we read with interest, but which come not within the circle of our personal experience. There are homes here and there among us — few, much fewer than they should be — in which may be seen the vacant seats of husbands, sons and brothers, who have gone to the tented field; and this is all we feel of the miseries of war! Compare our condition with that of the friends of the Union living in the regions where Treason and Secession are rampant. Think of the sufferings endured by the loyal inhabitants of Missouri, Kentucky, Tennessee and Virginia, compelled as they are to witness the destruction of their property, the burning and sacking of their dwellings, the violation and murder of their families; and to wander famishing and shelterless over their once happy domains, which rebellion has made a desert. Oh! must we not acknowledge that the God in whom we live has distinguished us by His special protection and blessing? In view, then, of the striking manner in which He has been pleased to mitigate to the North, and so largely to ourselves, the burdens and calamities of war, shall we not lift up to Him the voice of reverent praise, and say with the inspired singer of old, " Though war should rise against me, in this will I be confident " — thankful, rejoicing?

We have reason for trust and gratitude, in view of the great and salutary lessons which the war is teaching us. God is the Instructor of nations. He appoints the bounds of their habitation, ordains the part which they are to perform in the world's history, and by His dealings toward them so shapes their training as best to subserve His high and beneficent designs. That vast and far-reaching purposes, bearing on the progress of liberty and civilization throughout the earth, are connected with the destinies of this Republic, no thoughtful man can doubt, who studies the Hand of God in our Past, or reads aright its beckonings in our Future. For this our fathers were borne across the stormy sea, to found, on the bleak New England shore, "a church without a Bishop, and a State without a King." For this their infant colonies were fostered and strengthened up to manhood. For this their independence and autonomy were achieved. For this, under Divine superintendence, a government was established for them, the freest and the best which the human race has ever seen. For this has been our wonderful expansion, our rapid increase in population and territory, our onward strides in national greatness, ever faster and stronger, up to the level of the chief Powers of the earth. Our history, our institutions, our geographical position, our complex nationality blending the elements of many lands, all proclaim that this country has a grand work to do for humanity and for God.

But prosperity is as trying an ordeal to communities as it is to individuals. In our astonishing advancement, we were in danger of becoming so corrupt and emasculated as to be unfit for the noble sphere which Providence had assigned us. Greed and Selfishness were fast gaining an uncontrolled ascendency over all ranks and classes. Love of country, love of freedom, the fear of God, respect for His laws, honor, integrity, benevolence, every public, every private virtue, were overborne and stifled by one all-absorbing passion — the accursed thirst for gold. Materialism, like some monstrous fungus, was rapidly spreading its abnormal growth over the whole body of the nation, poisoning its heart, eating out its vitality, and presaging its sure decay. Money, money — the successful pursuit of wealth, material development — this was the Moloch at whose shrine everything precious and sacred was to be offered up. On rolled the iron car of our national Juggernaut — on over the Bible, the Sabbath, and the Sanctuary—on over Eternal Right and Justice—on over the crushed limbs of the weak, and the body and soul of the slave. A little longer, and we should have been the scorn of the civilized world, and the abomination of Heaven.

From this peril of self-destruction, the same overruling Power, that has been our Guide and Protector in all the eventful epochs of our former history, has mercifully interposed to save us. It is not against foreign invasion, not against alien hosts seeking to conquer and enslave us, but against ourselves, against the consequences of our own suicidal folly, that this watchful guardianship is now put forth. And the discipline which He has seen fit to employ for this purpose, though severe, is eminently suited to the case, and indispensable. Nothing less potent could have startled us from our ignoble ease, and called back the manhood of earlier days. So debased had the nation become in its worship of Mammon, so deadened in all its moral perceptions by the influence of Slavery, that only some tremendous convulsion, like that which now shakes the continent, could dissolve the spell, and restore the public mind to health and vigor. It is with such a view that God has permitted the whirlwind of domestic strife to break loose, and rage in all our borders. As the commotions of Nature, the tempests and hurricanes which she breeds in her long periods of calm, refresh while they desolate, and, in purifying the air from noxious ingredients, more than compensate for the ravages they inflict; so the fierce civic storm that is beating upon us is intended to be less our ruin than our redemption; less the waster than the restorer of the land. It is just the shock that was needed to break up the fatal sluggishness in which all but present gain was forgotten; and to clear the national atmosphere of the deadly malaria with which politics and Slavery had infected the national life. The timorous and faint-hearted may fear lest the nation should die under a remedy so harsh; but the wise see clearly that the nation must have died had the remedy been withheld. No, no, the war will not kill us. But a few more years of deceitful peace, purchased by the surrender of every principle dear to freedom and humanity, would have killed us, and left us to rot in the sight of the nations, a warning and a stench through all time.

In the great teachings of the hour, and in the rich fruit which those teachings are beginning to bear, we are more than repaid for all which the war has cost us. God is speaking to us—speaking to us out of the thick darkness, and in tones so clear and awful, that none can mistake His meaning, or scorn His counsels. By placing us in circumstances which require the furnishing of vast means to sustain the Government, He rebukes our avarice; and by bringing us into the death-grapple, not for national aggrandizement, but for national existence, He is teaching us that there are things more valuable than material prosperity; that courage, manliness, unblenching devotion to the welfare of our country, the willingness to give treasure and blood in its defence, are more precious than all the sordid triumphs of inglorious peace. He is waking up the dormant patriotism that had long slumbered under the pressure of business, or been smothered in the mire of political corruption; and is kindling in the young men of to-day the same noble fire that animated their fathers in the struggle for Independence. Oh! it is a glorious manifestation which is now gladdening our eyes! I thank God that I have lived to see it. The Pilgrim stock has not degenerated. "There is sap in the old tree yet." The sons of Massachusetts dishonor not their pedigree. Those who fought and fell at Ball's Bluff are worthy to have their names inscribed on the same immortal roll with those whose blood consecrated the fields of Bunker Hill and Lexington. And God is teaching us this—this grand spirit of self-sacrifice in a grand and righteous cause.

And other lessons, equally important and timely, He is reading out to us in the mighty eloquence of passing events. He is showing us that collective bodies of men cannot, any more than individuals, violate His laws, and trample His authority under foot, without bringing down the bolt of His vengeance; and that if we would be delivered from the awful chastisement which we now suffer, we must repent of the sins which have provoked Him, put away our infidelity, our irreligion, our worldliness, and return to the paths of faith and obedience. But, most solemnly, most emphatically of all, is He impressing on us the truth, that a great social iniquity, incorporated into a system of government, defended, cherished, perpetuated with blind obstinacy, against all the claims of justice and all the pleadings of philanthropy, must, at last, work the destruction of that government. As surely as powder, touched by the kindling spark, will burst the rock that incloses it; so surely will a mighty wrong, embosomed in a Commonwealth, explode, and shiver it into fragments.

Such has been the experience of this country with slavery. Always a source of weakness and peril, always a smouldering fire threatening to break out into a conflagration, it has, at length, defied all control, and wrapped the whole fabric of the Union, from corner-stone to pinnacle, in one broad sheet of flame. To this cause all our present troubles are to be ascribed. From the fatal admission of slavery into the Constitution by its framers, and the yet more fatal spread and strengthening of the institution by their descendants, have sprung the wreck and ruin which we now see.

When the ship of the Republic first came from the stocks, she was a sight beautiful to behold, the wonder and the joy of the world. Her model was perfect, her workmanship skilful and thorough, her fastenings stanch, her rigging complete; and, thus furnished and equipped, she spread her canvas on the broad ocean of the Future, cheered by happy auspices, and hailed by the god-speed of the admiring nations. But ah! there was one rotten plank in her hull; and that plank was slavery. Her builders knew it was there, for they put it there. But they trusted that the defect would not prove serious; and that the sound timbers, when they had been long enough in the water, would swell and crowd out the rotten one. And so the proud ship went on her way over placid seas, wafted by favoring breezes, with a merry crew on board, and streamers flying from peak and mizzen. But, hark! what fearful sound breaks in upon their mirth, and is passed by pale lips along the deck? *The ship has sprung a leak!* Yes, the rotten plank begins to do its work. The officers and crew make frantic efforts to stop the leak. They stuff into it the old rags of Compromise. They plaster it up with the tar of Concession, and the pitch of "Dred Scott Decisions." And then, finding all such attempts futile, they resolve to ignore it.

They turn their backs upon it. They strive to forget it in the engrossments of work or of pleasure. They will not believe there is any leak. They pronounce it to be only bilge water. They declare the ship safe, and call its rottenness its strength, its danger its security. But their labors and their sophistries, their mending and their letting alone, are alike vain. From watch to watch, the cry goes forth, *The leak is gaining on us!* From watch to watch, the breach grows wider, and the intruding tide more strong and furious. And now the end has come. The ship's side is burst in, and the mad flood of Rebellion rushes through the opening. Oh! the ship must go down, or slavery must go out! We must take her back into dock. We must cast forth the treacherous plank, destroy it with axe and fire, and close up the crevice with solid oak. Then may the good ship, sound from truck to keelson, and freighted with the happiness of unborn generations, shape her course in safety, victorious over the storm and the wave.

Such are some of the lessons which God is teaching us by this Rebellion. They are momentous lessons, involving our highest welfare. And though we are but slow scholars, we are beginning to learn them. Their influence on the tone of public thought and feeling is already visible. We are nobler men to-day than we were a year ago. We stand more erect. We are more patriotic. We love our country better, and are more willing to make sacrifices for it. We have broken away from the trammels of party. We have done with upholding slavery. We have done with compromises and half measures. We see our foe, and are prepared to wrestle with him to the death. And it is my firm hope and belief that this improvement in our character will go on, under the same tuition that began it, until the nation shall be redeemed, and Slavery and Treason are expelled from all its borders. Then shall our country be indeed free. Then over all its wide territories shall float the Banner beneath whose folds no bondman shall cower — the Banner of universal Liberty. And then, rising to a higher type of civilization than history has yet known, we shall fulfil our glorious mission in holding forth an unblemished example of self-government to all the down-trodden races of the earth. What thanks do we not owe to our all-wise Instructor for teachings so full of present good, and so pregnant with benign results yet to be developed!

We have grounds for grateful confidence in the issue of the conflict in which we are now engaged. I am not insensible to its difficulty, nor to its magnitude. I underrate not the strength and resources of the foe. I know his vast preparations, his multitudinous levies, his terrible earnestness. I know that we have to contend with an antagonist fertile in expedients, treacherous, cruel, who will shrink from no artifice, however base, that may further his impious ends. I know that the Catilines of the South, conscious that if they fail in their atrocious purpose, infamy and death await them, will cling to it with the energy of desperate men, and strive to drag down in their fall the country which they can no longer rule. The struggle must be severe, it may be long. But we cannot for a moment doubt what the final result will be. Strong as the rebels are, they are unprovided for a protracted contest. They have exhausted themselves by their first effort. They have done their utmost at the beginning. In all the necessary means of carrying on the war, in food, clothing, money, credit, they are fatally deficient. And when the power of the Federal Government, with its unlimited supply of men and treasure, is once hurled upon them in its full strength, and in downright earnest, they must be swept before it like chaff before the whirlwind.

But apart from the assurance of success founded on our superiority in numbers and resources, we have another yet stronger, in the wickedness of their cause, and in the rectitude of our own. The annals of human guilt furnish no instance of a crime so enormous as that with which the Southern conspirators stand charged before earth and Heaven.

It admits of no justification or even excuse; and the conspirators themselves do not pretend any. Not a right has been assailed; not a privilege infringed. They have suffered no wrong, no oppression. All the guarantees and engagements of the Constitution have been scrupulously observed toward them, grievous as some of these were to the Northern conscience. They have had their bond, even to the pound of flesh. So far from having been damaged by the Union, they have been the chief sharers in its benefits. For more than half a century, the administration of the Government has been in their hands, or has been controlled by their influence; and they have uniformly wielded it in the interest of slavery. Their will has dictated every law of Congress, and shaped every public measure. Theirs have been the highest offices, the fattest emoluments; theirs the most potential voice in the Senate and on the Bench. And while thus favored and caressed by the Government, with its bounty in their pockets, and the oath of fealty to it on their lips, they have all the while been plotting its overthrow; threatening and intriguing to dissolve the Union, whenever any check has been offered to their insolence or their ambition.

During all these years of their pride and power, they have heaped insult and wrong on the free North. They have claimed to be our masters;

have declared it their birthright to rule, and ours to serve; and, in the frenzy of their arrogance, have commanded us to bow down and do homage to their hideous idol, and surrender speech and thought, principle and conscience, into the keeping of the lords of the plantation. To appease these bloated chattel-drivers, what has the North not done? It has cringed and bent; it has truckled and fawned; it has grovelled, aye, crawled in the very dirt. But no amount of subserviency has been able to satisfy them. Conciliation has but led to bolder demands, and to humiliations more disgraceful. Believing from former experience, that the North would yield everything to their menaces and their bluster, they have, at length, set up the monstrous claim that the Constitution should be so changed or so interpreted, as to make slavery national, a universal right, to be held sacred wherever the flag of the Union may float. And because the North has been compelled to resist this claim, or submit to be itself enslaved, they are now in open revolt against the Government, and laboring with might and main to break it up. Such is the grievance which they put forth in defence of their treason. It is, however, only a pretext. The real purpose, underlying all their movements, and reaching back of all irritating antagonisms, is to destroy the heritage of Freedom which our fathers left us, and erect, in its place, a vast Slave Despotism, the vilest and most abominable that ever cursed mankind. For this they have struck at the pillars of social order, and plunged the nation into all the woes of intestine war.

And shall such transcendent villany succeed? Shall this "throne of iniquity" be established? Will a righteous God permit it? Will He ally Himself with a scheme so at war with human happiness, so abhorrent to His justice and benevolence? Will He suffer the blood-stained miscreants that now rule the South to cut short our national career, and disappoint the oppressed of all lands who have looked to our shores as the refuge of persecuted Liberty? No, no, we cannot believe it. Every attribute of God, every unfolding of His will in His word and in His providence, assures us that He is on our side in this awful exigency, and will bring to our aid the succors of His omnipotence. The wheels of His chariot may tarry. He may try us by delay. He may humble us by temporary defeats and reverses, in order to deepen our feeling of dependence upon Him, and to render us more obedient to the leadings of His hand. But He will not forsake us. Our cause is His cause, the cause of Civilization, the cause of Humanity, the cause of true Religion — and must triumph. His arm is bared against the oppressors, and their doom is certain. He will make their own horrid sin, and the insane fury with which they cling to it, the means of their punishment. Into the pit which they have dug for the Union, the Rebellion shall go down, and Slavery with it. The besom of destruction, which they have made ready for the North, shall sweep their own fields from the Potomac to the Gulf. On the gibbet which they have reared for Liberty, they themselves shall hang, and with them the broken fetters of the last bondman. Such is the awful retribution prepared for slavery and the slaveholder.

No, no — God will not let the foul tyrants of the South prevail. He will not permit them to sunder this glorious Republic, and plant a Slave Confederacy on its ruins. Not long will He allow the banner of Secession, the vile emblem of the whip and chain, to flout our American sky. He made us one nation, and He means us to continue one through all time. The form of the Continent, the encircling of the oceans, the course of the rivers, the trend of the mountains, all proclaim that He has ordained for us one Country, one People, one Government, from the St. Lawrence to the Rio Grande, from the rocky headlands of Maine to the golden shores of the Pacific. Yes, the Rebellion will be put down, and with it Slavery and the Slave Power; and we shall come forth from the present appalling crisis a stronger and a better people, prepared to take a higher stand and to do a nobler work on the platform of history, than have ever yet been allotted to a nation. "In this may we be confident."

Such are some of the reasons which we have for reliance and thankfulness, even amidst the public perils that encompass us. Let them awaken trust in God, courage, hope. And remember that whatever may be the state of national affairs, whatever events may occur on the broad theatre of the world, you have private blessings, without number, and beyond price. You have life, food, raiment, homes, friends, the means of intellectual and spiritual culture. Your cup of personal mercy overflows. And, crowning all, infinitely more precious than all, you have redemption by the blood of Christ, and the offer of immortal blessedness. Oh! give thanks unto the Lord, for He is good. Thank Him in His house, thank Him at your firesides, thank Him in your hearts, thank Him by a penitent faith, and with holy deeds. Then, when your pilgrimage is done, your ransomed souls shall soar far above these scenes of war and tumult, to the regions where gratitude and joy are perfect, and peace is eternal.

CHAPTER III.

GREAT ERAS MARKED BY GREAT JUDGMENTS.

"BY TERRIBLE THINGS IN RIGHTEOUSNESS WILT THOU ANSWER US, O GOD OF OUR SALVATION."—*Psalm* lxv. 5.

THIS whole psalm is throughout a magnificent description of the sovereignty and universal providence of God. There is nothing in the Bible more striking and sublime. It is replete with the loftiest inspirations of poetry; while, at the same time, it glows with the most fervid breathings of devotion.

The writer commences by addressing Jehovah as the supreme Object of reverence and worship, for whom praise and adoration were waiting in Zion, and to whom the vow of fealty and obedience should be performed. This thought — the thought of the homage so constantly and so rightfully rendered to God — suggested the closely related thought of God as the Hearer of prayer, and the Dispenser of pardon; bending from His seat of awful majesty to accept the confessions and listen to the requests of all who seek His face; forgiving their sins, and achieving their deliverance, by manifestations of His power and mercy. "O Thou that hearest prayer! unto Thee shall all flesh come. Iniquities prevail against me; as for our transgressions, Thou shalt purge them away."

He then proceeds to consider the grounds on which the friends of God may repose the fullest confidence in His faithfulness, in His willingness to receive their petitions, and in His ability to perform them. These he finds in the supreme and all-pervading government which God exercises over the world, and in that watchful superintendence which He maintains in every department of human affairs. With a rapid and glowing pencil, he traces the workings of this government as they are displayed alike in the realms of matter and of mind; in the vicissitudes of the seasons; in the products of the earth; in the bounties that supply man's physical wants; and in the political changes and convulsions which affect his social condition. Everywhere he sees the controlling agency of God. Every object, every event, speaks to him of God. The turmoil of Nature in her agitations and upheavings; the calmness and beauty of Nature in her repose; the tempests and earthquakes that ravage and lay waste; the genial showers, the fructifying dews, the life-awakening sunbeams, which call forth the springing corn, and clothe the valleys with food for man and beast; the peace and order which foster the industrial arts, and give prosperity to nations; and the tumults and revolutions, the wars and the carnage which change the face of empires, and fill continents with mourning — all these are in his view equally under the direction of the Almighty, equally obedient to the behests of His providence, equally fulfilling the mission which He appoints.

But amidst these diversified operations of Jehovah's ever present energy, there is one feature which seems to stand out before the eye of the Psalmist with peculiar prominence. It is the justice and holiness which characterize the Divine administration. While he recognizes the consoling fact that God is infinitely gracious and long-suffering, and that He will surely accomplish, in His own time and way, all the desires of His people for succor and protection, and for the final establishment of truth and goodness upon earth, he yet clearly perceives that the Most High often does this through the ministry of afflictive judgments, and brings to pass great and beneficent ends by means of events, which during their continuance appear to be fraught with disaster. Hence he exclaims, "By terrible things in righteousness wilt Thou answer us, O God of our salvation."

These words contain a general truth of vast significance, and of wide application. It is a truth which relates not merely to the personal experience of the Sweet Singer of Israel, nor to any particular exhibitions of Divine power in his behalf; but to the whole history of God's procedure toward His Covenant Church, and to the grand principles which underlie His work of overthrowing evil, and advancing His kingdom in the world. There is here announced to us the broad and comprehensive fact, that in all periods of time God has answered the prayers of His people for the suppression of Wrong and the vindication of Right, by dispensations of correcting wrath, as terrible in their progress as they were righteous in their character, and benign in their results. And, in illustration of this fact, we shall find that those great conjunctures in human affairs, which have exerted a commanding influence on the well-being of our race, and shaped anew the course of its destiny, have ordinarily been heralded by dread forthputtings of Jehovah's hand, attesting His presence, delivering His friends, and recompensing His enemies.

Ever since depravity found place on the earth, and began to assail the prerogatives and to insult the authority of its rightful Lord, the prayer of all who have truly loved Him has been, that He would put forth the resources of His omnipotence to defeat wickedness, to uphold His own glory, and to make holiness universally triumphant. And this He has all along been doing — not always, however, in the manner which His people had marked out for Him — not always by slow and silent changes — not always by the mild and sweetly purifying influences of Truth and Love, as noxious vapors are melted and exhaled by gentle breezes and soft sunshine — but often by appalling interventions of His just displeasure, destroying the wicked; punishing the good so far as they have participated in the sins which call down His vengeance; and thus sweeping the field clear for fresh victories of His grace. There are states of the atmosphere in which hurricanes and tornadoes are necessary to expel from it malarious elements, and restore its salubrity. So there are times when the social atmosphere becomes so charged with moral poison, that nothing but God's thunder can clear it, and make it a medium in which holiness can live.

True it is that mercies and blessings constitute the chosen method by which the Almighty carries on His moral administration. He seeks to draw men from their sinful courses, and to win their hearts into allegiance to Himself, by the force of instruction, by the power of light, by the persuasive ministry of loving-kindness. This is the normal character of His dispensations. But when individuals or communities have become so sunk in degeneracy, or so wedded and sold to enormous vices, as to be insensible to every motive derived from His goodness; and, especially, when from wicked laws, institutions or governments, obstacles stand in the way of His purposes which ordinary appliances fail to remove — then it is that He makes bare His arm for judgment; then it is that "by terrible things in righteousness," He answers prayer, and annihilates the barriers that oppose the going forth of His salvation.

Having thus developed and explained the principle announced, we shall occupy the remaining part of this discussion in showing how that principle has been brought out in the past dealings of God with nations; and how strikingly it may be seen in His dealings with our own country and with ourselves.

The first example, embodying the truth before us, may be drawn from the method by which Divine Wisdom saw fit to deliver the people of Israel from their bondage in Egypt, and conduct them into the land appointed for their inheritance. This was indispensable in order that revealed Religion might find expression and perpetuity in the establishment of the Mosaic Economy; and the transactions which attended it are pregnant with momentous lessons to all the ages.

God had given to Abraham, as the reward of his faith and obedience, a solemn promise, often repeated, that the goodly hills and valleys of Canaan should be the permanent home of his posterity; that there they should become in number as the sands of the sea, and dwelling in safety under His inviolable guardianship, be distinguished above all other nations by miraculous communications of His will, and by peculiar tokens of His favor. And the fulfilment of this promise was hardly less important to the welfare of the world at large than to that of the chosen Tribes themselves. The countless races of the Gentiles, though not expressly named in the covenant, had nevertheless a vast interest in the higher benefits which it was intended to convey. The grand design of God in electing the descendants of Abraham to be His peculiar people, planting them in the spot set apart for their abode, and placing them, by restrictive laws, in holy isolation from the darkness and pollution that covered all the earth beside, doubtless was that through them the true knowledge and worship of Himself might be retained amongst men, and a lineage furnished for the Messiah, the future Restorer of the world. Beyond the narrow limits of the Hebrew family, the whole world had lapsed into idolatry; and He, who made and upheld it, saw, as it rolled round in His hand and under His eye, no light breaking through the gloom, and no incense ascending to His throne, save where dimly burned the sacrificial fires on the altars of the patriarchs, or where the homage of the One Creator still lingered in the tents of Goshen. And if the single line in which the knowledge of the true God yet survived, were to continue, as in the days of its founders, a mere horde of nomadic herdsmen, wandering from place to place without any settled habitations, the truth which they held as a precious deposit in trust for the world — guarded by no fixed institutions and no regular observances — would soon die out and be forgotten amid the necessities and the fluctuations of a mode of life so uncertain.

In like manner, if after the Children of Israel had gone down into Egypt their exile had been perpetual, they must have lost, in the lapse of years, their very existence as a distinct people. Crushed into utter annihilation under the iron heel of slavery, or absorbed into the nationality of their oppressors, they would have adopted their customs, imitated their vices, accepted their religion, bowed down to their gods. Whatever of divine illumination they possessed would have been swallowed up and extinguished by the predominant power of surrounding heathenism; celestial Truth would have been driven from her last home on earth; and the one lone point of light that still broke the universal darkness, would have disappeared from our world, and left it to the shadows of a night that could know no morning. And, therefore, the settlement of the Tribes in their promised heritage was an event involving not only their own national life and their future greatness, but the spiritual destinies of the human race as well, and the preparatory processes of its coming redemption.

Now, there can be little question that the Hebrew fathers, instructed as they were by personal communion with God, regarded this great fact in the broad and momentous relations which we have ascribed to it. Nor is it extravagant to suppose that its realization formed the burden of their addresses to the Throne of Infinite Mercy. It must have been always present to their thoughts, whenever they pondered the Promise that in their seed should all the families of the earth be blessed, and gazing down the vista of the ages, strove to grasp the glory they were to unfold. And well may we believe that each dying patriarch, as he bade farewell to earth, turned his last look to Canaan; while on his aged lips trembled the prayer, that God would fulfil His covenant to the sacred seed, establish them in their destined possession, reveal to them His will, and teach them by His ordinances; and thus prepare the way for the coming era of Christian light and salvation.

With equal confidence may we believe that the same prayer was constantly offered up by all the pious among the Israelites, during their protracted exile in Egypt. As the slow years of their bondage dragged heavily over them; as their chains grew more galling, and the exactions of their taskmasters more severe; as they trod the clay, and shaped the bricks, and crouched down under their hard service, and writhed and groaned under the lash of their haughty oppressors — how often and how earnestly must their cry for deliverance have ascended to Heaven! Oh, yes! while Egypt increased in wealth and splendor by the toil wrung from her bondmen; while her princes and nobles rioted in luxury, and mirth and rejoicing filled her palaces — from the hovels in which the Hebrews dwelt, and from the fields where they wrought, were heard the ceaseless wail of suffering, and the loud pleading of the enslaved, going up into the ears of the God of Sabaoth.

At length the answer came. Yet how different from their expectations was the way of its coming! If they speculated at all upon the method of their predicted emancipation, they probably believed it would be brought about, not by violent changes, and sudden outgoings of Divine power, but by gradual and almost imperceptible ameliorations of their state, coming in as naturally and as noiselessly as day succeeds to night, or summer to winter. Perhaps they hoped that time might soften the bitterness of their vassalage; or that faithful service and patient endurance might by degrees win the respect of their masters, and mitigate their cruelty. Possibly, too, they dreamed that even in the bosom of Pharaoh might be found a dormant conscience and a better mind, which, awakened by the remonstrances of Moses, would prompt him to listen to the Divine summons, and let the people go. And thus they imagined, it may be, that they should depart out of their bondage with the consent and good will of their former lords, leaving the land of their exile unscourged by any visitation of wrath — the oppressed and the oppressors mutually grateful and happy. And, questionless, all this might have been. Had the infatuated monarch yielded to the command of Jehovah, and broken the fetters of the enslaved, the fearful calamities, which his obstinate wickedness brought upon his reign and country, might have been averted. The exodus of the Israelites, instead of being made memorable forever by wonderful displays of Almighty vengeance, would have been only a peaceful emigration of a particular class of the population to new and more eligible seats. And so the hope of centuries would have been realized amid universal harmony, and the rejoicings alike of those who conferred the boon, and of those who received it.

But such magnanimity is seldom to be looked for in this fallen world. All history shows that power rarely gives up its prey, except from the compulsion of events which it can no longer resist. The king of Egypt, in binding faster the chains of his victims, the more he was importuned to unloose them, but followed the course of human tyranny in all lands and ages. He doubtless deemed the extorted labor of the Hebrews, employed as it was in furnishing materials for the construction of cities and public works, to be of vast importance to the development and prosperity of his empire; and he was resolute that no voice of priest or prophet, no behest of Israel's God, or of any god, should prevail on him to relinquish the control of muscles that had proved so valuable. His refusal to release the captives necessitated the intervention of that grand law of the Divine procedure to which we have adverted. The merciful intentions of Jehovah with regard to His chosen people were not to be frustrated by the greed or the obstinacy of their enslavers. Commands and expostulations having failed, a mightier agency was called in. The ministry of wrath — the stern efficacy of "terrible things in righteousness" — was commissioned to undertake the work which milder means were unable to accomplish.

In pursuance of this design, the rod of Divine vengeance was stretched out over all the habitations of the spoilers. Blow followed blow in swift succession, and with crushing effect. Appalled by the severity of the visitations, the king and his princes seemed at intervals to relent, and often promised obedience to the mandate so fearfully enforced. But no sooner was the punishment withdrawn, than they became as obdurate as before. Then the scourge was again lifted up; and the awful series of inflictions went on, growing more destructive at every step; reaching all ranks; carrying dismay and woe into all places; turning into desolation all the pride and glory of the land; till its avenging work was consummated in that dread midnight hour, when "the Lord smote all the firstborn of Egypt," and every dwelling of Israel's foes wailed its dead. Subdued by this last overwhelming calamity, and by the cry of anguish which it woke throughout his dominions, the trembling despot pronounced the decree of emancipation, and commanded the people, whose God was so terrible, to depart at once from beneath his sway.

Yet how the love of domination infatuates men! How it blinds their reason, and renders them reckless of consequences! Even when compelled by the judgments of Heaven to set free their thralls, how unwillingly they surrender them! How furious are they to recover them; how full of hatred and rage against them, when they have gone beyond their power. The children of Israel had scarcely crossed the border of Egypt on their journey into the wilderness, before the frantic monarch and his equally frantic satellites began to regret their departure, and to take measures for dragging them back into bondage. How could they be so besotted — so insensible to the terrible chastisements to which they had just been subjected? How could they so soon forget the waters turned to blood, the all-wasting hail, the darkness that could be felt, the sword of the destroying Angel strewing the whole land with corpses? They could not but know that God was on the side of Israel, and that, in attempting to re-enslave those whom He had delivered, they must fight with Omnipotence. Nevertheless, while the most startling evidences of this Divine interposition were still fresh in their minds — while they beheld, wherever they looked, field and city, palace and temple, scarred and rent by the hurricane of vengeance that had swept over them — they determined to pursue the fugitives, and return them by force to their shackles. With this fell intent, they mustered the entire military strength of the kingdom — chariots and horsemen in almost numberless array — and pushed forward on the track of the fleeing bondmen. They soon came up with them, encumbered as they were with flocks and herds, with wives and little ones, with the aged and the infirm. And now these man-hunters thought themselves sure of their quarry. The Hebrews were encamped in a narrow defile, with steep mountains on either side, the deep, impassable sea before them, and the fierce legions of their pursuers pressing behind them. Retreat was cut off. Escape in any direction seemed hopeless. What could this multitude of lately emancipated serfs, debased by centuries of oppression, unskilled in arms, and accustomed to regard the Egyptians as a superior race, do in a conflict with the collected might of the most warlike nation then on the face of the earth? What possible fate awaited them, but to submit to their infuriated persecutors, and bow down once more under the yoke; or, pent up and helpless, to be slaughtered without mercy? That one or the other of these catastrophes must befall them, was looked upon as certain both by their enemies and by themselves. And so shorn of all manhood were they by the long years of servitude which they had endured, that they were ready to go back to their prison-house, rather than encounter danger and death in a struggle for freedom.

But God had not brought them forth with such signal displays of His interference, to desert them in their extremity. He heard their cry for succor, and answered it by an outputting of His almightiness more stupendous than any which they had yet witnessed. The Pillar of Cloud and of Fire, that had hitherto gone before them, now moved from their front, and stood between them and the Egyptians — its bright side shining on their own ranks, its dark side frowning on their foes — the token of deliverance to the one, of overthrow to the other. At the same time, Moses, by the command of the Lord, stretched his rod over the sea; and lo! its waters were parted asunder to their lowest depths, leaving along their uncovered bed a dry passage for human feet. Down into that miraculous chasm went the millions of Israel, tribe after tribe, column after column; the radiant Pillar lighting their way, and the liquid walls rising up straight and high on either hand. And down after them poured the Egyptian host, madly bent on following the escaping slaves into the very jaws of Hell. On, on they hurried, the pursued and the pursuers — on through the long night — on over the secret places of the deep, over coral hills, and valleys that never saw the sun. Strange march! stranger marching-ground! Type of the race between lord and vassal throughout the ages! The heaven-defying audacity of the oppressors had now reached its climax, and the hour of their destruction was come. In the morning watch, Jehovah looked out upon them from the angry face of the Cloud that hovered between them and the objects of their rage. At the glance of that awful Eye, their hardihood forsook them; consternation spread from squadron to squadron; and with broken lines and disabled chariots they turned to flee from the Almighty One that fought for Israel. But the attempt was vain. The rod of Moses was again stretched over the sea, and the watery mountains, which God's hand had held divided, rushed together, burying king and noble, horse and rider, chariot and charioteer, under the swift-meeting billows. The proud array of Egypt was no more. And while, on the safe shore, the rescued Tribes sung hymns of triumph, and with harp and timbrel celebrated the praise of their omnipotent Defender; in the cities of the Nile was heard the voice of lamentation, and Misraim, through all her provinces, wept her fallen chivalry, and her glory departed.

It was thus that, by dispensations as just as they were appalling, God responded to the prayer of His people, and led them forth from the house of bondage. But the operation of this great principle did not cease here. The froward and rebellious conduct of the Hebrews themselves often demanded its exercise. A brief trial of their character proved them wholly unfit for the high destiny which the Divine purpose had assigned to their race. With a few striking exceptions, the entire nation was so corrupted by slavery, and so deficient in physical and moral stamina, that, had it been conducted at once to Canaan, it would have shown itself utterly incompetent to drive out the peoples by whom it was occupied, and found a stable commonwealth. Or, if celestial aid had supplemented this weakness, and placed the descendants of Abraham in possession of the land which God had given to him, their waywardness, their idolatrous leanings, their imbecile habits, their want of all elevating impulses, must have rapidly induced a state of degeneracy and disorder, that would have made them the easy prey of surrounding kingdoms. In either case, the design of God in reference to the establishment of His truth in the world, would have been defeated. He, therefore, saw that a course of severe and protracted discipline was required to shape such worthless materials into the instruments which He needed. Hence he held His promise in abeyance; visited their frequent disobedience with frequent correction; and compelled them to traverse the wilderness for forty years, in a series of aimless marches backward and forward, till the track of their wanderings was studded thick with the graves of all who came out of Egypt. And then, when a new generation had arisen, a generation born in the desert and vigorous with its fresh life — a generation born free, and educated under the influences of freedom — when such men stood in the place of their feeble sires, He consummated His assurances to the patriarchs, and bestowed on their offspring the heritage which He had ordained for them.

At this point, also, we witness corresponding manifestations of retributive Holiness. The land of Canaan was then inhabited by numerous races of

Phœnician origin, who were intruders upon the soil, which the All-Owner and Disposer had allotted to the children of His Covenant. Their obscene idolatries and enormous wickedness had long recked up to heaven, and Divine justice had decreed their extermination. The future developments of God's providence, in relation not merely to His chosen people, but to the whole human family, required the expulsion of these heathen trespassers from the central position into which they had thrust themselves, and its transfer to the nation selected as the conservators of the knowledge and worship of the One Jehovah, till the Light of the Gentiles should appear, and the lost brotherhood of man be restored by Christ. For the carrying out of this arrangement, the Almighty clothed His arm with terror. At His command, the hosts of Israel passed into Canaan, routed its armies, sacked its cities, ravaged its territory with fire and sword, slew vast numbers of its population, reduced the remnant to submission, or forced it to seek new settlements. In all this they were but the agents of the universal Sovereign, to whom the whole earth belongs, and who has a right to apportion it as He pleases. His will was their authority; His aid the source of their triumph. Guided and supported by Him, they took possession of the land set apart as the birth-scene of the world's

Salvation, and cleared it for the waiting wonders that were in reserve for it.

From this rapid survey, how clearly do we perceive in the Hebrew Exodus the ministry of judgments! How thickly along its path stand the "terrible things," which bring about the purposes of the Most High! Nor were these the outburstings of mere arbitrary vengeance. They were righteous in their infliction, and compensative in their end. The blessings which they prepared transcended a thousand fold the sufferings which they occasioned. It was only through them that God could introduce the era of Organized Religion — the era in which His Truth, no longer homeless and a wanderer, should be established in a permanent abode, and be embodied in a national worship, reflecting its light on the surrounding darkness, and serving as the precursor of that broader and more spiritual economy which was ultimately to embrace the world. The scourging of Egypt, the afflictions of Israel in the wilderness, the conquest and extrusion of the idolatrous hordes of Canaan, stood in intimate and necessary connection with the fulfilment of the promise, that in the seed of Abraham all the families of the earth should be blessed. And so it was, that from miseries narrow in their range, and transient in duration, sprung Hope and Happiness for the human race.

Analogous events marked the inauguration of Christianity. This epoch, the most important which the earth has seen, was waited for with intense desire, from the hour of its first announcement in Eden, down through all the slow-moving centuries that preceded its introduction. In every land, in every period, under every form of social existence, it was the one bright expectation which cheered the travail of the darkling generations. Even among pagan races, however ignorant and barbarous, there prevailed an indistinct, yet strong and universal impression, arising from the intuitive feeling of need, or from dim traditions of the original Promise, that some Divine Personage would appear, to remedy the disorders of humanity, and usher in the golden age of purity and joy. The Jews, instructed by revelation, possessed clearer views, and cherished a hope more definite and assured. They knew that the Celestial One, for whose advent the world thus vaguely longed, was to be their own Messiah, the King and Saviour of Israel. They knew that the covenant of God with their fathers, the predictions of their prophets, the ceremonial of their religion, and its whole spirit, pointed to His coming as their consummation and fulfilment. To the dawning of His day they looked forward with eager yearning. For its arrival the devout among them incessantly prayed. And in all their changeful history, in weakness, in exile, in the humiliations inflicted on them by their foreign conquerors, they were upheld and consoled by the never-wavering faith, that the mighty Champion who was to arise for their deliverance, would avenge every wrong, and heal every sorrow.

Yet, though right in their belief as to the fact of Christ's mission, they were utterly in error as to its nature and objects. The ideas which they formed of the relation which He was to sustain to them, and of the work which He was to accomplish, were altogether carnal. They had no conception of the moral bearings which His manifestation was to assume — of its vicarious and expiatory character — of its grand scope in putting away sin by the Sacrifice of the Cross, and erecting, through the power of that sacrifice, a spiritual empire over the hearts of men. A political redemption, a material sovereignty, engrossed their thoughts, and kindled their anticipations. They looked for a temporal Messiah — a Prince wearing an earthly crown, wielding earthly weapons, leading invincible armies — a Divine Hero, who should break the Roman yoke, vanquish the heathen in battle, raise Jerusalem to the seat of a universal monarchy, and, infusing new life into effete and dying Judaism, make it the religion of the world.

Doubtless there were contingencies in which some

of these expectations were possible. Had they recognized, in the coming of the God-man, the completion of their national Hope; had they comprehended the true meaning of His office; had they yielded to the evidence of His Divine authority, acknowledged His claims, received His words, and embraced His salvation — they might have escaped the tremendous doom which subsequently befell them. Accepting Jesus of Nazareth as their Deliverer from spiritual bondage, they would have found in Him the Guardian and Uplifter of their social condition. Their existence as a people would have been preserved. The dispensation of the Law would have melted into the dispensation of the Gospel as silently and as serenely as the orb of night disappears before the rising of the sun. The land in which they dwelt, endeared to them by so many glorious memories, would have remained the inalienable heritage of their race. And their Holy City, the renowned centre of Hebrew worship, would have been no less hallowed in all future times, and among all kindreds of men, as the birthplace of Christianity, and the radiating point from which its light first went forth to dispel the darkness of the nations.

But their obstinate unbelief blasted all these splendid possibilities, and evoked, in their place, public and individual ruin, as certain as it was utter. The unpretending manner in which the Redeemer entered upon His ministry, His humble origin, His lowly demeanor, His recoil from all schemes of ambition and aggrandizement, shocked their prejudices, and ran counter to the whole current of their opinions in reference to the Messiah. His humility offended their pride. The holiness of His doctrines condemned the corruption of their lives. The method of justification which He unfolded, overthrew their self-righteousness. They clearly saw that if the divinity of His character and of His teachings were admitted, the national religion in which they gloried, with all its legal observances, and all the puerile additions with which they had disfigured it, must be swept away and superseded by this new system of truth and worship. Hence they clung to their sensual views, and rejected Him whom prophecy and miracle, the converging of events, His own forthputtings of infinite power, and the concurring witness of Heaven, pointed out as the Only Begotten of the Father. Fired with jealousy and hate, they heaped on Him scorn and insult and contumely, and, at last, compassed His crucifixion, crying out in their awful blindness, "His blood be on us, and on our children." And when He had risen from the dead, and they knew that He had risen, and had thus given the crowning proof of His Messiahship, they persecuted His followers, and endeavored, by threats and imprisonment, to restrain them from preaching the Name which they detested and feared.

From that hour their destruction was sure. They had put themselves into antagonism with Omnipotence. In their opposition to Christ and His Gospel, they strove to block the path of Jehovah's purposes, and so came within the sweep of that dread law which crushes the enemies that mercy cannot subdue. The Judaism to which they adhered, distorted, debased, and shorn of all its primal virtue, false to its Founder and false to its design, instead of welcoming Christianity, and opening the way for its triumphs, stood forth as its chief and most envenomed foe; and, therefore, the cause of human salvation, no less than the voice of outraged Justice, demanded that it should be driven from its place of power, its home made desolate, and its abettors scattered over the face of the earth. In accordance with the usual course of Divine dealing, by which national crimes become the means of national punishment, the final ruin and dispersion of the Jews, and the complete uprooting of their state and polity, were the consequences of their own act. The same ecclesiastical bigotry which led them to repudiate and murder their Messiah, incited them also to rebel against the authority of Rome, and brought upon them its swift and terrible vengeance. The fierce legions of Vespasian strode over the land, filling it with carnage and woe, turning its fertile plains into deserts, storming its fortified places, laying its towns level with the ground, and driving the houseless inhabitants before them, till nearly the whole nation was shut up in Jerusalem. Then commenced a siege, memorable through all time for its duration, for the vigor with which it was pressed, for the desperation with which it was resisted, for the horrors that attended it — a siege in which more than a million of Jews perished by the sword or by famine. So fearfully was their own imprecation verified! At length, the city was taken, its walls demolished, its very foundations razed, its temple laid in ashes, its surviving population given up to slaughter, or borne away as slaves by their conquerors. Hebrew nationality was extinguished. The land, stained with the blood of the Crucified, was surrendered to perpetual desolation; and the race that committed the awful deed were to be evermore wanderers and outcasts, abandoned of Heaven, and abhorred of earth. Thus, by a visitation as necessary as it was stern, as righteous as it was overwhelming, the All-Ruler swept from the pathway of His Gospel the mightiest obstacle that impeded its introduction and progress.

Similar revealings of His hand may be seen in

all the great epochs that have signalized the march of Christianity along the track of the centuries. History abundantly shows that whenever organized wickedness, whether that of governments, hierarchies, or institutions, has opposed the advance of His kingdom, striking exhibitions of His power have come forth to remove the obstruction. But we cannot now trace out and describe each instance in detail. The brief space which remains to us will barely suffice to present the working of this law in our own time and country.

The period in which we live is distinguished preeminently as the Era of Freedom. We do not so designate it because freedom is yet either perfect in its nature, or universal in its extension. But there is everywhere a growing appreciation of it, a more earnest struggle to secure it, a stronger conviction of the right to it which belongs to all, and of the deep wrong involved in the violation of that right. This feature is so prominent in our day as to constitute its leading characteristic, and determine its place in history. And God has stamped this feature on the age with a view to the promotion of His work of Grace in the world. It is the grand intent of His mercy to recover the lost children of earth from the degradation and misery into which sin has plunged them, emancipate them from moral thraldom, elevate them in civilization, knowledge, comfort, and render them holy and happy under the peaceful sceptre of His Son.

Among the external hindrances to this redeeming process, the tyranny of man over his fellows is the most unyielding and potent. Even the Gospel, with all its heaven-born energies, cannot uplift masses held down by the iron clutch of despotism, till that clutch is rent away. It may save from final perdition the souls that truly receive it, however shrouded in ignorance, and imbruted by vassalage; but it cannot exert its high and transforming influence on social welfare where thought is fettered, and every faculty lies benumbed and paralyzed under the incubus of oppression. Nor can its more spiritual work be successfully prosecuted in such a field. It may reach here and there an individual among the benighted and down-trodden; but the wide, dead waste of debasement will remain unaffected by its power. The spirit of the Gospel is a free spirit, and can hold no alliance with absolutism, whether civil or ecclesiastical, whether that of king, pope, or oligarch. Hence we might well expect that the Providence which rules in all terrestrial affairs, would direct its operations with special reference to the removal of this greatest barrier to the spread of truth and righteousness. And the going forth of its agency to this end is manifest, not only in the overturning or liberalizing of despotic governments, but more emphatically still in the tremendous conflict with slavery which now convulses our own land.

Human bondage, so long dominant in this otherwise favored country, has been the chief impediment to the growth of a pure Christianity at home, and to the efficiency of our labors in the cause of evangelization abroad. It has been the nation's blackest sin, and its deadliest curse. A monstrous crime and a blighting pest wherever it exists, its enormity has been more flagrant here than elsewhere, from the fact that it has here assumed its most ruthless form, and also on the ground that it has been upheld and cherished in direct antagonism to our republican principles, and to our noble antecedents. Inscribing on the organic framework of our national government the great truth, that God has created all men free and equal, and proclaiming it as the corner-stone of our political system, we have held in chains millions endowed with the same natural rights as ourselves; have robbed them of their manhood; have bought and sold them like brute beasts; have dishonored and defiled the proud banner of Liberty by making it the protector of the man-stealer, and the symbol of chattelhood. What wonder is it that an infamy like this should have exposed us to the contempt of the civilized world? Who can marvel that our vaunted freedom has been the scoff of aristocrats and monarchists throughout the earth; or that we have been branded as a nation of hypocrites, whose philanthropy tolerates injustice, and whose religion is linked with the foulest iniquity on which the sun ever looked?

This glaring blot on our character and on our institutions has not only been reprobated by the general voice of humanity; its evils have been felt and deplored by ourselves. We have long viewed it as our country's guilt and bane. We have seen it debauching the public conscience and the public morals, entering into all the walks of business, contaminating our literature, corrupting our churches, and pervading every department of society with its fatal poison. For its removal wise and good men have labored during many years with patient zeal, and in the unblenching faith, that argument, and expostulation, and the reforming forces of the Gospel, would finally eradicate and banish it from the land. And there was a time when this faith seemed to be well founded. The giant curse appeared to be losing strength under the moral stress brought to bear upon it. Slaveholders themselves began to grow weary of it, to acknowledge its baleful tendencies, and to contemplate the possibility of its future extinction. There were few so blinded by prejudice and passion, as to pronounce it a good in itself — few so lost to all sense of right, as to assert its rectitude. The almost unanimous verdict even of slaveholding society declared it to be a system of labor wasteful, unremunerative, an injury to the master, and a wrong to the slave — a system whose longer existence could be justified only by the fact, that it was so interwoven with all the habits and interests of Southern life as to render its sudden withdrawal productive of wide-spread industrial derangement. The sentiment was general that slavery was not a blessing to be perpetuated, but an evil to be removed as soon as it could be done with safety. And so extensively did this sentiment prevail, that in some of the slaveholding States incipient steps were taken for so changing their constitutions as to provide for gradual and final emancipation.

That was the day of grace — the probation-hour of the South. Then she had a Conscience. Then her heart was tender. Then the Spirit of God moved upon the minds of her people, convincing them of righteousness. Then all that was Christian in her condemned on moral grounds the making merchandise of men, and all that was patriotic desired its abolishment as a great social mischief. Oh! had she known, in that day of her merciful visitation, "the things which belonged to her peace" — had she seen that a fungus so deadly was to be cured, not by delay, but by prompt and instant excision — had she obeyed the voice of Providence, the voice of history, the voice of her own convictions, and broken at once the fetters of her bondmen — the devastating wrath which she has called down upon herself and upon the nation would not have been inflicted!

But the propitious season was not improved. Soon a marked change occurred in the financial aspects of the question. A wider market for cotton, and new facilities in the growth and preparation of the staple, led to increased production, and thus created a demand for slave labor, and greatly enhanced the price of human bones and sinews. Then a complete revulsion of opinion and of feeling passed over the South. All thought of emancipation, present or future, was laid aside. All consciousness of the wrong of involuntary servitude was overborne and extinguished by the dazzling rewards which it promised. Slavery, no longer deemed unprofitable, but a source of boundless wealth, seemed to undergo a wondrous transformation. The demon became an angel; the destroyer a saviour; the essence of barbarism a grand agent of civilization; the blaring scandal of the age, detested by God and man, a sacred and holy thing, the twin sister of Christianity. The population of the slave States declared itself a unit in support of the institution, in maintaining its equity before Heaven and earth, and in claiming for it universal and perpetual dominion.

From that moment, the fate of the oligarchy was sealed. From that moment, it passed within the sweep of the retributive law which we have described. From that moment, its punishment was as fixed and determined as it is now. A just God gave it up to the power of an infatuation, which was as certain to plunge it into the abyss of ruin, as a boat, set adrift in the rapids of Niagara, is sure to go over the cataract. The abettors of Slavery were smitten with judicial blindness. In attempting to make the Bible an apologist of their accursed system, they blasphemed the Holy Author of the Bible, and perpetrated the sin for which the All-Merciful has no forgiveness. Thenceforth, every ministry of Grace forsook them. They had crossed the line which separates trial from doom — had left the region in which their redemption was possible, and madly entered the dread realm over which wrath and judgment alone preside. Return was barred to them forever. There was no longer any place for moral appliances. Reason, and Conscience, and Remonstrance, and Persuasion were recalled from the field; and Nemesis became the sole actor. To its red hands the work was committed. Yet we knew it not. We still thought that Light and Love might prevail in the struggle, and continued to marshal their superseded forces. But the more we looked for a peaceful issue, the farther it receded into distance. The more we trusted that the clouds would break away, and the glad sun of Freedom shine out, the louder the thunder muttered, and the blacker grew the gathering tempest.

> "We prayed and hoped; but still with awe
> The coming of the sword we saw;
> We heard the nearing steps of doom,
> And saw the shade of things to come."

And now the hurricane is upon us. He, who employs even the wild passions of the reprobate as instruments of His benign decrees, has permitted the Southern oligarchs to rush into treason and rebellion, for the purpose of destroying the Union, and rendering the empire of slavery permanent and supreme. He has thus made their own madness the occasion and the means of their overthrow. In the mighty battle which we are compelled to wage in defence of the nation's integrity and the nation's life, we are but the ministers of His vengeance. He appoints our task, and His hand beckons us onward to the utter annihilation of the fell iniquity that has defied His laws.

True it is, that in this fearful conflict we ourselves suffer, as well as the doomed ones against whom we are called to execute the sentence of Heaven. God is chastening us for our participation in the sin which He is visiting with such signal outgoings of His anger. We have shared in the guilt of slavery. We have bowed down before it. We have compromised with it. We have legislated for it. We have given it scope and verge. And it is for this very reason that God has laid on us the work of its destruction. He intends that we shall expiate, with rivers of blood and oceans of treasure, our part in riveting the chains of the bondman. Not otherwise could our political regeneration be accomplished. Through tears and agony lies the nation's way to its new and higher life. The flame must scorch deep, that renovates and purifies.

> " We wait beneath the furnace-blast
> The pangs of transformation;
> Not painlessly doth God recast
> And mould anew the nation.
> Hot burns the fire
> Where wrongs expire;
> Nor spares the hand,
> That from the land
> Uproots the ancient evil.
> What though the cast-out spirit tear
> The nation in his going?
> We who have shared the guilt must share
> The pang of his o'erthrowing!
> Whate'er the loss,
> Whate'er the cross,
> Shall they complain
> Of present pain,
> Who trust in God's hereafter? "

No, no — the furnace will not consume us, seven times heated though it be. It will burn up our league with death, and our covenant with hell. It will burn out from us whatever is mean and false, and burn in all that is great and true. As the glowing oven expels from the porcelain the stains left on it by unclean hands, at the same time that it fixes and deepens the beautiful tints with which the painter has adorned it; so the fiery purgation to which we are subjected will burn away from us the smut of greed and selfishness, and bring out in brighter and more indelible colors the lineaments of justice, love of freedom, and love of country, which the Divine Limner imprinted on the nation at its birth, but which the foul touch of Slavery, and the attrition of material interests, have since well-nigh obliterated. Nothing but our weakness, our sycophancy, our subservience to wrong, will perish. All that is strong, and firm, and noble, and vital in the land, will come forth purer, grander, mightier for the trial. Where the fire is hottest, where the anguish is keenest, there walks by our side the form of Him who has decreed the ordeal, who determines its process and its continuance, and who, when its work is done, will lead us out to the cool waters and halcyon airs of peace and prosperity.

But the guilty cause of all our woe — the poison tree that has borne such deadly fruit — will be destroyed, root and branch. No efforts of its worshippers, no forbearance toward it on our own part, can save or even prolong its abhorred life. Its hour has come. The death-fiat has been spoken; and the only choice left us is, to help kill it, or die with it. The same avenging law, and the same almighty Hand, that wrought a clear path for the great eras of former times, are revealed, in a manner yet more impressive, for the rescue of suffering millions, and the ushering in of the new age which shall bring right and deliverance to all.

> " A redder sea than Egypt's wave
> Is piled and parted for the slave;
> A darker cloud moves on in light,
> A fiercer fire is guide by night."

And in the destruction of slavery will perish the remorseless faction that has so long ruled the land, and is now deluging it with fraternal blood. We mean not that the people of the South will be utterly swept away; that all her sons will be slain in her unholy battle; though myriads will doubtless fall, as myriads have fallen, dying bravely yet ingloriously for the bad cause on which God has set His curse. But the South as once we knew it — the slave-holding South, the arrogant, dominating South, the soul-selling, woman-whipping South, the world-scorning, heaven-daring South — will never live again. Her insolent aristocracy, her fire-eating lords of the plantation, will be gone, rotting in traitors' graves, or wandering landless and beggared, as unpitied in their day of adversity as they were pitiless in their day of power. Let them go. They are the enemies of God and man; and the world will be the better when they are no longer in it. Another race will stand in their places — a race fitted to the new conditions that will arise from the downfall of slavery; and the sunny regions, over which the tempest of civil war now rages, freed from the scourge of bondage, and sheltered once more under the banner of the Union, will become the home of industry and happiness. The old South, impenitent, incorrigible, will be swallowed up by the billows of the bloody sea into which she has cast herself. The new South, transformed by the awful baptism, will emerge to a fresh life and a magnificent destiny.

So conspicuous in our own land and day is the operation of that principle of the Divine government which we have reviewed. Demolition and re-construction are now pre-eminently the work of God "in the midst of the years." "The Breaker has come up." He is hurling down obsolete or corrupt systems of civilization, and building nobler ones on firmer foundations, and with better materials; laying low the mountains, and exalting the valleys, in preparation for the final triumphs of Righteousness and Peace. American Slavery reared its huge bulk, frowning defiance, directly in the track of the advancing chariot of Salvation. Though warned by countless voices from earth and heaven, we refused to take it away, but sought, instead, to make it more impregnable by the bulwarks of compromise, and the buttresses of iniquitous legislation. The season of forbearance and of admonition having passed, the Breaker lifts His hammer, and the dark, towering barrier comes toppling to the ground, dragging its defenders with it, and spreading terror and havoc in its fall. The world reels under the concussion.

Changes and revolutions less startling in their aspects, but not less clear in their meaning, are going forward over the whole face of this apostate globe. Everywhere dissolution and re-adjustment follow the steps of Providence. Everywhere the All-Governor is extirpating ancient abuses; modifying laws, customs, institutions; unbinding fetters, lifting off burdens; and thus inaugurating the era of universal Equality and Justice, as the forerunner of Time's last and greatest era, the era of universal Evangelism. The crowning victories of the Gospel must be won,— the enthroned Mediator must be King over all the earth,— whatever political and social upheavals the glorious consummation may involve. Where the indications of God's will are recognized and obeyed, there the process will be silent and peaceful. But wherever human organizations, whether civil or religious, are blind to His purpose, and fail to mould themselves into harmony with it, there the resistless hammer of the Breaker will descend, crashing through all their defences, and shivering them into fragments. If the nations are in his way, He "will shake the nations, and overturn, overturn, till He shall come whose right it is."

Convulsions will yet rend the Old World as fearful as that which now rocks the New. Opportune reforms and ameliorations may place some of its peoples beyond the line of the Avenger's march. Russia, autocratic as she is, in her sympathy with progress, in the liberation of her thirty millions of serfs, and in the bestowal of equal franchises upon all classes of her population, gives evidence that she comprehends the hour which the clock of history is striking, and is putting herself in a posture to meet its demands. And Austria even, long the very centre and stronghold of Absolutism, manifests a similar movement in the direction of coming events, and similar auguries of immunity from the visit of the Destroyer. But England, Constitutional England, Christian, Protestant England, is mantled with foreshadowings of another hue. Of the same blood, the source from which we drew our nationality, her crimes resemble our own. The Mother is as wicked as the Daughter, and may expect as severe a chastisement. We, while chanting pæans to Liberty, boasting a pure Gospel, and sending out troops of missionaries to preach it to the heathen, doomed the children of our own soil to a servitude more cruel and debasing than the worst form of paganism ever knew. In this guilt she has been our pattern and leader. She first brought slavery here, and entailed the evil upon us. And though in later years she emancipated the slaves of other people in her colonies, she has never emancipated her more than slaves at home. To this day she tramples her toiling masses in the dust, loads them with civil disabilities, and keeps them in a state of ignorance and helplessness that differs in nothing but the name from the lowest vassalage. Her domestic and her foreign record is characterized by oppression, insolence, selfishness, perfidy. She acknowledges no law but interest, no honor but profit, no Bible but the ledger, no creed but wealth, no conscience but fear. A bully and a coward, she insults the weak, and truckles to the strong. What inconsistencies glare out in her protean policy! Her churches christianize barbarians, her merchants sell them idols, her armies slaughter them. Hypocrite of the nations, how piously she lectured us a little while ago on the sinfulness of Slavery! And now, when we are fighting to destroy it, how infamously she ignores her past teachings, aids the slave-power, supplies it with the means of carrying on the war, covers the sea with pirate ships to ravage our commerce, and does all that she dare do to establish the vile Confederacy whose corner-stone is human bondage! With what a sanctimonious air she preaches to us on the magnanimity of mercy to rebels and traitors, while blowing sepoys from the muzzles of her guns in India, and hanging and shooting thousands of unarmed negroes for a trifling riot in Jamaica! In all the broad earth, there exists not a government so false, so treacherous, so shameless in wrong, so dead to the very perception of justice, as the government of England. And shall such a government draw down no bolt from heaven? When our sins are so fearfully punished, shall her greater transgressions go without rebuke? If she take warning from our example, and repent in time, repair the injuries which she has inflicted, cease the aggressions of her greed and her ambition, and lift the iron hand of caste and prescription from her groaning millions, she may escape the wrath which is preparing for her. But unless she does this, and does it soon, then, as surely as a righteous God reigns above, her doom and its lesson will be the most awful which the world has ever seen, or ever will see again.

In the great crisis through which we are passing, and in the yet wider and vaster commotions which the near future is bringing to the nations, there is no reason to tremble for the issue. The cause of Humanity will assuredly triumph in the end. It will triumph with us; and it will triumph wherever its battle is fought. The conflict must be terrific. It may be protracted, fluctuating, and to mortal view long barren of any definite result. The down-treaders of men will summon all their strength to hold them in subjection. The blows of Truth, and the shocks of Providential dealing, may appear to make little impression on the solid front of crystallized Wrong. Decades, centuries, may roll away before the conquest is complete. "The mills of God grind slow;" but they never stop, and their work never fails. Victory will come at last. Every shackle shall be broken. Arbitrary rule, priestly usurpations, despotism in all its manifold shapes, the fetters that bind the limbs, the degradation that imprisons the soul, shall be scattered and annihilated by the breath of the Omnipotent. Free labor, free thought, free speech, free government, shall be the heritage of the human race. In the process of the material creation, when the uproar of primeval Chaos had ceased, the expanse of waters lay still under the wings of the brooding Spirit, and the new-born world, calm and silent, waited the omnific word of the world's Maker, "Let there be light." So, in the moral creation, repose and expectancy will succeed to the turmoil of change and the heavings of struggle. Then, on the hushed and prepared earth the energies of the all-quickening Paraclete will descend, pervading it with life from heaven. Then, over its whole circumference the Gospel will go forth without bar or pause, dispersing its darkness, restoring its beauty, and blessing it with universal holiness and joy. And then the Almighty Designer and Worker, looking back upon the long train of His purposes from their beginning to their fulfilment, will proclaim, IT IS DONE! the march of the Eras is ended; the grand, crowning Epoch, to which all the Past has pointed, and for which all the Past has been, IS CONSUMMATED FOREVER!

CHAPTER IV.

PIOUS MEN THE NATION'S HOPE.

"The holy seed shall be the substance thereof."—*Isaiah* vi. 13.

IN the preceding part of this chapter the solemn decree is announced, that the Jewish people, in consequence of their flagrant and persevering rebellion, were to be abandoned to national obduracy. And when the prophet inquired of the Lord, how long this general impenitence and disregard of the Divine threatenings would continue, he received the startling answer, "Until the cities be wasted without inhabitant, and the houses without man, and the land be utterly desolate"— national corruption thus bringing forth its legitimate fruit, national calamity. But across these portentous clouds of degeneracy and ruin there shone one beam of hope — lone and solitary, it is true, amid the encompassing gloom, yet clear, full, and bright with the promise of returning prosperity. It is found in the expressive and cheering words with which the prediction closes. "As a teil tree, and as an oak, whose substance is in them when they cast their leaves, so the holy seed shall be the substance thereof." Or, to adopt a more correct and lucid version, "As the linden, or the terebinth, though cut down, hath its stock remaining in the earth; so the holy seed shall be the stock of the nation." The figure here employed is one of great force as well as poetic beauty. In it the Hebrew people, scourged by their own wickedness, and brought almost to extinction by the righteous judgments of Heaven, are represented by a tree, stripped of its proud foliage, its spreading branches rent away, and even its lofty shaft levelled by the avenging axe. Still the living root remains, and, endowed by nature with the power of reproduction, will start up, under genial suns and showers, into its former glory. Thus the Jewish nation, though wasted and prostrate, and apparently given over to hopeless decay, should have in it "the substance," the undying germ of subsequent renewal, and of restoration to the Divine favor. And this indestructible element, so fraught with the principle of future life and vigor, was to be found in "the holy seed" connected with it. By "the holy seed" we are unquestionably to understand pious men — men who, amidst the prevailing apostasy, feared God, and were faithful to His laws. We are, therefore, taught that on this class alone all the hopes of Israel rested. By them, and for their sake, the utter ruin of the nation was to be prevented. From Jehovah's kindness to them its renovation would proceed. In the period of overflowing wrath, they were to be the sure depositaries of its interests. And through them, when the storm had passed by, were to spring forth recovered strength and happiness.

It is not, however, with the bearing of this prophecy on the particular instance before us, that I would now occupy your attention. In addition to this, it inculcates a grand moral lesson, fitted to all seasons and countries, and which no lapse of time can render obsolete. The government which God exercises over the world is regulated by immutable laws. The forms of its manifestation may vary. It may appear in sterner or in milder aspects. The springs and wheels which guide its movements may be now disclosed, and now hidden; and one part after another of its vast circle may come into view, and be withdrawn. But its nature and its great controlling principles are ever unchanged; and God acts toward the nations of the present day on precisely the same general rules as those which marked His dealings with the chosen Tribes three thousand years ago. We may, therefore, announce, as the teaching of our text, the broad and comprehensive truth, that PIOUS MEN — evangelical Christians — are the most efficient preservers and restorers of national prosperity.

To illustrate this principle, and to exhibit some of the obligations which grow out of it, will be my present endeavor.

Pious men are the best conservators of national welfare, because for them is exerted that upholding Providence, without which nations as well as individuals cannot exist.

In nothing, perhaps, is the spirit of practical infidelity more manifest, than in the views which are generally entertained respecting the connection of God with human governments. By many the very idea of any such connection, involving as it does the fact of His immediate control over them, and consequently of their public and absolute accountability to Him, is derided as the offspring of fanaticism or of folly. Multitudes, who acknowledge the existence of a great First Cause, — the Maker and Upholder of the universe, — virtually repudiate the truth that He superintends the affairs of nations, setting up one and putting down another, and dispensing to all their appointed destinies. Even those who admit the personal responsibility under which He has placed them, and recognize His law as the rule by which they are now to live, and by which they are hereafter to be judged, seem, in numerous instances, to forget that He exercises the same sovereign authority over man in his collective capacity, as in his individual condition and character.

If we would know the extent to which this denial of God as the Supreme Ruler actually prevails, we have but to cast our eyes over Christendom, to perceive everywhere the proofs of its mournful and guilty predominance. On the lands so denominated has shone the light of a dispensation that is full of God, and which sets Him forth as the omniscient Inspector and Judge of human conduct. In the hands of their population is found that inspired Volume, in which the Almighty has declared His will, and asserted His sovereignty; and by many of them Christianity, in a form more or less corrupt, is vauntingly proclaimed as the religion of the State. But where shall we look for the evidence that its power is felt and its precepts obeyed? Where is the government that is either founded or administered on principles strictly Christian? Of what nation can we pronounce, that in its structure, its institutions, its legislation, its internal polity, its foreign relations, in a word, its whole official character, it recognizes God as its Author and Defender, and bows with holy fear to His supremacy? There is not, properly speaking, a Christian government on earth. Whatever the profession they make, or the name they bear, they are all deeply pervaded by an impious disregard of the Divine authority and superintendence. The whole world has revolted from its rightful King; and nations, no less than individuals, have conspired to "break His bands asunder, and cast His cords from them."

And yet Revelation most clearly teaches that Jehovah is the absolute Disposer of national welfare, and the immediate Arbiter of national conduct. "The Most High ruleth in the kingdoms of men." "He is Governor among the nations." "He doeth according to His will in the army of heaven, and among the inhabitants of the earth, and none can stay His hand, or say unto Him, What doest Thou?" His supervision extends to the whole human family, alike in its separate members, and in its aggregate bodies. "He hath determined their times, and the bounds of their habitation." Whatever of civil freedom, of social advantage, of public security and happiness they enjoy, is all bestowed and continued by Him. And when disaster and ruin overtake them, it is His hand scourging them for their sins, and vindicating His insulted majesty. "When He giveth quietness, who then can make trouble? And when He hideth His face, who then can behold Him, whether it be done against a nation, or a man only?"

Now it is a great and solemn fact, that this government of God over the world is carried on solely in behalf of His redeemed Church. From the birth of time to the present hour, His Providence has been the auxiliary of His Grace. All its dispensations, whether of mercy or of judgment, have been conducted in subordination to that purpose of everlasting Love, according to which He is gathering His chosen ones from every kindred and tongue and people. For this the world was made. For this it is upheld. For this nations rise and flourish. For this they fall and give place to others. For this the sun shines on the good and on the evil; and the rain scatters its sparkling wealth on the fields of the thankful and the unthankful. For this all bounteous Nature unlocks her treasures, and pours from her teeming lap supplies for every living thing. The whole sphere in which we live is a vast spiritual laboratory, where Redemption is working out its high and glorious designs.

To give scope for the conversion, training, and religious development of those whom Christ has purchased with His blood, the civil compacts of men were ordained. With this view, their existence is prolonged; and, for the same reason, when they no longer answer the end of their appointment, they are removed and superseded. What can be more evident, from the light of all history, both sacred and profane, than that God establishes, preserves, and overthrows nations from a regard to His people and His cause? Had Sodom contained but ten righteous men, its fearful and ever memorable doom would have been averted. And even though its impiety was almost universal, the bolt of Divine vengeance could not descend, until the solitary man whose arms of faith and prayer held it back, had been removed from the devoted population. To provide a home for His Elect, and to furnish room for the operations of His mercy, He led the descendants of Abraham into Canaan, founded their Commonwealth, and sustained it amidst multiplied provocations, until these purposes were achieved. Often did their apostasy call forth His displeasure. Yet, on account of the "few faithful found among the faithless," He forbore utterly to extirpate them, but commissioned His servant to declare, "Thus saith the Lord, As the new wine is found in the cluster, and one saith, Destroy it not, for a blessing is in it; so will I do for my servants' sake, that I may not destroy them all."

But when, on the other hand, nations have wholly rejected His truth, or their connection with the objects of His grace has ceased, how rapidly have they passed away! No sooner had Judea completed the measure of her guilt by crucifying the Redeemer, and casting out His followers, than the day of her destruction came. When the region where flourished the Seven Churches of Asia — once the most populous and cultivated spot on the globe — torudd preach the Gospel of life into senseless forms and deadly errors, how speedily did all its prosperity depart, and leave it a silent waste. And Rome, the crowned empress of the world, glorying in the vain epithet of "Eternal," by exchanging Christianity for a baptized paganism, lost the palladium of her greatness, and fell from her glittering height into the mire of superstition and slavery.

There cannot, in short, be a question that God spares and blesses guilty nations wholly in reference to the piety that yet lingers in them, or the fulfilment of some design of mercy with respect to them which the future is to evolve. Who can doubt that if all the sincere followers of Christ were to be removed from a land, and the counsels of redemption required that no more of its inhabitants should be brought to the enjoyment of His salvation, that land would at once be destroyed? Or who, with the teachings of Inspiration before him, can doubt that when the last of those whom the Father hath given to the Son shall have been renewed and sanctified for heaven, the fires of the Judgment will blaze forth, and earth itself pass away?

It is, then, most evident that God administers His providence over communities and over individuals entirely for the sake of His people. They alone are in covenant with Him. They alone are the objects of His special favor and protection. If others share His overflowing munificence, it is because, in the present state of human affairs, His bounty cannot reach its chosen subjects without being in a greater or less degree diffused over all; and because the salvation of the redeemed requires that the framework of society should be preserved.

Viewed in this aspect, how important is the relation which pious men sustain to the land in which they dwell! They are, indeed, "the salt of the earth," not only as they pervade it with an element of moral health and purity, and thus preserve it from utter corruption, but also as they avert from it that storm of Divine wrath which would otherwise overwhelm it. The pointed rod that turns away the lightning is not more essential to the protection of our dwellings, than are Christian men to the safety of nations. And if this be so; if "the holy seed," through its union with God, thus becomes the guardian of civil communities, may it not well be called "the substance thereof"?

Pious men are the saviours of a land, because to them is intrusted the only remedy against national demoralization and ruin.

Philosophers and statesmen have speculated much on the means by which the social welfare of a people may best be secured. Some have relied on the force of armies, on the skill and prowess of commanders, on the wisdom of legislators, on the nice balance of constitutional powers, and on the harmonious adjustment of the various interests of society. Others, with better reason, have built their hopes on learning and culture, and on the spread of general education. But all these expedients, however valuable in themselves, and however necessary as subordinate agents, are wholly insufficient, when operating alone, to achieve the end in view. Many of the nations of antiquity, whose towering greatness overshadowed the world, and the crash of whose fall will echo to the latest time, were eminent for military talent, for political sagacity, for well-ordered governmental institutions, for wide intelligence, and for a high state of social refinement. But how strikingly has their history demonstrated the inadequacy of all such barriers! Their vices destroyed them. Over all the splendor of their civilization public and private corruption shed its withering power — eat through the bulwarks of their strength — sapped the foundations of their glory, and laid the whole fabric in the dust.

National virtue is the only national safeguard. The land in which this lives and reigns cannot be subdued. No matter with what fury the storm of invasion or the deluge of conquest may rage around it. They cannot overthrow it. The pillars of its defence will stand unshaken amid the shock of thrones and the convulsion of empires. Virtue is omnipotent. It inspires every bosom in which it dwells with the courage of a martyr, and the might of a host. It is insuperable — invulnerable — resistless. Treason cannot betray, nor ambition enslave it. It is that invincible, inextinguishable enemy, against which tyrants league in vain, and from which the pride of the oppressor recoils broken and vanquished.

But the virtue, so indispensable to national welfare, can be produced and maintained only by the influence of a pure Christianity. In lands where the Gospel is unknown, or where it has been shorn of its life-giving truths, and degraded into the mere handmaid of ignorance and priestcraft, there is no such thing as public morality. Individuals may occasionally be found rising above the common level in uprightness of character; but the masses of the population are in all cases sunk in debasing vices, imbruted by superstition, or frenzied with unbelief. In such communities there is no healthful principle in exercise, that can resist degeneracy, or act as a barrier against the encroachments of lawlessness on the one hand, and of despotism on the other. It is from this cause that France and Germany, after shaking off their old tyrannies, astonished the world by riveting anew the chains which they had broken. Their people, emasculated by profligacy, blinded by falsehood, insane with infidelity, were unfitted for freedom, and were therefore powerless to retain it. And never will any country long continue to be either free or prosperous, where the Gospel in its purity does not so thoroughly pervade all classes, as to become the governing law of public and private life.

Now, it is to true Christians alone that we can look for the diffusion of this vital element of social virtue and happiness. Our Lord committed the spread of His Gospel to His Apostles, and, through them, to the whole body of His followers in every subsequent age. This is the chief purpose for which the Church of Christ exists in the world. It was intended by its Divine Founder to be the grand Receptacle and distributing Centre of all holy agencies on earth — a moral light-house, throwing the rays of Truth far out over the dark and restless sea of human ungodliness — a mighty reservoir, receiving the water of Life from its Fountain-Head above, and dispensing it, by numberless channels, through the broad wastes of our sin-blasted globe. From age to age, under all forms of civilization, in all stages of intellectual development, in all epochs, all lands, this has constituted the one instrumentality by which God has been lifting our fallen race from the abyss of its degradation and misery. The ministers whom He appoints, and the people whom He sanctifies by His grace, are required, everywhere and at all times, so to teach to others, and so to illustrate in their own lives, the Word of Salvation which they have received, that the corrupt multitudes around them may be penetrated and transformed by its energy. This is their godlike work — a work in which none but they are fitted to engage. They only who have themselves felt the renovating power of the Gospel, are prepared to diffuse that Gospel among their fellow-men. They alone understand the Gospel. They alone love the Gospel. They alone know the real value of its blessings. They alone comprehend its momentous bearings on the interests of time, and on the destinies of eternity. And, therefore, they alone can be expected to enter with heart and soul into the labor of extending it. If, then, the Gospel, in its living influence, is indispensable to the weal of nations; and if God has committed the embodiment and dissemination of that Gospel to His regenerate Church — is it not evident that the Christian men of a land are "the substance thereof"?

Such men are the hope and strength of a country, inasmuch as they only are qualified to put forth in its behalf the power of prayer.

That there resides a wondrous efficacy in prayer, none can question who accord any credence to the declarations of Scripture, or regard the experience of the children of God in all periods of time as anything better than a conceit of enthusiasm, or a dream of delusion. In the economy of Grace, under which our Divine Sovereign has placed all terrestrial affairs, it is His ordinance, that every outflow of His beneficence and of His mercy should descend to men in answer to humble and earnest supplication, offered up through His Son, whom He has appointed to be their Mediator and Advocate. And this arrangement includes not merely spiritual blessings, but temporal; not merely the bestowal of benefits on individuals, but on communities, and on the world. "The effectual, fervent prayer of a righteous man availeth much." That it so avails with respect to public as well as private events; with respect to providential occurrences affecting the interests of this life, as well as with respect to those mysterious operations of the Spirit reaching forward into the life to come, is manifest from the example which the Apostle immediately cites in proof of his statement. He refers, for this purpose, to the fearful drought which desolated the territories of Israel, in response to the prayer of Elijah; and to the fact, that when the prophet prayed that the judgment might cease, "the heavens gave rain, and the earth yielded her fruit." In short, the whole teaching of the Bible, alike in its narratives and in its doctrinal announcements, proclaims prayer to be the chief means by which good is obtained, and evil averted.

But this instrument, so benign and so potent in its effects, the sincere friends of the Redeemer are alone competent to use. It is the prayer of the *righteous* man only — the prayer of the man justified by atoning blood, and sanctified in heart and life by the Holy Spirit — that is effectual. All real prayer is prayer in the name of Christ, — prayer presented in reliance on the merits of Christ, — and necessarily involves a cordial recognition of His office and His claims. Hence none can pray acceptably but those who believe in Christ, and embrace Him as the Saviour of their souls.

In the spiritual telegraph which prayer has established between earth and heaven, at man's end of the line Christians are the only operators. They alone know the mystery of its mechanism, the way in which it is worked, and the laws that govern its results. And their despatches alone will be regarded by the Great Superintendent, at God's end of the line. Upward along the celestial wires they send the plea of the sinful for pardon, of the wretched for comfort, of the wronged for redress, of suffering lands for deliverance. And when the answer comes back, though it is always *through* them, it is not always *for* them, but often for others — glad tidings addressed to millions; a word of power and of salvation for imperilled nations.

The evaporation from the earth's surface, which is returned to it in fertilizing rain, rises from places and from substances containing water. Little or nothing is given to it by the trodden and dusty highway, the barren mountain, or the broad reaches of the stony desert. It is drawn up, by the attractive forces of the atmosphere, from fruitful fields and gardens, from the foliage of the forests, from the springs that gush from the hill-sides, from the brooks that flash and sparkle in the glens, from the streams that enrich the valleys, from the oceans that carry health and plenty round the globe. Much of it is polluted. Some has been exhaled from stagnant pools, some from fetid morasses, some from loathsome sewers. But all goes into the air, and is there filtered and purified. The salt becomes fresh, the foul sweet, the turbid clear. And then the shower falls, — yet not alone on the spots whence its treasures came, but everywhere, — rushing and pouring in its fulness over the land and over the sea, on the thirsty plain and on the swelling river, on the low shrub and on the lofty pine, on the grain-clothed meadow and on the naked rock, on the hovel and on the palace, on the green lanes of the hamlet, and on the paved streets of the crowded city. How the earth rejoices! How the young leaves glisten! How the corn sings! How the valleys smile! How the hill-tops shout! How all nature laughs in its gladness!

So does the Spirit of grace and of supplication draw up prayer from the hearts of God's children — from hearts wet with the tears of penitence, and washed in the blood of Propitiation. Imperfect, indeed, that prayer is, and ever must be. The fountains from which it ascends are yet strongly imbued with remaining earthliness, often sullied by sensual passion, often roiled by the feet of worldly care. Still, however unworthy, it is borne aloft by its Divine Attractor into the presence of Infinite Holiness. There, cast into the alembic of Christ's Intercession, — its defilement taken away, its faith and sincerity accepted, — it is distilled into blessed rain — rain freighted with every mercy which man can need now and forever — rain descending not merely on the offerers of prayer, but on the undevout and godless; bringing grace to the sinner, freedom to the slave, respite to doomed nations; and travelling in its mighty sweep from continent to continent, till it has emptied its stores over all the world. If such be the power of prayer, such its place in the moral government of God, and such the relation which Christians sustain to it, who can hesitate to admit that praying men are the defence, the security, the very life of the land in which they dwell?

From this view of the connection of religious men with the public weal, we proceed to notice briefly the duties which that connection imposes.

They ought to manifest a lively solicitude for the welfare of their country. A Christian should be, in the most emphatic sense, a patriot. He should not feel that the Gospel, while relating chiefly to a future world, has nothing to do with this. He should not persuade himself that his religious profession requires him to stand aloof from the great social and political movements of his day. Still less should he imagine, as many seem to do, that when he goes forth to exercise his influence on these movements, he may leave his religion at home. His relations alike to God and to his fellow-men pre-eminently demand that he should take part in all those momentous public questions which concern the glory of the one, and the improvement of the other; engaging in the promotion of freedom, order, and righteousness; and doing what he can in his sphere to make his land wiser and happier. This is at all times sacredly binding on him, even in periods of national peace and prosperity. But the obligation becomes vastly more imperative when his country is encompassed with dangers; when adversity overtakes it, and the storm of invasion or of civil war threatens to sweep all its cherished institutions into one common ruin. Then it is that the Christian, beyond all other men, should meet the crisis with the noble courage of faith, and the utmost devotion of patriotism.

With what peculiar urgency does this duty press upon ourselves at the present hour! The government under which we live; the government founded in the wisdom and cemented by the blood of our fathers; the government which has been the shield of our civil and religious rights, and the source of our national greatness — this government, the freest and the best that ever blessed the world, is assailed by a rebellion as unprovoked as it is impious. A fierce and fanatical oligarchy, reckless with ambition, and madly resolved to rule or perish, is attempting to overthrow our glorious Republic, and erect in its place that vilest of all tyrannies, a slave-despotism. The tempest is upon us. The great deeps are broken up. The earthquake is let loose in all its fury. We look, and lo! the tall column of the Union, the bulwark of our strength, — the Pharos of the world, — is rent in twain by the thunder gust. Still the heavens grow blacker, and the conflict thicker and more deadly. Huge armies confront each other. Mighty battles heap the ground with their countless slain. The glories of the past, the hopes of the future, the very life of the nation, all hang trembling in the balance.

And while we are thus struggling in the death-grapple, our perils are intensified by the hostile attitude of European Powers, from whom we have a right to expect, if not aid, at least fairness and sympathy. France looks sternly and menacingly at us. England sneers and blusters. England — from whose blood we sprung, forgetting her own course in similar emergencies; ignoring her past words and deeds in condemnation of slavery — claps her hands, and hounds on the slave-power while its fangs are at our throats; assumes that the Republic is destroyed, and exults in the assumption; accords to rebels and traitors belligerent rights; gives them help and comfort in their work of riveting forever the chains of the bondman; furnishes them with military supplies and munitions of war; and builds for them a pirate navy, and mans it with pirate crews, to plunder our commerce and burn our ships on the high seas. O Hypocrite of the world! meanest, falsest of nations! Seest thou not that thy own day is coming? As surely as there is compensation with God for outrageous wickedness, so surely shall thy cup be the bitterest that kingdom ever drank. And when the dread reckoning arrives; when the measure of thy crimes is full; when thy daughters shall leave thee and strip thee bare; when ravaged India shall once more shake off thy yoke; when the myriads of China shall rise to punish thy greed and thy fraud; when Ireland's wrongs shall come up for judgment; when the volcano of thy crushed and starving masses shall burst forth, toppling over thy hoary

Establishments, and scattering like chaff King and Parliament, priest and aristocrat; and all the peoples whom thy insolence has wounded, and thy avarice overreached, and thy selfishness betrayed, shall gather as eagles to thy fall, and revel round thy dishonored corpse — then will avenging Heaven pay thee back for thy perfidy to us in this hour of our agony.

What, then, is the position demanded of religious men and of religious bodies at a moment so awful? Is it one of neutrality, inaction, silence? There are some who appear to think so. At a Convention lately held in New York, representing one of the most influential denominations among us, — a denomination claiming to be exclusively "*the* church," — a large portion of the delegates refused to utter one word of cheer for the Government, or one word of rebuke against treason, and even opposed the adoption of a prayer for the suppression of the Rebellion, on the ground that it would be leaving the service of God to serve Cæsar! Are such Christians "the stock of the nation?" Is this the way in which "the sacramental host" is to fulfil its mission in a juncture so terrible, and so big with stupendous issues? Oh, no, no! The cause of our country and the cause of religion, the cause of humanity, the cause of eternal Right and Justice, are so intimately blended in this crisis, that you cannot separate them. The triumph of the Government will be the triumph of order, the triumph of civilization, the triumph of freedom, the triumph of a pure Gospel. The triumph of the Rebellion will be the triumph of anarchy, barbarism, slavery, and of a Christianity so debased by slavery as no longer to deserve the name. If, therefore, you would meet your obligations as religious men, stand by the Union, stand by the Government, stand by the old banner, stand by the grand destiny which God has written all over our land, in the circling of the oceans, the course of the rivers, the trend of the mountains, — One Country, One People, One Government, One Flag, from the St. Lawrence to the Rio Grande, from the rocky headlands of Maine to the golden shores of the Pacific. To save the nation from dismemberment, give labor, give property, give your sons, your brothers, yourselves. For this live; for this, if need be, die.

As Christian men, we ought to bow in deep repentance for the nation's sins, and humbly implore the Father of mercies to remove the chastisement which they have drawn down upon the land. The calamities that now afflict us must be viewed by every thoughtful mind as an expression of God's abhorrence of the iniquities with which our history is stained. In these iniquities the people of the North are implicated as really if not as deeply as the people of the South. I do not mean that with respect to the slave-holding States themselves we of the North are guilty of any wrong which can justify or excuse their foul conspiracy against all that we deem precious and sacred. But while we have done nothing to deserve punishment at *their* hands, we have done much to deserve it at *God's* hand. Against Him, not against them, our offences have been committed.

It was said of Israel in the time of the Judges, "They chose new gods; then was war in the gates." Here has been the great crime of this country. We have denied to Jehovah His rightful place as the Supreme Governor, and substituted for His high, unchangeable law, the low maxims of the politician, and the varying dictates of expediency. We have chosen new gods. Mammon, "the least erected spirit that fell," has been proclaimed, by almost universal acclamation, god of the North. We have, indeed, sought to hide his more disgusting features, and to render his worship respectable, by clothing him in borrowed garments, and giving to him fictitious titles. We have applied to him the better-sounding names of "Business, Enterprise, Industrial Development, Material Prosperity." But, under all disguises and all designations, he is the same old shuffling, cringing, grovelling Demon still. On his altars we have laid our manliness and our self-respect; our principles and our consistency; the national character and the national conscience; the claims of the helpless, and the mandates of Heaven. Nothing has seemed to us too valuable or too sacred to be relinquished in his service. At his bidding, we have been ready to surrender justice and mercy; to submit to any degradation, and to plunge into any slough of meanness or wickedness, whence we might extract the glittering incense in which he delights. And while the North has been thus engrossed in its idolatry of Mammon, the South has paid its homage to Moloch —

> "Moloch, the strongest and the fiercest spirit
> That fought in heaven, now fiercer by despair.
> His trust was with the Eternal to be deemed
> Equal in strength, and rather than be less,
> Cared not to be at all. With that care lost,
> Went all his fear. Of God, or hell, or worse,
> He recked not."

In modern demonology, the name of this fiend is Slavery. His temple is built on robbery. His religion is the chattelizing of beings made in the image of God. His insignia are whips and chains; his ministers, cruelty, licentiousness, and murder. Such is the deity of the Southern oligarchs — the deity to whom they have sworn eternal allegiance; in whose interest they have inaugurated rebellion; and with the symbols of whose horrid worship their whole Confederacy is inscribed from corner-stone to pinnacle.

Now we may be sure that He who is King over all will not permit His authority to be thus usurped, without manifesting His displeasure; and, therefore, it is not presumption to affirm that the civil war, which now rages in all our borders, is Heaven's judgment, alike upon the money-worship of the North, and the slavery-worship of the South. God grant that both may be utterly consumed in the fire which His wrath has kindled!

With what emphasis, then, do these solemn circumstances invoke the pious to penitence and humiliation! We are all connected, directly or indirectly, with the sins which have provoked the Almighty. We have committed them, or we have countenanced them, or we have failed to rebuke them. So that each one is personally guilty, and has cause to humble himself before God. But there is more than this. The repentance of a nation is always the repentance of that part of its population by whom the motives and claims of religion are acknowledged and felt. And if this nation shall repent and be pardoned, it will be, not its ungodly many, but its godly few, who will repent, and for the sake of whose repentance the pardon will be bestowed. If all who fear God, in every city, and town, and rural neighborhood, were to prostrate themselves in lowly contrition at the footstool of Mercy, confessing the nation's guilt, supplicating the nation's deliverance, can any one doubt that the plea would be heard, and the nation saved? Has not God said, "If my people, which are called by my name, shall humble themselves, and seek my face, and pray, and turn from their wicked ways, then will I hear from heaven, and forgive their sins, and heal their land"? Do we believe this? Then why do we not act upon it? Why is there such worldliness in our churches, such languor in our places of prayer? Why are our sanctuaries almost deserted, and the fire on their altars left to burn dim and low? While we are so alive to the war, so eager for progress, so impatient of delay, why is it that so few turn to Him from whom alone success can come? With all that we hold dear at stake, why does not one universal burst of petition go up to that Almighty Power on whose decision the issue depends? Surely, among the many strange aspects of this strange time, there is nothing stranger, nothing sadder, than the spiritual apathy, the death-like slumber, that has fallen on the great body of believers, and stilled, as by an enchanter's wand, the stirrings of anxiety and the wrestlings of faith. An angry God is visiting us for our transgressions. Our very existence as a people is in jeopardy. Yet we laugh and are gay. There are no ashes on our heads, there is no sackcloth on our loins, no agony in our souls. The tree of our national greatness, like that seen in vision by the proud king of Babylon, stands in the midst of the earth, the height thereof reaching to heaven, and the sight thereof to the ends of the world. Its leaves are fair, and its fruit much, and in it is meat for all; the beasts of the field have shadow under it, and the fowls of heaven dwell in its boughs. But, ah! a serpent has coiled its deadly folds round it, strangling trunk and limbs, and blighting fruit and foliage with its venom. And, lo! a Watcher and a Holy One — Divine Omniscience watching our sins, Divine Holiness preparing to punish them — has come down from heaven, and cries, "Hew down the tree, and cut off his branches; shake off his leaves, and scatter his fruit; let the beasts get away from under it, and the fowls from his branches." Oh, men of God, awake! Kill the serpent, and grind it to powder; and beseech the Watcher and the Holy One to spare the tree, and make it in the future, as it has been in the past, the home of the free, the shelter of the oppressed, the hope and joy of the whole earth.

Finally; the great emergencies of the hour call upon Christians to cultivate an unwavering attachment to the doctrines and institutions of the Gospel. There is, throughout our country, a wide-spread unbelief, a growing dislike of evangelical truth, and neglect of its ministrations. Infidelity, profanity, and contempt for the house of God, are everywhere increasing. And while this abounding irreligion has had no inconsiderable share in creating the civil convulsion that now desolates the land, it has at the same time been vastly augmented in extent and boldness by the very evil it has helped to occasion. In the domestic, social, and moral dislocations inseparable from a state of war, men are breaking loose from the restraints of the Bible and the ·Sanctuary; and, casting off the principles which their fathers revered, are afloat on the tossing sea of error, with no compass but their passions, and no chart but the opinions of others as corrupt as themselves. The inroads which the war has made on the sanctity of the Sabbath, and the disregard of public worship which it has fostered, have broken down the embankments against vice, and caused the swelling waves of ungodliness to rush in upon us with unusual violence. At such a crisis, we are specially summoned to stand fast by the truth and the altar of God. This is no time for indifference and feebleness; no time to give to religion diminished support; no time to forsake the Ark of the Testimony, and shut up the Tabernacle; no time for silent pulpits and vacant sanctuaries.

These days of rebuke and disaster admonish the whole Church of Christ to rise to one united and earnest endeavor to bring the Gospel into living contact with all classes of society. Nothing but this can adequately meet the exigencies in which we stand. It is a departure from the Gospel which has brought upon us the indignation of the Almighty; and we can contribute most directly to its removal by enthroning the Gospel in our own hearts, and doing all in our power to enthrone it in the hearts of others. If the Christians of this land would but put forth the moral energies with which the grace of the Saviour has clothed them, the tide of disorder and anarchy that now threatens to overwhelm us would soon be rolled back, and the day of our regeneration come. The combined efforts of God's children, rendered effectual by His Spirit, would speedily evangelize and renovate every section of the Republic, till from our cities and villages, from our mountains and valleys, from our lakes, and rivers, and broad western plains, should ascend in universal chorus the song of praise to the Crucified One. Then would slavery, and rebellion, and political intrigue, and intestine strife, vanish like the fogs of night before the splendors of the morning. We should have no fear for the country nor for the Church in the present struggle, or in any other through which the providence of God may hereafter call them to pass. Upheavings and revolutions, emanating from Wrong, are but as torrents that rush from the hills after a summer storm — terrible, it may be, in their outbreak, yet soon dwindling away and disappearing. But great moral movements, founded on everlasting Truth and Right, can never die. Their going forth is like the sweep of mighty rivers to the sea. Small and unnoticed they may indeed be in their beginning. But, fed from innumerable springs deep down in the world's heart, they gather volume as they advance. Onward, still onward they flow, from generation to generation — never receding, never growing less — now gliding gently along through smiling meadows — now foaming over rocks — now thundering down cataracts — widened by affluents from all lands, and swelled by the tribute of all the ages, — till their collected waters expand at last into an ocean of PEACE, RIGHTEOUSNESS, and LOVE.

CHAPTER V.

THE MOVING PILLAR.

"AND THE LORD WENT BEFORE THEM BY DAY IN A PILLAR OF CLOUD, TO LEAD THEM THE WAY; AND BY NIGHT IN A PILLAR OF FIRE, TO GIVE THEM LIGHT; TO GO BY DAY AND NIGHT." — *Exodus* xiii. 21.

THE children of Israel, in their passage from the Land of Bondage to the Land of Promise, were preceded at every stage of their wayfaring by a moving Pillar — a Pillar of Cloud by day and of fire by night — that directed their course, and served at once as their guide and their defence. By its signals their whole march was ordered. When the Pillar advanced, they went forward; when it stood still, they encamped. And however long it continued at any time to hover over the Tabernacle, whether it were for a day, a month, or a year, they abode in their tents, and journeyed not, till the journeying Pillar again beckoned them on. Often its movements seemed to them intricate and involved; often divergent; often retrograde rather than progressive. But there was in it, as in Ezekiel's wheels, a Living

Spirit, governing with unerring intelligence alike its stoppings and its goings, and bringing it, and the favored host which it led, by the right way to the right destination.

They must have been dull indeed not to have regarded such a manifestation as a high honor, and an inviolable security. It was to them the visible Symbol of the Divine Presence. They knew that in it the Lord went before them as their Captain and Upholder. So long as they could see the Pillar, they had ocular testimony that He was in their midst, to superintend their way, supply their wants, and subdue their enemies. How safely might they follow wherever it conducted them, whether through the depths of the parted sea, or under the quaking brow of Sinai, or across the wide, dreary stretches of the burning desert! With what confidence might they trust it, in all its delays and turnings, assured that under its leading they could not go wrong! And how endeared must it have become to them during their long and devious pilgrimage! What precious memories of deliverance in the past, what hopes of blessing in the future, must they have learned to associate with it! Never was sight of pole-star or sun so grateful to the storm-tossed mariner, as the sight of that ever present Pillar to those ancient wanderers in "the great and terrible wilderness."

In our own circumstances, how natural is the wish for a similar token of Divine care and direction! Encompassed by difficulties and perils; walking through private trials and through public commotions; often in doubt where lies our way; often desponding as to the issue of current events on the destinies of the Church and the world, — how frequently are we tempted to desire that some God-infolding Pillar might move before us, and solve our perplexities!

We have such a Pillar — unseen, it is true, by the outward eye, but distinct and palpable to the vision illuminated from above. Throughout the whole progress of terrestrial affairs, — in every crisis of the Redeemer's kingdom, in every step of our individual experience, — the Pillar of God's Providence is the presiding Presence, arranging all, overruling all. Hence the startling changes that are passing around us, and the yet more startling ones which loom in the near future, are not to be ascribed to chance, nor to the independent action of human intellect and passion. Chance can have no place in a universe over which Infinite Wisdom presides. And human intellect and passion are but instruments in the hands of Him who sways the hearts of all men as He pleases. In every unfolding of the world's history Divine Providence is the controlling power, — a Providence which embraces the entire circle of sublunary events, and subjects them, however apparently adverse, to one vast comprehensive plan, by which Jehovah is conducting onward to their completion the sovereign purposes of His Grace.

Under the economy of the Gospel, Providence has been subordinated to Christ, and is now wielded by Him for the promotion of His cause. He has thus been the Leader and Guardian of His people in all periods, and through all the vicissitudes of their pilgrimage. As the Pillar of Cloud and of Fire went before the Chosen Tribes, and marked out their wanderings in the wilderness; so has the Providence of God marked the changeful track of the Church across the desert of the centuries. That Providence goes before us now, pointing out our way, and protecting us in it. The striking occurrences of the pregnant hour in which we live, are to the eye of faith only so many movings to and fro of the cloudy Pillar, showing the course of our march, and the direction of our efforts. To our imperfect vision these movings may appear to be at one time backward; at another, sideways; at another, whirled into aimless gyrations by the winds of strife or the storms of revolution. But Omniscience guides them still; and no force of unforeseen contingencies, no gale of popular excitement, no hurricane of political tumult, no roaring blast from the mouth of Hell, can carry the Pillar where Omniscience does not intend it to go, and where its going will not subserve some high and beneficent design.

How much of courage and of comfort may we draw from this truth, amid the civil agitations that now convulse our country! A fearful tempest is upon us. The great deeps are broken up. The earthquake and the tornado are let loose in all their fury. We look, and lo! the tall column of the Federal Union, reared by the sweat and blood of heroes, — the bulwark of our greatness, the Pharos of the world, — is struck by the thunder-gust, and rent in twain; its Southern half toppling away into scattered fragments. Around the mighty ruin, and in the deepening gloom that gathers over it, the fierce elements career and rage; while, mingling with them, black fiends of Discord flap their sooty wings, and yell forth their demon cries, — "Disunion, Secession, War." And there, too, in the very centre of the wild uproar, we see the Pillar, seemingly tossed amid the conflict, and borne hither and thither by the rush of encountering armies. But the Shekinah is within it; and as the darkness grows more dense, we see the Pillar of Cloud become a Pillar of Fire, beaming hope and strength into the hearts of those who struggle for the great principles of Freedom and Justice; but darting lurid and destroying flames on the traitors who, in their fanatical devotion to Slavery, would pull down the noblest government the world ever saw, and deluge the land with fraternal blood. In what manner He who dwells in the Pillar will overrule these events for the furtherance of His own glory and the interests of humanity, we know not. Yet we have the fullest confidence that He will so overrule them; that He will bring the nation out of the terrible shock and the scorching furnace, regenerated, purified, shorn of nothing but the mighty Wrong which has weakened and dishonored it; and that when the night of strife is past, and light and day return, we shall see the Pillar — changed to a golden Cloud — floating serenely above the scene of battle, and moving straight forward to Peace, Liberty, and a grander Civilization than the history of our race has yet witnessed.

And while we thus descry, beyond the black waves of desolation that now surge around us, a new career of prosperity and greatness awaiting the American people, the same vision reveals a bright future for the spoiled and trampled ones who have so long been the victims of our injustice. Slavery is the deadly source from which all our woes have sprung. Its enormous guilt, unforsaken, cherished, championed against natural and Divine law, against reason and conscience, against everlasting Right, against the moral sense of the world, has at length worn out the patience of all-suffering Heaven, and drawn down its thunder. Slavery is the true origin of the war. Slavery fomented, inspired it. Slavery sowed the seed, and ripened the red harvest. Slavery laid the train and kindled the explosion which shakes the continent. Slavery has filled the land with graves, and our homes with mourning. Slavery is the great criminal on whose head God is pouring the vials of His wrath. And all the intimations of His will, and all the outstretchings of His hand, declare His purpose utterly to destroy this giant iniquity, this "sum of all villanies," foul with hideous pollution, and steeped in the blood of innumerous murders. Whatever else of good the dread crisis may develop, its bearing in this direction is too plain to be misapprehended, too mighty to be withstood. He who sits above the din and turmoil of the storm is evidently so shaping its forces as to sweep away forever the curse of bondage, and eliminate the last vestige of its poison from the political and social life of the Republic. On, through our doubts and hesitations — on, through our victories and our defeats — on, ever on toward the goal of Universal Emancipation — goes the Pillar of His Providence. It marshals the way of the slave out of the prison-house, by manifestations as distinct and signal as those which of old led the exodus of the Hebrews. And across the Red Sea, whose gory billows are opening the path of his redemption, it points him, as it did them, to the happy bourn where manhood and equal rights shall be the heritage of all. This high and beneficent end solves the mystery of God's dealings with us. In it we read the design, for the attainment of which He has permitted civil war to break forth and rage in all our borders. He saw that the slave-demon could be cast out by no means less violent, and He deemed the blessings that would follow its extrusion more than compensative of whatever throes might attend it. And here, too, we may discover the reason of the slow progress we are making in putting down the Rebellion, and of the many reverses which our arms have suffered. Our cause is righteous — dear to Humanity, and to the God of Humanity. It is the cause of Nationality, Order, Constitutional Government, against Disunion, Anarchy, Despotism. Its final triumph is sure. But in our methods of conducting it, we are not working in harmony with the Divine intention. We are aiming to restore the Union as it was, with slavery in it. God is aiming to restore the Union as it shall be, with every trace of slavery expelled from it. Disaster will pursue us till we accept His plan. In the track of Providence, and there alone, shall we reach full success and durable peace.

If we turn our view to foreign nations, we there behold the Pillar heralding, not less visibly and directly than among ourselves, the cause of the oppressed, and the advancement of true religion. How straightforward it moves along the path of Italian Independence! We see it hanging over the bloody fields of Magenta and Solferino, giving victory to the patriot hosts, while it flashes defeat upon the legions of despotic Austria. Next we see it guiding the heroic Garibaldi straight to Sicily, and leading him straight onward from triumph to triumph, till the last chain is broken from that long enslaved land. Then we see it conducting him straight across the narrow sea to Naples, and the expulsion of the Bourbon from his sanguinary throne. Straight to Gaeta we see it pursue the flying tyrant, and having driven him thence into ignominious exile, it is now moving straight for the Vatican, to rend away the secular arm of the Papacy, thus breaking the horn with which the Beast has for ages gored the Church, and removing the chief obstacle to free thought and free speech throughout regenerate Italy.

Not less undeviating is its forward course in the abolition of Russian serfdom. Over all the broad steppes and mighty provinces that compose the empire of the Czar — from the fertile shores of the Crimea to the Frozen Ocean, from the plains of Poland to the newly explored regions of the Amoor in the utmost East — we see it taking its straight, swift way, sowing the seeds of improvement, planting liberal institutions, unbinding fetters, till thirty millions of slaves step forth from vassalage into the dignity and immunities of freedom.

Look where we will on the map of the world, we see the track of the Pillar clearly marked, and stretching in direct lines to definite ends. Everywhere we recognize the presence of a Power, working through human agencies, yet above them; apparently identified with their forces, yet separate and independent. We see it acting upon the varied populations, inspiring them with a sense of their rights, and the purpose to assert them. We see it modifying governments, abrogating or softening unjust laws, increasing the franchises of the subject, and rendering him more secure in their enjoyment. We see it controlling the rivalries of thrones and the ambitions of dynasties, and making kings and cabinets, Congresses and Parliaments, diplomacy and statecraft, unconscious pioneers in raising the valleys and levelling the mountains for the unshackled Word of God to enter in and conquer. So distinctly may we trace the movings of the Pillar in the political changes which are taking place on the earth.

Equally manifest is its influence in the extension

of commerce, the pushing forward of discovery, and the growth of the useful arts. Does the ever active spirit of trade, in opening doors for itself, open doors for the Gospel as well, throw down the wall of Chinese exclusiveness, and, breaking through the jealous insulation of Japan, bring to our shores ambassadors from those mysterious Isles which for untold ages have slumbered behind their ocean barricades, refusing all communion with the nations? The Pillar is there. Do Livingstone, Barth, and their associates, lift the veil from the heart of Africa, and show us, in place of burning Saharas roamed over by naked savages, wide and fruitful plains, covered with luxuriant vegetation, intersected by broad rivers, studded with cities, and thickly peopled by thrifty, intelligent races, already progressing in the industrial arts, and longing for the blessings of Christian civilization? The Pillar is there. In the improved state of navigation, and the means of rapid communication with all parts of the world, are we furnished with opportunities for spreading the knowledge of Divine Truth, such as no former times have seen? The Pillar is there. These are the beckonings of Providence, indicating to us what to do, and where to do it, and supplying the needed facilities. Follow the Pillar wherever it goes, whether to the frozen North, or the blazing South, to the old East, or the young

West, to the lost myriads abroad, or the equally lost myriads at home. You cannot err, you cannot fail under such a guidance. As the Shekinah was in the Pillar, so God is in Providence. And where God is, victory is.

But it is not alone on the high plane of public affairs that the Pillar moves. While it marches in the van of commonwealths and empires, it enters not less into all the walks of individual life and history. It goes before us in personal duty. The path of each one is strewed thick with intimations of his Master's will — with occasions of usefulness, and calls to lay himself out for Christ and the souls of men. Do you know a neglected child, growing up in ignorance, and ripening for crime? Do you know a young man led away by temptation, and falling into the snare of the destroyer? Do you know a family that keeps itself aloof from the house of God — a neighborhood destitute of religious instruction — a haunt of guilt — a home of want — a dwelling darkened by sickness and sorrow — a body crushed under burdens — a heart broken with misery? There is the Pillar pointing you to your work. You need no other voice to teach you what to do. Every opening for your activity, every appeal to your benevolence, every case of need, every object of pity, every votary of sin, that meets your view, is a command as authoritative and as clear, as if it were written on the sky in letters of fire, or thundered forth from the battlements of heaven by an archangel's trumpet. Go where the Pillar goes. No matter through what weariness of toil, and depths of self-denial, and severity of sacrifice, obedience to it may carry you. Peace with yourself, the approbation of God, the smile of the Comforter, will lighten every labor, and support you in every trial, till you reach the world of perfect compensations, receive the crown of Righteousness from your Saviour's hands, and hear from His lips the glorious words, "Inasmuch as ye have done it unto one of the least of these my brethren, ye have done it unto Me."

The Pillar goes before us in personal experience. The dispensations of the Almighty in relation to His people, are as wise as they are sovereign. With infallible foresight He adapts His appointments to the peculiar character and exposures of each, and so diversifies His dealing as most effectually to promote their salvation. Does He ordain for us poverty, affliction, loss? It is because He knows that we shall there walk most safely. Does He place us in higher positions, and surround us with wealth and honors, and all the seducing glitter of worldly prosperity? It is because He knows that such circumstances will furnish the fittest discipline of our faith, most successfully develop our spiritual energies, and best educate us for His service. Thus, whether our journey lie through grief or joy, through gloom or sunshine, through deserts parched with drought, swarming with serpents, and frightful in their desolation, or through scenes of peace and beauty, by the banks of bright rivers, along "the vale of Beulah," over the "Delectable Mountains"—in either case, we do but march after the Pillar in the path which it chooses as most suitable for us. Fear not to tread where the Pillar leads. Infinite Knowledge and Infinite Love determine all its movements. It cannot err; it cannot miss the true course, nor take you, in ignorance or in wantonness, over rugged ways, when more pleasant ones would have been as direct and sure. Submit your whole pilgrimage to its disposal. Keep it ever in sight. Follow it implicitly to the end. And when your toilsome sojourning in the wilderness is finished, and you stand, at length, on the brink of Jordan, the Pillar will be there, and the Shekinah will shine out upon the dark flowing river, and the Ark of the Covenant will go in before you, and as your feet touch the waters, they will cleave asunder, and permit you to pass dry-shod through the cold, heaving billows to the shore of Immortality.

CHAPTER VI.

THE FREEDMEN OF THE WAR.

"He bringeth out those which are bound in chains." — *Psalm* lxviii. 6.

THE history of the world is marked by sudden changes and startling evolutions. It is not a dead uniformity — an unvarying expanse. We cannot compare it to a vast prairie, where scarcely an undulation, and never a hill, breaks the view; where the streams all flow with a sluggish and leaden current; and where the same succession of low banks and monotonous plains forever repeats itself. Much more does it resemble portions of our own Atlantic scenery, where the traveller sees rugged mountains, jagged rocks, and tumbling cascades, interspersed with glimpses of fair and smiling valleys, and is surprised at every step by some new feature in the landscape.

Such is the aspect which the progress of our race presents. To a careless observer, surveying it through the dim haze of the ages, it may appear almost an unbroken level, with only here and there a salient point to arrest the eye. So when you look forth from some Alpine summit on a wide stretch of country over which the morning shadows are yet sleeping, its inequalities and roughnesses may be so toned down by distance and obscurity, as to render the prospect apparently tame; but, on a nearer inspection, the bold lines come out, and you discover lofty ranges, precipitous gorges, and rushing waterfalls, where before all seemed so smooth and placid.

In following back along the centuries the way of Divine Providence in the government of our world, we are often perplexed by its intricacy, often bewildered by its sinuosities, often confounded by its deviations from the course which we ignorantly judge to be the true one. We find that the ongoing of terrestrial events is not equable and regular, like the flow of a broad river rolling on in calm majesty, without a rift in its current or a bend in its shores. Instead of this straight and even movement, we perceive in it all the diversified windings and alternations of the mountain brook; now leaping wild and free from its rocky birth-place; now pent up and stagnant in its confined bed; now creeping about among the hills, and losing itself in deep, shadowy glens; now hurrying through volcanic chasms; now spreading out into a clear, still lake;

now roaring over rapids; now plunging down cataracts; yet ever pressing forward, swift or slow, through turmoil or repose, to its goal in the sea.

So it is with human history. It is full of abrupt turnings and unexpected vicissitudes. In fact, it would seem to be the design of God that the cause of man should go forward, not with a quiet and continuous progression, but by leaps and bounds — by forces brought to it at long intervals from great epochs — transition periods — when civilization and philanthropy enter upon new careers, and put forth their energies in new directions. Such an epoch was the Introduction of Christianity. It closed up the old channels of thought, and opened a new path of progress for the world. Similar epochs were ushered in by the Invention of the Art of Printing, the Reformation from Popery, and the Discovery of America. Each of these events changed the course of human opinion, and inaugurated a new scene in the drama of the world's life.

Now, as these grand crises powerfully affect the destiny of our race, so they modify in an equal degree the duties and responsibilities of all who would shape that destiny for good and happiness. And hence the highest wisdom, in times of social disturbance and upheaval, is to know the lesson of the hour, and to do the work of the hour.

We stand to-day at one of those momentous turning-points in human affairs, which change the face of history, and send down their influence to the latest generations. Consciously or unconsciously, we are actors in a struggle out of which the Future is to be born. Without our knowledge, and contrary to our desire, Jehovah has made us His instruments in a strange and terrible convulsion, through which it is clearly His purpose to prepare the way of righteousness and peace.

Long have the prayers of the pious and the humane been going up to the Eternal Throne, that this land might be purified from the guilt of Oppression; that it might be lifted out of the slough of wickedness into which Slavery had plunged it, to the high ground of fidelity to its own principles, and of justice to all; and that Freedom might grow and triumph, till not a chain should clank, nor a bondman cower, under the symbol of our nationality. We hoped, we believed, that hour would come. But we deemed the period of its coming to be far distant. And we looked for its dawning, not in thunder, and storm, and earthquake, but amid scenes of tranquillity — its golden beams flushing an azure heaven, and welcomed with the melody of songs, and voices of love and blessing. That day has come — sooner than we thought, and not in the way we thought. Its sun is above the horizon; but it rises on a sky red with blood, and lurid with the smoke and flame of battle. The nation is in the throes of its second birth. In the hot furnace of civil war its purification is being accomplished. And out of the consuming fire, out of the strife and the agony, out of the carnage and the woe, up from the gory fields where our sons and brothers have fought and fallen, up from their graves, springs the glorious form of our new National Life, waving aloft the banner of Emancipation, and "proclaiming Liberty throughout the land, to all the inhabitants thereof."

In the pride of our vain wisdom, we marked out for ourselves the way to political greatness. Across the shaking morasses of Expediency, over the bottomless bog of Compromise, we formed the track, and laid the rails, and put on the train, and got up the steam, and with rush and roar were sweeping onward in our self-confidence, heedless of the abyss which Slavery had dug in our path, and whose yawning depths lay just before us. But God put his hand to the brakes, and switched us off on a new track, which He laid, and not man. There was surprise, terror, outcry, at first. There are doubts, apprehensions, tremblings still. But the road is firm and straight, the engine sound, the cars stanch, the Conductor all-wise and all-powerful, and the end of our journey — a vindicated Government, a restored Union, a Free Nation — already in sight.

A period so eventful must be full of grave problems; and of these one of the gravest relates to the measures which should be adopted in behalf of those lately bound in chains, whom God, through the instrumentality of the war, is bringing out of bondage.

At the beginning of the fierce struggle that now convulses the land, the people of the North had but a dim perception of the stupendous issues which it involved, and no clear foresight of the consequences to which it would lead. They were animated by the single purpose of suppressing treason, upholding the Government, and maintaining the integrity of the Republic. The overthrow of Slavery was not their direct object; for with whatever feelings of abhorrence they may have regarded the system, and however unquestioned may have been their right to prohibit it in the Territories, they were precluded, by the compromises of the Constitution, from any forcible attempt to abolish it in the States where it had been established by law. But as the war went on and assumed unexpected proportions, — as the conflict grew thicker and more deadly, — as the Rebellion developed its real strength and its atrocious aim, it became more and more evident that we could conquer it only by destroying the institution in whose interest it had been commenced, and from which it drew its vitality and its chief support. Slowly and reluctantly we accepted this alternative. It required the protracted frown of an angry Providence, months of disaster and defeat, the sacrifice of countless millions of treasure, and of almost countless lives, to bring us to it. But we reached it at length. In obedience to the voice of the people, the President, recognizing military necessity as superior to all constitutional provisions, issued his proclamation, declaring forever free the slaves of the conspirators who were seeking to overturn the Government.

This fact, the grandest in our history, infused a new element of power into the conduct of the war. It revived confidence. It gained for us the suffrage of the world. It allied us with Heaven. It enlisted in our cause the invincible might of Eternal Right and Justice. It arrested the almost unbroken tide of reverses that had carried mourning into myriad homes, and ushered in those subsequent successes and victories which have filled all loyal hearts with rejoicing, and cast over the Rebellion the shadow of its approaching doom.

Since this potent word of deliverance was spoken, more than a million of slaves have obtained the blessed boon of freedom, partly by escaping within our lines from districts yet held by the rebels, and partly by the progress of our arms in restoring the authority of the Government over large portions of the revolted States. And these are but the advance-guard, the forerunners of millions more who will follow them out of the prison-house of bondage, as the victorious forces of the Union open the way, till Slavery and Secession — foul mother and foul child — shall be driven forever from our shores.

With what glowing interest and sympathy must we contemplate this multitude, thus led forth, by the hand of God himself, from life-long vassalage to liberty and the possession of those personal rights which Heaven ordains as the inalienable heritage of all! And as we behold them struggling up into the light of a better day, — stamped with the brand of chattelhood; scarred with the lash of the task-master; all covered with the traces of the degradation and misery to which they have been subjected, — how impressively must these questions present themselves to every thoughtful and benevolent mind! What is their condition? What are their most pressing needs? What must be done to prepare them for the new circumstances in which they are placed? In what way can their welfare be most effectually secured? And what are the reasons which render this the great work of our time, and summon us to give to it our utmost zeal and energy?

Of the million already freed, about two hundred and thirty thousand are in the military service of the United States; one hundred and eighty thousand as soldiers, organized into regiments and brigades, and so armed and drilled as to be highly efficient; and fifty thousand as army laborers, workmen on fortifications, wagoners, and hospital servants — thus releasing an equal number of white troops for active duty in the field. The remaining seven hundred and seventy thousand, though more or less dispersed over the whole territory recovered from the rebels, are chiefly to be found at Port Royal in the Department of the South; at Newbern in North Carolina; at Norfolk in Virginia; in the District of Columbia; on the Mississippi from Helena to Vicksburg; and in New Orleans. The peculiar circumstances attending the early days of their exodus exposed them to much suffering from the want of food, clothing, and shelter. But through the care of the Government, their own industry, and the prompt aid of societies and individuals, these necessities have been so far supplied, that the freedmen are now, for the most part, in a state of comparative physical comfort. This statement, however, is not to be received as absolutely and universally true.

Among the liberated bondmen, as among all other classes of our population, examples of indolence and unthrift may be found. Many, too, have recently escaped from slavery, and have not had time to redeem themselves from the rags and beggary which they brought with them. Such cases of distress, we are happy to say, are now chiefly confined to the region of the Mississippi. Owing to the unsettled and insecure state of that Department, and the consequent greater difficulty in organizing labor on the plantations, large numbers there are still in great destitution. But, leaving out of view these sad instances of suffering,—instances exceptional in their character and rapidly passing away,—we recognize everywhere the broad and cheering fact, that the condition of the freed slaves as to employment and subsistence is far more satisfactory than even the most sanguine could have ventured to predict. So well provided are they in these respects, that, as a general thing, they may be said no longer to require our aid, or call for our solicitude. It is in reference to their intellectual and spiritual wants, that the most urgent appeal now comes to us.

In studying their needs under this aspect, it is important to bear in mind the fact, that hitherto they have been debarred from all means of education, and from all correct religious teaching. Despotism always endeavors to keep its victims in ignorance, in order that they may be more patient and submissive under its control. This has been its aim in all lands and ages. In whatever form it exists, — whatever name it bears, whether that of hierarchy, monarchy, aristocracy, or oligarchy, — it seeks ever to perpetuate its power by holding in darkness the minds it would subject to its will. The motive which induces the ruling classes of Great Britain to withhold free schools from her crushed and imbruted masses, is precisely the same as that which led the oligarchy of the South to prohibit the instruction of the slaves. The English aristocrat dreads the diffusion of knowledge among the common people, lest it should diminish their subserviency to the privileged orders. His brother, the Southern oligarch, feared to permit his slave to be educated, knowing well that an educated slave would soon be a slave no longer. Hence in all the slave-holding States the most severe laws were enacted against teaching the slaves to read. Little better were the opportunities allowed them for religious instruction. They were, indeed, permitted to hear what their oppressors called the Gospel, dispensed by such lips as their oppressors chose. But it was the Gospel of the trafficker in human flesh — the Gospel of the child-seller and the woman-whipper — a Gospel which nullified marriage, denied their manhood, trampled on their God-given rights, and held forth obedience to their masters as the essence of all grace and virtue.

Coming out from such a condition, with the impress of generations of servitude and darkness upon them, is it surprising that they should be ignorant, superstitious, degraded; or that the most energetic endeavors should be demanded to fit them for the new position into which they have been so suddenly brought? What else could we expect? To suppose that men, born and reared under the debasing influences of slavery, will become, by the mere act of emancipation, intelligent, self-reliant, and competent to their own welfare, is to hope for that of which the annals of civilization afford not a solitary example. There is needed for them — as once there was needed for every race that has emerged from barbarism — the guiding hand of a wise philanthropy, to lead them on to knowledge, independence, and happiness. This necessity the Government has felt strongly from the first, and has done all to meet it which the overwhelming burdens of the war have left it the ability to do. Numerous voluntary associations are also co-operating in the work with a liberality and an earnestness that are full of promise. The noble enterprise is begun; and it is only requisite that the Christian sentiment of the North should be deeply imbued with the feeling of its importance; and thoroughly roused to its prosecution, in order to put in action an array of agencies that shall pour the light of education and of a pure Gospel upon those millions of immortal minds, which long years of chattelhood have benighted and brutalized.

A single glance at what is being done, even in this incipient stage of the movement, is enough to inspire us with confidence and joy. For the freedmen in the District of Columbia a village of neat, comfortable homes has been built on Arlington Heights, formerly the residence of the rebel General Lee. Who sees not the righteous retribution of Providence in the fact, that the princely estate of the man who has been the ablest champion of a rebellion undertaken for the perpetuation of slavery, should have been converted into an asylum for negroes whom the crushing of that rebellion has set free? What a striking instance of that poetic justice which, though often portrayed in fiction, is so seldom witnessed in real life! Into this village the freedmen have been gathered from the various camps around Washington; and there the problem of their social amelioration is in process of successful solution. The men are employed on work for the Government, and in cultivating the adjoining farms. They labor regularly and earnestly. And although the season was far advanced before operations were begun, the experiment has already more than repaid the expense incurred. The charge of their mental and religious training has been assumed by the Tract Society at New York, under whose auspices a commodious building has been erected, intended for the double purpose of a chapel and a school-house; and at its opening, a few months since, cabinet ministers, members of Congress, and high officers of the army, made congratulatory addresses. And well they might, for never did statesman or warrior utter words on a nobler theme or at a grander hour. In this house a day-school for children has been commenced, with hundreds of pupils; and also an evening school for adults, which is numerously attended. The capacity of the learners, their desire for improvement, and their proficiency, are eminently encouraging. In the formation of provident habits, in domestic economy, in moral culture, they manifest an equal progress. Indeed, the whole population is represented as evincing, in its industry, its thrift, its sobriety, strong indications of soon becoming an intelligent, self-supporting, well-ordered community.

Similar accounts come to us from almost every point where any attempt has been made to succor and benefit the freedmen. In the neighborhood of Norfolk, large numbers of them have been placed on the plantation of Henry A. Wise, where they are now sustaining themselves by their own labor, and are being rapidly educated by the churches and schools which have been established among them. A short time ago in New Orleans, a lady, a native of the city, — perhaps one of those whom General Butler converted, — felt herself moved in spirit to open a school for colored children. The first day she had three pupils, and the third, three hundred. A movement was then begun to increase the number of schools, which has since been carried forward, partly by governmental and partly by individual patronage, until now there are ten schools, thirty teachers, and two thousand pupils under instruction. A prominent citizen of West Virginia informs us, that when that portion of the Old Dominion became an independent State, there were in the city of his residence several thousand slaves who were then emancipated; and that since that period, they have built, chiefly with the avails of their own labor, comfortable dwellings for their families, erected two chapels and four school-houses, and are now supporting their own pastors and teachers. In North Carolina there are twenty-three schools, forty-six teachers, and three thousand pupils.

At Port Royal and the adjacent islands the experiment has been longer in operation, and the results are correspondingly more decisive. When this portion of South Carolina came under our control, the Secretary of War immediately instituted measures for the protection and welfare of the negroes who had been abandoned by their owners in their hasty flight from our victorious army. The population of the Sea Islands has always consisted almost entirely of colored people; and since their occupancy by our forces, this population has been largely increased by slaves who have fled thither from all parts of the State, to find freedom and safety under the flag of the Union. Over these growing numbers the Government has exercised a watchful and paternal care. Superintendents have been assigned to the plantations, and the freedmen encouraged to work by the offer of suitable wages. And so fully has the effort succeeded, that the plantations are now in a good state of cultivation, and the laborers well supplied and contented. Many have even been able, from their surplus earnings, to purchase land of the Government, and are now working it on their own account; and instances have occurred of individuals realizing for their crop the past season, two or three thousand dollars beyond what was needed for the support of themselves and families. Nearly the whole town of Beaufort has thus passed into the hands of freedmen, who now hold as owners the mansions in which they once crouched and trembled as slaves. If we take into account the derangements which a change from compulsory to voluntary labor must at first inevitably create, the interruptions incident to military occupation, and the shortness of the period during which the new order of things has existed, we cannot but acknowledge the cheering character of the results. One important step has at least been gained. It has been demonstrated that the negro will work, and work well, under the stimulus of compensation. He has got over the idea that freedom means immunity from labor. He has tasted the luxury of wages, and is eager to acquire property and a home which he can call his own. And when once this desire has been awakened, the ground has been won for higher influences, that will enter in and complete his elevation.

Accordingly we find that while this improvement has been going on in the industrial character of the freedmen, there has been a similar progress in their intellectual and religious development. Various philanthropic associations have sent out teachers and organized schools, which are filling those dark places with the light of intelligence and truth. In the Department of Port Royal, there are now about fifty schools, with fifty teachers, and nearly four thousand regular attendants, besides a like number who are receiving occasional instruction. Little more than a year has passed since the educational arrangements were in such forwardness that these schools could begin their work. Then, not one among their pupils knew a single letter. Now, nearly all of them can read with ease almost any chapter in the Bible, and such plain pieces as are found in ordinary school books. They have acquired some knowledge of writing and arithmetic; can answer simple questions in geography; give the names and boundaries of the different States; and point out on a map the oceans, continents, and principal countries of the globe. Their memories are quick and susceptible, and they learn as readily, and give as much evidence of capacity for intellectual attainment, as children of any race whatever. They are docile and affectionate, fond of going to school, and delighted at being free. And, as an expression of these feelings, they take great pleasure in the singing exercises of the schools, and love to roll out with the full strength of their voices,

> "My Country, 'tis of thee,
> Sweet land of Liberty,
> Of thee, I sing;"

or those beautiful lines of Whittier, written expressly for the school on the Island of St. Helena:

> "The very oaks are greener clad,
> The waters brighter smile,
> Oh, never shone a day so glad
> On sweet St. Helen's isle.
>
> For none in all the world before
> Were ever glad as we;
> We're free on Carolina's shore,
> We're all at home, and free."

Let any one visit the plantations where these freedmen live; let him note the evidences of increased comfort which gladden their homes; let him mark the new-born dignity, the look of recovered manhood, with which they ply their voluntary toil; let him go into their schools, and watch those dark minds brightening and expanding under the beams of knowledge; let him listen as they sing the songs of Freedom; let him enter their crowded places of worship; let him contemplate their churches with thousands of members, which fresh accessions are constantly augmenting, — let him ponder all this, and he cannot but be convinced that a social and moral transformation is here going forward, mightier than human sagacity ever contrived or human statesmanship ever wrought; and that never, since the light of the Gospel first broke on the hill-sides of Judea, has the earth presented a spectacle so fraught with sublime and inspiring auguries.

Such is the field which now invites our culture, and such are the bright signs of promise which it everywhere displays. There is room here for all; and the Providence of God summons all to enter in and reap. The whole Christian strength of the North could not suffice to gather a harvest so wide and so ripe. To the Baptist churches, however, the appeal addresses itself with peculiar significance and emphasis. The pious among the freedmen are largely of our denomination. At Port Royal they are almost exclusively so. And everywhere throughout the South, vast multitudes of the colored people profess our faith, or harmonize with us in sentiment. They naturally look to us for their religious teaching. We can most readily gain their confidence and sympathy. Hence it is clear that on us the care of their educational and spiritual interests pre-eminently devolves. If we neglect the trust, God will transfer it to more faithful hands; but this will not alter the fact that to us the work appropriately belongs. Others may help us; and most gladly do we welcome their co-operation. Yet let us never forget that ours is the chief and foremost place in this godlike undertaking.

What, then, as Baptists, are we called to do in this matter? The first and most urgent demand that meets us — a demand that cannot be neglected a single day without incalculable injury to the cause of Christ — is to supply these broad wastes with missionaries and pastors, at least in sufficient numbers to occupy the central points, superintend the churches that still exist, gather new ones, and direct the general work of evangelization. We cannot longer defer this duty on the plea that the South is inaccessible to our efforts. The brazen wall which Slavery had built around it has been beaten down by our victorious cannon. Already wide regions invite our occupancy; and the whole land will be open to us sooner than we shall be prepared to go up and possess it. In those parts of the rebel territory which the advance of our armies has brought back under the control of the Union, there are many vacant houses of worship once belonging to our denomination, and many desolate altars on which the fire still feebly burns amid the ashes of devastation and the deluge of war. These the national authorities have placed in our hands, with the guaranty of military protection, and the promise of similar facilities in all the revolted States, whenever they shall have been reclaimed to their allegiance. Thus does the Providence of God summon us to the mighty task of reconstructing, on a Christian basis, the religious institutions of the South. In place of a Gospel so corrupted by false views of human rights, so distorted by the selfish greed of the oppressor, as to stand forth an abomination to heaven and earth, we must plant there the Gospel which He taught who came to save the poor and to lift up the fallen — a Gospel which proclaims liberty to the captives, and the opening of the prison doors to them that are bound. And as an evidence of the pressing necessity that we should engage in this work at once and with the utmost vigor, and as an incentive to our zeal, it will be sufficient to cite the history of our operations in the Sea Islands. Here was the beginning of our labors for the spiritual welfare of the freedmen, and here they have been most thoroughly and earnestly prosecuted. And what is their actual amount? How large is the supply which we have sent to this our earliest and most favored field? On these Islands there are sixteen thousand liberated bondmen, all needing our aid, all placed within the reach of our Christian sympathies. In this population there are three Baptist churches, comprising an aggregate of thirty-three hundred members. The church at Beaufort contains, with its five branches, fifteen hundred members; that on St. Helena Island nine hundred; and that at Mitchelville, near Hilton Head, a similar number. In these churches thirteen hundred and fifty have been baptized during the two years since missionary work commenced among them. And yet at this important point, so peculiarly our own, and so rich in promise, there are only three ordained Baptist ministers, two white, and one colored. Of the former, one is there merely for the purpose of regaining his health, and will soon return to his home in the North, if he has not already done so; and the other, worn down with exhausting toil, and unsupported, is also expected ere long to leave the field. So that, unless reinforcements are speedily sent, there will be only one colored preacher of our denomination for sixteen thousand souls. And if such is the destitution in the spot where we have done most, how great must it be throughout the vast regions in which we have done nothing! Oh, how thrilling, how importunate is the cry which comes to us from all parts of the recovered South for men to break to these famishing multitudes the Bread of Life!

But the preaching of the Gospel does not comprehend our whole duty in relation to this momentous matter. These degraded and outcast masses need to be educated for this world as well as for the next. Along with an adequate number of competent ministers, we must send out a host of teachers, qualified not only to take charge of the business of secular education, but also to assist in organizing and sustaining Sunday schools, and in the various departments of Christian labor. This is a want which has been greatly felt. A large proportion of the teachers now on the ground, however competent to instruct in the week-day schools, have little fitness for the duties of the Sunday-school. Many of them are rationalists, deists, skeptics; and instead of seeking to instil into those clouded minds the knowledge of Christ and of His salvation, are laboring to infect them with the gospel of Theodore Parker and Wendell Phillips.

Here is our work; and this is precisely the relation in which the Baptists of the North stand to the Freedmen of the South. God has pointed us out as their guides in the upward course which he is opening before them. What Moses and Joshua were to the Tribes which Divine Power, with mighty signs and wonders, delivered from the thraldom of Egypt, we should be to the myriads whom the same Almighty hand, by manifestations not less startling, is bringing out of a more cruel bondage. On us rests the obligation to lead them into the Land of Promise—to train them for freedom on earth, and for immortality in heaven.

Let the vastness of the work rouse us. Here are a million of human beings, just risen from the black night of Slavery, now waiting to be enlightened, elevated, and prepared for the rights of manhood and the heritage of salvation. And behind them are three millions more, yet lingering in the prison-house, from whose limbs the fetters are breaking, and are destined to fall utterly away, when the design of God in this civil war shall have reached its triumphant fulfilment. And, following these, are eight millions of white men, who, when the curse of bondage is removed, will rise up from their darkness and degradation, to claim the franchises of which a tyrannical oligarchy has robbed them, and ask for the blessings of education and of true religion. Where in all the ages is there a movement so stupendous as this? On what page of the world's annals can you find anything so majestic as the moral uprising which will pervade the entire South, when once the Rebellion has been suppressed, and its authors and leaders have fled to the sheltering arms of foreign despots; or, like Judas, their great prototype, have emigrated to their "own place!" Oh, what a day of redemption will that be for the South, when over her sunny fields, now blasted by slavery, and ravaged by the fury and the despair of a merciless usurpation, free labor, free schools, a free press, and a free Gospel shall pour their living energies, renovating the whole land, and covering all its fertile plains and valleys with a thriving and peaceful population! This is to be the great social revolution of our day, and the grandest of all the days. Whose heart is so dead as not to kindle at the thought of taking part in an enterprise so mighty in its scope, and so benign in its results?

There are some, perhaps, to whom the force of this appeal may be lessened by the imagination that an undertaking so immense, requiring such large expenditures of men and of means, must necessarily cripple our endeavors for the evangelization of the West, which they have been wont to regard as our sole, particular sphere. Even were this objection well founded,—were it indeed true that we should be compelled by the inadequacy of our resources to neglect either the new West or the new South, — I hesitate not to affirm that wisdom and benevolence would alike justify us in leaving the West for the present to take care of itself. The West is free. The West is strong. No burdens have weakened her gigantic youth; no chains have clogged her swelling muscles. She has at her command all the requisites and appliances of her own intellectual and moral progress. Her soil, from the surface of the earth to its centre, is one huge treasure bed. Her plains are granaries, her hills mines, the sands of her rivers richer than those of old Pactolus. Her power of self-help is limited only by her inclination. By the munificence of His gifts God has made her the mistress of her own destiny. And the boundless energies which she has displayed in this hour of the nation's peril, show her sufficient for the trust, and equal to all the exigencies of her magnificent future.

But the trampled and crushed ones for whom we plead have hitherto had no agency in deciding their condition. No opportunity for better things has ever been theirs. Their darkness and their debasement have been forced upon them by circumstances beyond their control. Slavery, and not their own free choice, has made them what they are. And now as they come forth, in countless throngs, from the pollutions and the horrors of their involuntary bondage, and with outstretched arms implore us to succor them, must not humanity, and "the mind that was in Christ Jesus," prompt us to take them by the hand, stanch their wounds, wipe away their blood, and raise them up, even though in doing so we should be obliged for a time to let go of others less exposed, or less helpless?

There is, however, no necessity that in responding to this special call of God we should withdraw from other fields of labor on which He has led us to enter. If we faithfully use the resources which He has conferred upon us, we shall find that we have ample ability to do all that needs to be done for the freedmen and for the South, without setting aside the claims of any Christian enterprise whatever. We have means enough and men enough to meet the sudden and large demands arising from the downfall of Slavery, and at the same time to plant the banner of Christ throughout the destitute West and the pagan East. Nevertheless, we cannot but recognize, in the magnitude of the cause we advocate to-day, in its momentous bearings on the public weal, in the solemn emphasis of its claims, in the fearful hazards which indifference to them involves, the clear handwriting of Heaven, marking it out as the paramount interest of the hour, and invoking us to comprehend and earnestly promote it.

The hopeful aspects of the work should inspire zeal and confidence. Let us not be kept back by the cry of slavemongers and their upholders, that the negro belongs to an inferior race, and is incapable of improvement. That he is at present low down in the social scale, may be admitted. It would be a miracle if centuries of servitude and debasement had left him in any other condition. But he is no lower than God's chosen people were when He brought them out of Egypt — no lower than any portion of the human family would be, if subjected for the same length of time to the same deteriorating influences. We hesitate not to affirm that whatever of defect there may be in the character of the freedmen is to be ascribed, not to poverty of intellectual or moral endowment, but to the circumstances in which they have been placed. They have bent all their lives under burdens. Is it strange that they cannot at once stand erect? They have just come up from the foul dungeon of Slavery, with the scent of its abominations yet clinging to them, and its deadly vapors still paralyzing every sense and every faculty. And shall we marvel that they do not walk forth with the strong step and uplifted brow of those who have always trodden the mountain tops, breathing the free air, and basking in the glad sunshine? Notwithstanding the disadvantages which surround them, — disadvantages springing alike from their past deprivations and from their present unsettled state, — they nevertheless manifest qualities of mind and of heart which prove their capacity for better things, and prophesy well of their future. Even through the deep gloom that overshadows them, flashes of a noble nature gleam forth, indicating that they need only opportunity and culture, to emerge from their depression, and take their place by the side of the more favored races.

When the policy of emancipation was inaugurated, its enemies, both at home and abroad, assailed it as inviting the slaves to insurrection, and as tending to produce among them wild disorder and outbursts of brutal ferocity. And even its friends feared that a measure, for which so little preparation had been made, might leave its objects helpless through indolence, or lawless from sudden liberty. But the event has justified none of these predictions. The liberated bondmen have shown no unwillingness to labor wherever employment has been furnished them, and no disposition to avenge the insults and wrongs heaped upon them as well by loyal as by rebel hands. And those who yet remain in slavery are waiting for the deliverance which they know to be near, with a patience and forbearance actually sublime. That this calm endurance of injuries, this quiet demeanor under hope deferred, springs merely from constitutional timidity, or from lack of spirit to assert their rights, no one can believe who has witnessed the manliness with which they bear themselves as soldiers. Their firmness and courage in many a bloody field have silenced forever the taunt that the negro is a coward. The glorious dead of Port Hudson, of Fort Wagner, and of Olustee, who fell bravely fighting for a country which gave them no citizenship, and which, even in accepting them as its defenders, dishonored and robbed them, prove that dark skins may cover souls as heroic and patriotism as unselfish as the world has ever known. It is idle to deny that a race exhibiting such examples of magnanimity and valor, possesses elements of greatness which require only to be developed, to raise it to a high order of civilization.

Equally promising is the strong religious tendency so manifest in the negro character. Grant that his piety is often deeply tinged with superstition; that it sometimes resembles more the wild Fetishism of his ancestral Africa than the soberness of the Gospel; that it is a thing of emotion and excitement rather than of holy living; and that even when apparently most ardent it is not seldom dissevered from morality. These peculiarities are accidental — the fungus growth which the poison of Slavery has spread over his moral life. Nevertheless, the tendency is there, vital and potent in his nature, and, when purified and rightly directed, will become a powerful auxiliary in his uplifting.

These striking capabilities, displayed by the colored population of the South under circumstances so adverse, viewed in connection with the wonderful unfoldings of Divine Providence in their behalf, are full of encouragement to those who would seek their welfare. Nor is it an extravagance to say, that nowhere on the face of the globe is there a department of Christian labor so rich in presages of success, or where the reapers may gather sheaves so abundant and so precious.

The elevation of this race is as important to ourselves as it is to them. Their home is upon our soil. Our destiny is bound up with theirs. Their numbers forbid their removal. And even were this possible, it would be a disaster, and not a blessing. The industry of Spain was ruined for a century by the expulsion of the Moors, and that of France by the banishment of the Huguenots. And the productive power of our own country would be crippled, if not destroyed, by the colonization of the negroes in other lands. While all sections would suffer from such an immense loss of labor, there are vast regions which would become a desert, were the brawny arms that now till them withdrawn. They are here, and they are needed here. We cannot expatriate them if we would; and it were suicide to do it if we could. The only choice left us is, to allow them to remain in their degradation, a blot on the nation's fame, a gangrene in the body politic, a festering mass of ignorance and vice, imperilling alike the present and the future; or to rouse ourselves, and put forth instant and vigorous efforts to fit them, by all the appliances of Christian truth and Christian education, for the new sphere into which God is so unexpectedly conducting them. Patriotism and humanity, the command of Christ, and the finger of Heaven, all beckon us forward to the work. Interest, duty, consistency, benevolence, unite to intensify the summons. We have prayed — we have battled — for the freedom of the slave. And now that God is suddenly breaking his chains, how tremendous will be our guilt, if by neglect we turn the blessing into a curse! What dishonor will such neglect bring to the cause of emancipation among all the struggling peoples of the earth! What woes will it entail on the generations that are to come after us! If we fold our hands in listless inaction while the day of decision is upon us, and events big with the fates of unborn ages are rushing on, how shall we answer it at the bar of conscience — at the bar of posterity — at the bar of the world — at the bar of that Omniscient and Holy One, who will judge us for our not doing as for our misdoing; and who has declared that "to him that knoweth to do good, and doeth it not, to him it is sin?"

Followers of Jesus! you see the path of duty and of labor to which your Master points you. Whatever you do must be done now, and done with your whole strength, or the succor will be too late and too feeble to avail its objects. They are afloat on the wild sea of uncertainty, and will perish if left to their own guidance. Helpers of the helpless! hasten to their rescue. Let not the All-ruling Hand wave before you unheeded. Let not the blood of sons and brothers slain on the high places of the field be poured out in vain. By your country's peril, by the woes of the down-trodden, by the pity of Christ, so meet this solemn crisis, that the verdict of the ages shall bless you, and eternity confirm the award, "WELL DONE!"

CHAPTER VII.

THE LAND CARING FOR ITS DEFENDERS.

"TAKE NOW FOR THY BRETHREN AN EPHAH OF THIS PARCHED CORN, AND THESE TEN LOAVES, AND RUN TO THE CAMP TO THY BRETHREN; AND CARRY THESE TEN CHEESES TO THE CAPTAIN OF THEIR THOUSAND, AND SEE HOW THY BRETHREN FARE." — 1 *Sam.* xvii. 17, 18.

ON one of the islands that stud the broad bosom of the Pacific, there is a region scarred by wreck and havoc. A volcano, whose fires never slumber, rises in its centre; and all around are strewed lava rocks, and the still smoking cinders of recent eruptions. There are no trees, no verdure, no vegetable life. The whole scene is black and drear — traversed by yawning fissures, and covered with masses of scoria. Yet, amid this desolate expanse, at the very foot of the heaving and belching mountain, a spring of pure water gushes up; and from it a clear, sparkling brook flows off through the blasted waste, with many a playful winding and jocund ripple, down to the sea. And wherever it flows a belt of soft green appears, glinting joy and brightness upon the encompassing gloom. Strange union — beauty allied with horror — coolness and refreshment bubbling from a soil hot with flame and vomiting death!

How like to this is the spectacle which our country now presents! A fearful civil war is raging through all our borders — a war unexampled in its magnitude, in the gravity of the questions it involves, in the energies it develops, in the wide sweep of its destructive power. Loyalty and Rebellion have met in fierce and deadly encounter, and the whole land reels with the shock. A moral volcano, more wrathful than Vesuvius when it shook and roared in the battle of the demi-gods, now rocks the nation with its convulsive throes, and disgorges its molten floods, shrouding the heavens in sulphurous clouds, and pouring devastation on the earth. Broad commonwealths are ravaged, vast industries submerged, untold treasure and life swallowed up. The entire continent seems one huge crater spouting fire and blood.

But in this appalling view there is one feature on which the eye may linger with delight. Welling up from the deep heart of the people, a stream of patriotic beneficence winds through the lurid landscape, visiting every scene of carnage and suffering, and spreading health and gladness in its course. A tiny rill at its birth, it has become a mighty river, fed by countless affluents, and sending its healing waters by a thousand channels wherever the exigencies of the strife demand their presence.

In this remarkable war, unprecedented in so many of its aspects, there is nothing more remarkable, nothing more unprecedented, than the promptitude and fulness with which the individual contributions of the country have flowed forth to minister to the needs of its soldiers. That a people so young, so wedded to the arts of peace, so unpractised in military operations, should have been able, in an emergency so sudden, to raise and equip armies whose muster-roll registers millions, is one of the most surprising facts of history. How, then, must the surprise and the wonder grow upon us, when we see that same people not only sustaining such a tremendous drain of men, and the equally tremendous cost of their mobilization, but following them to the field, in outgoings of personal kindness and munificence, which, for system, comprehensiveness and extent, are without a parallel in the annals of war! Other nations have created great armies. But what nation ever cared for its armies as we are caring for ours? What were the paltry and ill-regulated attempts of England to lighten the miseries of her troops in the Crimea, compared with the vast, harmonious, all-embracing movement that now stirs the patriotism of the North to its profoundest depths, uniting every heart and every hand in the work of succoring the brave men who are enduring peril and privation in the cause of freedom and justice? Nor has this movement been necessitated by any neglect or deficiency on the part of the military authorities. No government ever paid its troops so liberally as ours; and none ever furnished such ample supplies for their subsistence and comfort. But the nation, in its intense solicitude for its defenders, cannot be content with what it is doing for them through the Government. It longs to do more; to pour out its bounty with a copiousness that shall meet all their wants, and satisfy every requirement of the camp, the hospital, and the battle. For such sympathy it must find its own modes of expression.

And it has found them. The anxiety for the welfare of the soldier which animates all classes, has crystallized in the Sanitary and Christian Commissions, — the one intended to relieve his physical sufferings, the other combining with care for the body the higher care of the soul. Having thus established appropriate vehicles for dispensing their gifts, what zeal, what abounding liberality, do the inhabitants of the loyal States everywhere exhibit in filling those vehicles, and keeping them ever in motion! All ranks, all conditions, unite in the blessed service. The dwellers in towns and the tillers of the soil, men and matrons, youths and maidens, gray age and rosy childhood, find here a common interest and a common object. The rich give their wealth; the poor, their labor and their prayers. Votaries of fashion, devotees of idleness, gay frequenters of the opera and the ball-room, turn from their wonted pursuit of pleasure to the stern tasks of the hour; and soft hands, that never knew toil before, busily ply the needle for those whose strong hands are plying the musket. Woman, ever foremost where pity calls, brings out all the warmth and enthusiasm of her nature in this benevolent work. In such ministerings lies her peculiar sphere, and nobly she fills it now. What words can do justice to the patriotic fervor, the untiring self-devotion, which the loyal women of the country have displayed in this solemn crisis of its destiny? Their hearts have listened to the eloquent appeal addressed to them by one of themselves, and eloquently have their deeds responded.

> "In hospitals, and in camps, so thickly crowded,
>   They are wasting life away,
> With no blessed touch of Home to balm and soften
>   The pain which maketh gray!
> Oh ye daughters! Oh ye sisters! Oh ye mothers!
>   Are ye haunted by their eyes?
> The weary, dying look of sons and brothers,
>   Who shall never more arise!
> Let us help them! We, who sit in careless comfort,
>   In our happy, cheerful homes —.

> Shall we leave our brave defenders pining, dying,
>   For the help that never comes?
> Oh! remember that the quiet of each hearth-stone
>   Is purchased by their blood;
> And for us they wear the cross and thorns of Christhood,
>   In their noble, martyr mood."

A voice of woe, a voice of pleading, a cry from thousands wounded in battle, from thousands perishing in pestilential swamps, from thousands starving in rebel prisons, goes swelling over the land; and swift feet and swift fingers move in answer, and husbands must give when wives entreat, and lovers must work when loved ones command, and "monster Fairs" spring up as by magic, and help is on its way. It is a sublime, a thrilling sight. The war is giving us new and loftier views of the grandeur of woman's mission. And when the triumph is gained, as gained it surely will be, the historic pen that records the heroism of the sons of the North, will record, on a page equally imperishable, the heroism of its daughters.

Not less deserving of grateful eulogy are the agencies through which these benefactions find their outlet and distribution. The Sanitary and Christian Commissions, what soldier does not bless them? What one does not regard them with emotions of thankfulness like those of the parched wanderer in the desert, when he hears the murmur of the fountain, and sees before him the cool verdure of the oasis? What angels have these organizations been to our suffering heroes! How often have their kindly offices cheered them on the weary march, revived them after the exhaustion of the fight, soothed them in sickness and pain! Such is the perfection of their arrangements, such the breadth and amplitude of their scope, that they reach the most distant point to which our forces have penetrated, and cover the whole expanse of the war. Wherever want is to be found, there their ministrations extend. Hundreds of earnest, self-denying men, acting as their delegates and representatives, carry supplies to the wounded on the field of battle and in the hospitals, comfort them with words of holy cheer, and point the dim eye of the dying to Christ and heaven. No language can adequately set forth the value of the merciful work thus performed, and no arithmetic can grasp the full measure of its results. We know that, in this way, eighty millions of dollars, the free gift of the people, have been expended in relieving our sick and wounded soldiers. But who shall reckon up the number of precious lives which this expenditure has saved, or estimate the amount of suffering it has prevented or assuaged? Go to the bloody field of Gettysburg. Survey the frightful scenes which followed the Battles of the Wilderness. See hosts of helpers flocking from every part of the land to these high places of Slaughter, — clergymen, lawyers, physicians, merchants, — all eager to render aid; searching for the wounded among heaps of the slain; bearing them to the hospital-tents; administering cordials; distributing food; watching by the couch of agony; consoling the departing with prayer and Christian hope, and receiving their farewell messages to the dear ones they will see no more. In such humane labors we have but a specimen of what these institutions have been doing all through the war.

But the most important feature of this noble work may be seen in its religious bearings. The efforts which have been made, in connection with it, for the spiritual good of the soldiers, constitute its chief interest, and its brightest renown. Here the Christian Commission has found a wide and open door. Here has been its special province. It was the felt need of more direct labor in this department that led to its formation; and faithfully has it sought to fulfil the purpose of its originators. By its means, the army has been largely supplied with Bibles and religious books; Sabbath schools have been established, and meetings for preaching maintained, whenever the state of military affairs would permit. Every delegate has been a missionary, dispensing, along with comforts for the body, the richer comforts of heavenly Truth. Churches of every denomination, all over the land, have sent their pastors to visit the soldiers, and carry to them the Bread of Life; and many an eloquent apostle has preached the word in the camps of the Potomac or of the Tennessee, to larger and more eager gatherings than ever listened to his voice in the thronged temples of the city. By these varied and continuous labors, superadded to those of the regular chaplains, the Gospel has been brought into direct contact with every division, and brigade, and regiment; and it is not extravagant to affirm that to multitudes the means of salvation have been furnished more abundantly, during their connection with the army, than in any period of their former life.

As a consequence of this fact, a strong religious element pervades the great body of the Union forces. We say not that there are none among them who are insensible to spiritual things. Many desperate characters have entered the service; and these have been rendered more reckless and obdurate by mutual influence and example. But it is far otherwise with the majority. The constant presence of danger and death has produced an abiding seriousness, and brought nigh the thought of God and eternity. Never since the days of Cromwell's Ironsides has there been an army with so much of true piety in it — never one in which the sanctions of the Bible were so generally revered, and the authority of the Divine law so fully recognized. There is many a Havelock among the officers; many a devout Christian in the ranks. From many a tent may be heard, in the still evening hour, the voice of prayer and the hymn of praise. Many a sentinel, as he treads his lonely beat under the watching stars, lifts his heart to God. And many, very many, can face the hottest fire with a courage as steadfast and serene as that of the noble commander,[1] who, as he led his division up the heights of Fredericksburg, along which the rebel batteries poured their terrible hail, being asked by a brother officer if he felt no fear, gave this sublime answer: "I never go into battle without seeming to see Christ above me in the sky."

When the instrumentalities of the Gospel are brought to bear upon masses of men in which such elements exist, special displays of converting grace may well be expected. Nor has this expectation been disappointed. In instances not few, the power of the Divine Spirit has been signally manifested, awakening great numbers from their carelessness, and bringing them in penitence and faith to the feet of Jesus. During the period of inaction that preceded the final advance on Richmond, an extensive revival prevailed for months in the Army

[1] Gen. Couch.

of the Potomac; and hundreds, who afterwards fell in that fearful battle-march, were among the subjects of the work, and had found eternal life through the blood of the Lamb. Who but the All-Knowing can tell how many souls went up, amid the roar of earthly strife, to the realms of everlasting peace, guided thither by the instructions which they had received from the Christian teacher; or how .many, left mangled and bleeding in the dense thickets of the Wilderness, cut off from mortal succor, and slowly perishing with thirst and hunger, were thus enabled to gaze with trustful eyes upon the calm heaven above them, till death dismissed their spirits to the rest of the glorified? One such instance would more than repay all the efforts that have been devoted to the moral welfare of the soldier. What, then, should be our estimate of the work which the Commission has accomplished, when we consider that thousands are now among the saved on high, and thousands among the renewed below, who were rescued by its agency from guilt and ruin?

The cursory view which we have taken of what the nation is doing for its armies, naturally suggests the inquiry, by what principle, or combination of principles, a result so great and beneficent has been achieved. It might, perhaps, on a hasty glance, be deemed sufficient to ascribe it to the humanizing influence of Christianity alone. Yet, to those who look deeper, this answer will not appear entirely satisfactory. Countries, whose Christianity is as active and as controlling as our own, have carried on wars without any such accompanying manifestations of wide-reaching care for those whose blood has been shed in their defence. Doubtless, the desire to do good which the Gospel inspires, underlies this whole movement, and gives to it impulse and vitality. But there are subsidiary causes which must not be overlooked. While the Christianity of the land is at once the originating and the upholding power in the grand exhibition which we witness, it is Christianity, not as we see it under despotic or monarchical governments, but as it develops its benign tendencies in connection with republican institutions, and amidst influences that harmonize with its spirit, and afford scope for its broadest workings. In the military systems of the Old World, the soldier is a mere machine, — a vitalized clod. He comes from a class that has no political rights, and no interest in the questions about which nations contend. He fights for his government because he is hired to fight for it, or because he is compelled to do so by authority against which he has no resource. His thews and sinews are regarded in the same light as cannon and muskets and other munitions of war; and when he falls by disease or in battle, his death is regretted only as the loss of so much fighting material. But the men who compose our armies are citizens, — our sons, brothers, neighbors, — men who are fighting to defend a Government which their suffrages helped to create, and who have the same stake as ourselves in the stupendous struggle. They have gone out from us to save the nationality in which we and they have equal franchises; and when their task is done, they will return, and be with us and of us again. Hence the peculiar relation which the soldiers sustain to the country has had no inconsiderable share in awakening the general concern felt on their behalf, and in calling forth the overflowing generosity with which their wants have been met. Christian philanthropy has been quickened and intensified by the claims of civic brotherhood. Patriotism blends with religion; and devotion to freedom expresses itself by showering benefits on the champions of freedom. How significant the fact! We hail it as the fruitage and the sign of advancing civilization, showing that no people is so humane, no land so just and noble, as that in which a pure Gospel walks hand in hand with Liberty.

But however highly the country may value and cherish its heroes, its munificence cannot surpass their deservings. Our glorious Volunteers! What words can do them fitting honor! What tribute of sympathy and love can equal the debt which we owe them! Among all the mighty legions of mighty empires on which the ages have looked, never has so grand a host rushed to arms, in a cause so holy, under an inspiration so exalted. As the Roman matron, when commanded to show her treasures, presented her sons, saying, "These are my jewels;" so, with greater truth and emphasis, may America point to the vast and stalwart array of young men thronging beneath her banner, and proclaim, These are my Ornament, my Bulwark, my Hope! Under whatever aspect we view them, — whether in regard to their personal qualities, their sacrifices, or their deeds, — their claim to the gratitude and admiration of the present and of coming generations, will appear manifest and indisputable. Contemplate their character. The traitors of the South, and their English abettors and allies, have asserted that the armies of the Union are made up chiefly of "base hirelings," the "scum" of our great cities and of foreign countries. Lying lips never uttered a viler falsehood. A few of this class, gathered from the slums of vice and the haunts of debauchery, have been sent forward as substitutes, in the vain expectation of manufacturing them into soldiers. But they have proved far more expert at deserting than at fighting; and their number is so small in comparison as not to affect the general estimate. The main bulk of our troops is composed of the best blood of the land—its very bone and sinew—farmers and farmers' sons, mechanics, tradesmen—choice contributions of youthful vigor from every industrial pursuit, and from every social condition. And while representatives of other nationalities stand by their side, nobly battling for the country of their adoption, yet the overwhelming majority in all our armies are natives of the soil. "Hirelings" are they! Mercenaries, fighting only for pay and plunder, and caring nothing for the great principles at issue! Away with the foul slander! Had money been their object, they could have found it far more abundantly and safely in civil avocations than in the gory fields of war. No, no! Human records contain no instance of devotion more unselfish, of patriotism more unbought, than that of the men who are waging the deadly strife with treason and rebellion. They have heard their country's call; they have seen their country's danger; they have comprehended the magnitude of the crisis; and, with purpose as high as their hearts are brave, they have hastened to the rescue. For this they have left homes and altars, fathers and mothers, brothers and sisters, wives and children,—all that they love, all that love them,—to encounter the privations and diseases of the camp, and face death in its most hideous forms. The motive that impels them is not gain nor ambition, but reverence for Justice, consecration to the Right. Freedom, Humanity, the wrongs of the lowly—these nerve their arms in the fierce heat of the conflict; and these, when they fall, mingle with their last thought of home, and their last prayer to the All-Righteous One in whose cause they die. "Hirelings!" Not Leonidas and his Spartans, not Tell and his Switzers, were truer and loftier of soul. Honor to the Volunteers, living or dead! May their patriotic zeal and their martyr spirit never be forgotten!

The hardships which they are undergoing for their country's sake merit all, and more than all, the country can do for them. Who but a soldier can fitly describe the toil and discomfort of the soldier's life? The very nature of his calling subjects him to incessant labor and sacrifice. Exposed to all changes of weather and all vicissitudes of climate, to scorching suns by day and chilling damps by night; often without food or shelter, harassed by fatigue, and drenched by tempests, how are his powers of endurance tasked to the utmost! Now, out on the distant picket, he watches through the long and dreary night, shivering with cold, and pelted by the driving hail; nor dares once to close his eyes, lest the lurking foe should steal on him by surprise. Now, in some hurried march, he struggles forward, over mountain and gorge, through tangled swamps, and swollen rivers, and deep mire, sweltering under his heavy musket and haversack, till darkness falls, and, famished and exhausted, he sinks down to rest upon the bare ground. Now he mingles in the stern tumult of battle—rushing from point to point in the rapid evolutions of the fight—up the cliff, down the ravine—in the charge, in the retreat, in the pursuit—amid smoke, and roar, and flame—faint with hunger, parched with thirst, stifled with heat and dust—till his strained energies can bear no more. Now, wounded and bleeding, he is left on the field to wait, through weary hours and days of anguish, for the help which is so long—oh! so long—in coming. And now he is stretched on a narrow cot in the hospital, racked with pain and fever, with no loved voice to cheer him, and no hand of wife or sister to wipe the death-drops from his brow. All this he endures for us. He goes to the war that we may remain at home; toils that we may rest; sleeps on the frozen earth that we may sleep securely in our beds of down; braves danger that we may be in safety; invades the enemy that the enemy may not invade us; dies that we may live. And shall we not care for them who thus care for us, and are preserving, at such fearful cost, all that we hold precious? Must not every manly, every Christian sentiment invoke us to a just appreciation of their sacrifices, and to earnest endeavors to alleviate, as far as we may, their sharpness and severity? Withered be the hand that opens not to their needs, and palsied be the tongue that is silent in their praise!

With an emphasis not less potent, the achievements of our defenders demand from us the tribute of grateful regard. Do you ask what they have done? Done! They have saved the nation,— saved it from a death of violence and shame,— and opened before it a new life, and a brighter career than nation ever trod. Done! They have saved the Union from dismemberment, and established it on a broader and more impregnable basis. Done! They have saved Freedom and Constitutional Government to us, to our children, and to mankind. Done! They have struck and shivered with their bayonets the chains of four millions of slaves. Done! What have they not done that the awful exigency required? But for them, vain would have been the wisdom of the statesman, vain the zeal of the patriot. But for them, all would have been lost; Treason would have triumphed; and our national unity, our material progress, our political and social blessings, our industry, our wealth, our rights, our altars, our homes, would have sunk together in the gulf of anarchy or of despotism. They have grappled the giant might of the Rebellion. They have hurled it back. They have laid it prostrate at their feet. Their work is nearly finished. One blow more, and it will be complete — complete in stupendous victory and everlasting fame.

And then they will return to their old places among us, and mingle again in the scenes and activities of peace. Let the nation spread wide its arms to embrace its deliverers. Receive them with thanks and honors, with high festival and loud rejoicings. With ringing bells, and waving banners, and pealing artillery, ye celebrated their outgoing. With demonstrations more glad and exulting, celebrate their "Welcome Home." Study to promote their interests. Open to them avenues of employment. Cherish them ever as the saviours of their country, its strength, and its glory.

They will return — but, alas! not all. A mighty host will come back no more. They lie in bloody graves all over the Southern land, guarding the soil which their swords have won, and holding it in trust for Freedom. But their memory can never die. It is with us — a holy charge — an immortal legacy. It was a beautiful fancy of ancient Paganism, that the good and brave were changed at death into stars; and that, whenever a hero left the earth, a new star blazed out in the firmament. So is it with our fallen sons and brothers. They have not perished. They are translated — fixed in the shining arch of the moral heavens, among the illustrious ones, of all climes and ages, who have died for the

Right. And there they are — four hundred thousand stars in the sky of Liberty — stars never to set, never to grow dim — a glorious galaxy for generations to gaze at and worship, while centuries revolve.

> "Four hundred thousand men,
>   The brave, the good, the true,
> In tangled wood, in mountain glen,
> On battle plain, in prison pen,
>   Lie dead for me and you!
> Four hundred thousand of the brave
> Have made our ransomed soil their grave,
>   For me and you!
>   Good friend, for me and you!
>
> "On many a bloody plain
>   Their ready swords they drew,
> And poured their life-blood, like the rain,
> A home, a heritage, to gain,
>   To gain for me and you!
> Our brothers mustered by our side,
> They marched, and fought, and nobly died,
>   For me and you!
>   Good friend, for me and you!
>
> "In treason's prison-hold,
>   Their martyr spirits grew
> To stature like the saints of old,
> While, amid agonies untold,
>   They starved for me and you!
> The good, the patient, and the tried,
> Four hundred thousand men have died,
>   For me and you!
>   Good friend, for me and you!

"A debt we ne'er can pay
 To them is justly due,
And to the nation's latest day
Our children's children still shall say,
 'They died for me and you!'
Four hundred thousand of the brave
Made this, our ransomed soil, their grave,
 For me and you!
 Good friend, for me and you!"

CHAPTER VIII.

THE DEEP PLEADING FOR ITS HEROES.

"THE DEEP UTTERED HIS VOICE."—*Hab.* iii. 10.

"THE deep uttered his voice!" Aye, the deep has a voice, and a meaning one too; a voice of many tones, and of various import. Who that has stood beside it, on a still summer night, while stars were shining above it, and soft breezes floating over it, and gentle waves rippling to the shore, has not heard its voice, low and sweet, yet full of power, coming up from its far abysses, whispering of hope and peace, and telling of that glorious Being, of whose repose, infinitude and eternity it is the emblem? Or who that has looked on it when the tempest was abroad, lashing it into wild tumult, has not felt, as he listened to its roar, the force of the inspired words, "The floods have lifted up their voice"? Oh, eloquent is the sea! In all its ever-changing aspects, in calm and in storm, flashing with sunshine, silvered with the moon's milder beams, or rolling dark and mountainous in its hour of wrath, it speaks a language alike solemn, mysterious, sublime — preaching of Immensity, declaring the Omnipotent.

But the sea has another voice, less majestic indeed, but not less impressive to the philanthropist and the Christian — the appeal which it sends forth in behalf of its children. To a benevolent mind the ocean is interesting, not only as it is in itself a world of wonders, the grandest mirror of the Creator's power; but also as it is the home of myriads of human beings, whose lives are spent in traversing its pathless solitudes. It is their sphere of labor, the theatre of their exploits, the scene of their cares, and joys, and sorrows. Its winds and waves are their companions; its soundless depths too often their sepulchre. For these, its foster sons, "the deep uttereth its voice."

Poets have told us that, on the far Indian coast, there is a shell which, when held to the ear, repeats, in low breathing murmurs, all the sounds of its native ocean. Such is the design of this chapter. Its object is to respond to the sea — to echo the cry of the sailor. Let us, then, draw near, and listen to the message which it brings from the expanse of waters.

There is a voice of Complaint from the sea. No class of men have conferred higher benefits on society than mariners; yet none have received from it so little appreciation and reward. The men of the land, engrossed by the busy activities of their own sphere, and living in immediate contact with the course of human development, are apt to regard themselves as the chief agents of social progress, and to look upon their brethren of the sea as bringing to it no important contributions. But so far from this being true, it may be asserted with confidence that seamen have borne their full share in those great achievements of peace and of war, which have wielded so potent a ministry in improving the condition of our race. Who, with incredible hardships and perils, amidst polar ice, and beneath tropic suns, has explored the briny waste, and given new continents to man? The sailor. Who, connecting nations otherwise separated by impassable barriers, has diffused the light of arts, science and civilization, and poured their blessings over the world? The sailor. Who bears to distant lands the surplus products of our soil, and brings back in return the riches of all climes — sweeping every coast, from the frozen North to the golden South and the spicy East, to gather whatever can increase our wealth, or enhance the comfort and luxury of our homes? The sailor. Who, when the invading foe hung on our shores, covering every bay and harbor with his fleets, encountered him on his own element, and bore "the star-spangled banner" in triumph over the waters? The sailor. And in the gigantic Rebellion of the South, which has cost us such a fearful expenditure of wealth and of blood to subdue, our obligations to the sailor have been unspeakably augmented. It is true that the position of the revolted States necessarily confined the chief theatre of strife to the land; and hence the naval forces employed, though vastly larger than at any former period, have been small compared with the immense armies in the field. Nevertheless, they have accomplished magnificent results. No portion of the nation's defenders has surpassed them in zeal and daring, and none have rendered more effective aid in the overthrow of treason, and in the final triumph of freedom and justice. All through the war, the record of the navy has been full of patriotic enthusiasm and noble deeds. Had it done nothing else, its vigilance and success in maintaining the blockade, shutting in the Confederacy from outside help, and thereby hastening its fall, would alone have entitled it to the lasting gratitude of the country. This, however, is but an insignificant part of its achievements. To its prowess we owe the splendid victories of Fort Henry, of Port Royal, of New Orleans, of Mobile, of Fort Fisher, and a long list of others that have contributed materially to bring about the grand consummation in which we rejoice. How often, when our sky was the darkest, and disaster after disaster had shrouded the land in doubt and gloom, has some telling blow struck by the navy broken through the cloud, and restored hope and confidence! When the tidings flashed over the country, that the terrible Merrimac had entered Hampton Roads, sunk two of our finest ships of war, and, having proved herself invulnerable to the fire of all our batteries, was waiting only for morning to renew the attack, destroy our entire fleet, dismantle Fortress Monroe, and plough her way out to sea, carrying destruction to our cities, what anxiety and fear oppressed every loyal heart! But how great was the relief, how jubilant the exultation, when fast upon the news of evil and the omens of dread came the cheering intelligence that, during the night, the little Monitor had crept into the bay, met the iron-ribbed monster, and driven him back wounded and crippled to his lair! This is but one, out of the many instances that might be cited, in which the timely presence and the dauntless courage of the sailor have averted impending danger, and changed defeat to victory. In all the gulfs and estuaries that indent the rebel territory, on all the rivers that intersect it,—wherever a gunboat could swim or a launch could penetrate,—sailors have borne the Stars and Stripes, scattering the foe with their huge artillery, turning the tide of battle, and co-operating with our armies in re-establishing the authority of the Government over all the insurgent domain.

Such and so important is the relation which seamen sustain to the public weal. So marked is their influence on the prosperity of the country in seasons of quietness — so faithful and strong the shield which they interpose for its defence in seasons of peril. And what, in most cases, has been their reward? Abuse, degradation, on the sea; neglect, scorn, robbery, on the land. A few, placed in situations of command, have been caressed and honored. But the common mass, the real authors of all these benefits, the men by whose patient labors Discovery has visited every green isle of the ocean, and social improvement spread itself over the earth, — from whose sacrifices and dangers Commerce has drawn its life — from whose blood Victory has plumed her eagle wing, — have been undervalued or forgotten. Satisfied with reluctantly doling out to them their scanty wages, or the trivial remnants of prize-money left from the hands of lawyers and courts and officials, society has felt itself absolved from all further obligation, and has quietly abandoned them to the caprice of tyrants on board, and to the mercy of sharpers on shore. Paltry and feeble are the efforts that have been made to redress their wrongs; to improve their physical condition; to elevate them intellectually, socially, morally; or to render them, in any respect, a return suited to the magnitude of their services. Even during the war, while the navy has been covering itself with glory, and the brows of commodores and admirals are crowned with laurel, and their names celebrated in song, and their deeds justly extolled by the plaudits of a grateful people, how little has been thought of the sailor, the toiling, fighting sailor, through whom they have won their renown? Who has rehearsed his exploits? Who has told how he trained and pointed his heavy guns on the bloody deck, and stood fearlessly at his post, while shot and shell were crashing around him? Here and there an instance of heroism may have awakened public regard, like that of the brave tars on the Cumberland, who, when the ship was sinking, and most of her guns were under water, refused to leave her till they had fired another broadside at the enemy, and so went down with her into the engulfing waves. But over the vast multitude of such acts the silence of oblivion has been suffered to fall; and the only guerdon which their authors have received is the consciousness of having performed them. There has been a similar indifference with respect to their necessities and their sufferings. For the welfare of our soldiers the sympathies of the whole nation have been enlisted. Treasure has flowed forth like water to supply them with comforts which the regulations of the Government did not provide. Sanitary and Christian Commissions have been organized to care for their wants, with a breadth of design, and an amplitude of resources, never before seen in the history of the world. Fair hands, and countless hands, have toiled day and night to furnish them with clothing. Women have left their homes, physicians their practice, clergymen their flocks, to nurse the sick, tend the wounded, and preach the Gospel in the camps. The benevolence of the land has poured itself out in a mighty stream to minister to the needs of the army. And the army has well deserved it. Too much has not been done, too much cannot be done, for the men who have gone to the tented field in obedience to their country's call. But by what strange oversight is it that the sailor, equally self-sacrificing, equally meritorious, has found no place in these demonstrations of kindness? Why has he been shut out from the solicitudes and benefactions of the nation? Why have no earnest, comprehensive endeavors been put forth to mitigate his privations, and promote his temporal and spiritual well-being? However this remissness may be explained, it cannot be excused. Nor can we evade the responsibility which rests upon us to do what we can to repair it. We owe a vast debt to sailors — a debt which it is high time we should begin to pay. And to enforce this claim, the sea, in every swelling gale and sounding billow, sends forth its summons. By the dead that sleep in its bosom, by the living that wander upon it, by the memory of their glorious deeds, by all the benefits which the children of the Deep have lavished on the children of the Land, it calls upon us to cancel the long arrears which ages of neglect have run up against us.

There is a voice of Want from the sea. It has been supposed by many, that mariners can have no necessities but such as are common to mankind at large, and that the general benevolence which seeks the good of the whole, is adequate for them. But the sailor is a peculiar being. He resembles no other. The very nature of his pursuits renders him unique in all his habits, thoughts, and feelings. He has mental and moral characteristics, social and religious privations, intellectual and spiritual needs, incident to himself alone. Even his physical state is not only inferior to that of the humblest denizen of the land, but in some essential features different from it. Compelled to feed on the coarsest fare, served in the rudest manner; exposed, in the vicissitudes of his changeful life, to all the extremes of heat and cold, thirst and hunger; the victim often of oppression and violence from arbitrary power,—a power against which he has no remedy at hand, and but an uncertain one in prospect,—he has a special claim on us for relief and protection.

But it is pre-eminently for his mind and his heart that our sympathy should be enlisted, and our energies called into action. Taken perhaps when a mere child from the fostering care of the parental roof, or from the neglect and desolation of orphanage, and committed to the companionship and training of men as wild and rough as the winds they encounter, what could you expect him to become but the brutal and reckless creature which he frequently is? Is it wonderful that Ignorance should mark him for its own, Superstition bind its fetters round him, and Defiance, uniting with Despair, render him dead to all self-respect, and heedless alike of the interests of this world and of that which is to come? What else could be looked for from the tuition to which he has been subjected?

Will it be said that he may, by his own unassisted efforts, or through ordinary aids, ameliorate his condition, and raise himself in the scale of intelligence and happiness? But how is he to do this? Where are the means appropriate or accessible to him? What avails it to him that sources of instruction, temples of worship, and all the appliances of mental and religious culture, are multiplied throughout the land? Lone and insulated, he stands apart from them all. He is not a dweller on the land. The greatest portion of his existence is passed in buffeting the surge and the storm, far away from these benign instrumentalities. When, at intervals, he does visit the haunts of men, it is only to be cheated and plundered, seduced into worse temptations, and made more depraved and wretched than before. And, to crown the evils of his lot, Hope, the grand Uplifter, — Hope, the inspirer of high thoughts and noble endeavors, — is an exile from his breast. He cannot rise, for he cannot hope.

In behalf of this isolated class specific exertions are demanded. It is our imperative duty to provide and sustain in operation a series of agencies adapted to their circumstances, and commensurate with their wants. In every naval station, in every resort of seamen, fitting accommodations should be furnished, where they may be safe from the arts of those who, for their own purposes, would lead them to ruin. Schools and Libraries should be established for their improvement. Places of worship should be set apart, and a competent ministry maintained, whose labors shall be devoted to their especial service. In a word, all the apparatus of benevolence and of piety must be brought to bear directly on their present and their eternal well-being. Nor should we limit our solicitude to the periods of their transient residence on shore, but seek to supply them when on the deep with every means of religious instruction which it is possible to place within their reach. Thus ought we to follow with the tokens of our zeal and of our love the path of those who are "separate from their brethren."

There is a voice of Sorrow from the sea. Ardent youth in the spirit of rash adventure, and poets who have a license to misrepresent all things, love to paint a sea-faring life in colors of unreal beauty. Thus Byron makes his Corsair exclaim,

> "O'er the glad waters of the dark blue sea,
> Our thoughts as boundless, and our souls as free,
> Far as the breeze can bear, the billows foam,
> Survey our empire, and behold our home.
> Ours the wild life in tumult still to range
> From toil to rest, and joy in every change.
> Oh, who can tell, save he whose heart hath tried,
> And danced in triumph o'er the waters wide,
> The exulting sense, the pulse's maddening play,
> That thrills the wanderer of that trackless way?"

But had Byron, with all his instinctive fondness for the sea, been a sailor before the mast, his verse would have borne a very different burden. It is, indeed, a kind ordination of Providence, that the human mind, however painful the situation in which it may be placed, becomes at length familiar with its ills, and in a measure insensible to their pressure. And it is also true that sailors, as a class, are proverbially thoughtless and void of care. Still, it may be confidently asserted that "life on the ocean wave," notwithstanding the charm which novelty may throw around it, is, in most instances, replete with hardships. The very banishment from society, the severance from domestic ties and enjoyments which it imposes, is in itself a source of constant and severe affliction. The sailor may be vicious and degraded; but he is never unfeeling. On the contrary, his affections appear to be rendered even more keen and active from the deprivations to which they are subjected. What, then, must he not suffer in that continual separation from kindred and home which his calling demands? Forced to part from all the cherished objects of his love,—uncertain what may befall them in his absence on the long and dangerous voyage,—how must his heart bleed, as the winds bear him away! And when the storm comes down in its wrath, and death yawns beneath him, with what agony must he think of the dear ones whom he may see no more! Or if, with no such connections, he is cast solitary on the waters, to float, like a lone weed, wherever the breeze and the tide may carry him, what isolation, what desolateness, must he not feel!

Add to these trials the physical sufferings which fall to his lot. Now, drenched and shivering, he keeps the midnight watch. Now he climbs the frozen and slippery rigging, amidst driving sleet and the howling of the tempest. Now he endures the extremity of famine. Now, wasted with wounds or sickness, he lies in the dark forecastle, or in some gloomy hospital, with no mother's or sister's hand to smooth his pillow, and wipe his fevered brow. Now he is shipwrecked, and thrown destitute among strangers, or exposed in an open boat, without food or drink, to scorching suns by day, and piercing cold by night — drifting on and on, over the wide, wide ocean — vainly watching for some friendly sail — and proving, in its fullest bitterness, that sickness of the heart which springeth from "hope deferred." Oh, "there is sorrow on the sea."

But there is a sharper grief which sometimes rends the bosom of the sailor. It is the sting of Conscience, the pang of undying remorse. He often becomes dissolute and abandoned, and plunges into the lowest depths of debauchery. But he cannot so steep himself in forgetfulness as to lose all sense of his guilt and shame. The days of his early innocence, of his father's counsels and his mother's prayers, come back to him, like accusing spirits from the grave. Regret for what he was, loathing of what he is, dread of what he may be, fill him with indescribable anguish. Oh, think not, as you see him wallowing in licentiousness, raising the shout of drunken revelry, and giving play to all his unbridled passions, that he is too callous or too besotted to know and feel his ruin. A man lying among scorpions, or encircled by fire, is more at ease than he. His breast is the abode of torturing thoughts and secret woes, which it needs but a touch to call forth.

By all these manifold sorrows we are invoked to come to the help of the mariner. In tones of piercing entreaty, they conjure us to commiserate his griefs, to relieve his distresses, to pluck him from the grasp of the destroyer, and, by pouring on his mind the light and hopes of the Gospel, seek to bring him, when his stormy voyage is ended, to that secure and blissful Haven, where every pain will be forgotten, every joy consummated, in eternal Peace.

There is a voice of Danger from the sea. In no calling is life so precarious as in that of the sailor. Its average term is shorter with this class than with any other. Not even to the soldier in the field of war does death come with so swift and sure a step as to the mariner on the deep. Destruction threatens him in a thousand shapes, and pursues him, with relentless purpose, through all his career. The diseases of the various climates which he visits stand ready to seize him as their prey. The slightest miscalculation of his course — the fall of a mast — a sudden leak — a hidden rock — fire, wind, or the lightning of heaven — may at any moment cut short his existence. Afloat on a treacherous element, with only a frail plank between him and the abyss, he has death ever beneath, above, and around him.

All this should incite us to do quickly whatever is to be done for his good, lest, while we linger, he pass beyond our sight to the scene of everlasting retribution.

But these dangers that so thickly beset him are only a type of the far greater moral perils by which he is encompassed. Indeed, the critical position in which his own "home of oak" is often placed, will furnish the fittest emblem of the hazards to which his immortal interests are exposed. See that ship, rocking in the hurricane, on a lee shore, with quicksands under her keel, and breakers on every side! Her anchors may be strong, her timbers stanch, her bearing noble and gallant. But, unless some mighty deliverance interpose, she must inevitably perish. Similar is the spiritual jeopardy that environs the sailor. Like all his fellow-men, he is by nature a sinner, and liable as such to final condemnation. Nothing can avert from him this doom but faith in the blood of Christ — faith wrought in his heart by the Spirit of Grace, and leading him to repentance and a holy life. But how many obstacles combine, in his case, to prevent such a result! From the ordinary means of salvation he is, for the most part, withdrawn; while, at the same time, he is brought into close and peculiar contact with the agencies of evil. On ship-board, there may be no teacher of truth to whisper in his ear the word of advice and warning. But he is sure to have vicious companions, ready to infect him with their poison, and lure him into sin and profligacy. On shore, few may be found to guide him to the house of God, and point him to the Fountain of Life. But deceivers are certain to lie in wait at every corner to ensnare and betray him. Here, the siren voices of Pleasure allure him to her deadly embrace. There, Infidelity hangs out its false lights, to draw him on the shoals of Doubt and Delusion. Here, the vender of intoxicating drinks throws open his moral pest-house, to invite him to taste the cup of madness and woe; and there, the theatre, that vestibule of Hell, solicits him to enter its polluted inclosure, and witness scenes whose catastrophe is the loss of the soul. Thus, while angels of grace and ministers of mercy seldom come within his sphere, the black demons of seduction and ruin constantly hover about his path, and flap over him their death-distilling wings. Oh, how terrible is the state of the poor sailor, with all these engines of destruction at work upon him, and conspiring with his own depravity to drag him down to the pit!

But the greater his danger, the more earnest should be our effort to save him. If you saw him on the point of being plunged into the waves, or dashed on the rocks, how eagerly would you fly to his aid! And the more imminent his peril, the more prompt and vigorous would be your endeavors. Such is our duty now. Men of God! to the rescue. Your brother of the sea is ready to perish. He is falling. He is overboard. Man the life-boat. Ply the oars. Throw out to him the Gospel. Cease not, till, by the blessing of God, he is brought to the firm ground of scriptural safety.

There is a voice of Hope from the sea. Signs of promise greet us, heralding the dawn of a brighter day for the sailor. The gloom of neglect and debasement, that has for centuries hung over him, is passing away. Philanthropy, instead of regarding him as a Pariah, sunk by his vices below her reach, has awoke to a sense of his needs, and is devising plans to elevate and bless him. Christian benevolence and Christian zeal have stretched out their arms to embrace him. Many hearts mourn his degradation. Many hands are striving to lift him up. In all the chief centres of Commerce, in every rendezvous of ships, instrumentalities are at work for his recovery. Beside the Custom House and the Exchange, beside the Navy Yard and the Receiving Ship, stand the Seaman's Home and the Seaman's Chapel; and Bethel flags, like Banners of Salvation, are streaming over the waters. The happy effects on his condition and on his character are already manifest, and are full of encouragement. On the distant main, he hears the glad tidings; and joy kindles in his eye, and on his weather-stained cheek ·glistens the tear of gratitude. He rises up from his despondency. He no longer feels himself an outcast, cut off from the sympathies of his species — wandering ever with the ban of exile upon him — toiling for all — owned and cherished by none. As he walks the deck, in the deep hush of night, beneath the stars of other zones, he thinks of the friends far away who watch for his welfare; and, in the consciousness that there are those who love him and would do him good, the rock melts from his nature, and despair leaves his soul. And we cannot doubt that, through the exertions now made, and the more comprehensive and energetic ones which, we trust, will yet be made, this whole forsaken class shall be gathered into the fold of the Universal Shepherd. The docility, generosity, frankness, and warm sensibility, which so strikingly distinguish the sailor, render him peculiarly accessible to Christian influence, and a most hopeful subject for its exercise. And, more than all, the Word of inspired Truth has expressly foretold his redemption. It is announced, as one of the earliest links in that sublime series of events which is to usher in the final triumph of the Church, that "the abundance of the sea shall be converted unto her." The fulfilment of this prophecy is already begun. Already have the laborers in this field brought home the first ripe sheaves with rejoicing. And we believe that what we now see is but the commencement of a long chain of efforts and successes, that shall go on ever increasing, until the empire of the sea shall be conquered for Christ.

Then shall the sons of the ocean unite with the sons of the land in spreading the knowledge of the Saviour's grace. Hitherto, one of the greatest obstacles in the work of evangelizing the Heathen has been the vicious conduct of seamen from Christian countries, and the unfavorable impression which they have given of the Gospel. Thus, as in the Apocalyptic Vision, "the flood has warred against the Church." But when mariners shall be converted, "the flood," as well as "the earth" shall "help her," and extend her reign. The multitude of those that go down to the sea in ships, and do business in the great waters, shall become messengers of mercy, publishing on the wings of every wind the news of salvation. And oh! what victories will the Gospel win, when navigation shall thus be consecrated to its service; when every dockyard and harbor shall be holy ground, every sailor a missionary, and every vessel that swims a Bethel, waving from its mizzen peak the Flag of Redemption, and bearing the name of Jesus over the world-encircling deep! Gloriously will the Cross then triumph: and swift, swift will be the flight of the

Angel, proclaiming its atoning Sacrifice to all the kindreds of men. And when the blest consummation shall at length arrive; when Messiah shall receive His appointed kingdom, and introduce the Jubilee of this long scourged and groaning creation, banishing from it every stain of sin and every sound of woe; then shall the voice of the ransomed Sea, and the voice of the recovered Earth, combine with the voice of a holy heaven, to swell the grand, eternal chorus, "ALLELUIA, FOR THE LORD GOD OMNIPOTENT REIGNETH."

CHAPTER IX.

MEMORIES AND LESSONS.

"I WILL REMEMBER THE YEARS OF THE RIGHT HAND OF THE MOST HIGH."—*Psalm* lxxvii. 10.

IN following the course of a river, we often find it flowing on for many miles with a smooth and uniform current, and without any striking increase of volume or change in its direction. Nor is there any marked difference in the scenery through which it passes. We meet along its banks the same succession of soft meadows and gently sloping hills — the same expanse of cultivated country, dotted with farmhouses and villages, and presenting a picture as serene as its own placid waters. But, after a time, we enter a wilder region. The mountains come nearer, and rise up in rugged grandeur. The river grows narrower, deeper, swifter. Instead of gliding peacefully on its way, with a surface so calm and still that a child's boat might venture upon it, it becomes rough and turbulent, lashing the shores in its wrath, dashing against rocks, foaming among rapids, till it plunges, in spray and thunder, down the cataract. Looking at it now, as it shoots like an arrow through the gorge, or leaps in its noisy might over the precipice, we can scarcely believe it the same which a little while ago we saw moving so slowly and silently. Yet not only is it the same, but it was back among those tranquil scenes that its flood gathered strength for the conflict which we witness. Every falling shower, every spring breaking out from the hillside, every little brook stealing through the valley, fed and replenished it, till it acquired a body and a force whose impetuous ongoing nothing can withstand. We wonder at the power of the angry torrent. But the power was in the river before; the cliff and the defile have merely called forth and displayed it.

So in the stream of Divine Providence there are long stretches of repose and quietness. The tide of events, perhaps for centuries, moves on with an even and almost imperceptible progress. There are no upheavals, no abrupt turnings, no sudden hastening forward to great social and moral revolutions. To mortal view, God seems to have forsaken the earth, and left the current of human affairs to pursue its course, without change and without disturbance. But such a conception, however natural, is utterly unfounded. Jehovah has not abandoned His cause, nor ceased to fulfil His purposes in the world, when our unbelief can discover no visible proofs of His interposition. Even in those very periods of apparent inaction, when we think His hand withdrawn, He is but preparing to stretch it out with more resistless vigor — collecting the instruments by which He works — turning into one channel all the scattered rills of influence that permeate society, and directing their united contributions toward the coming issue. And then, when the river of His power is full, we see the stir, the commotion, the rush of the accumulated waters to their appointed outflow.

These great epochs of the world's history, in which the interference of the Almighty has been signally manifested, are referred to by the Psalmist, as "the years of the right hand of the Most High." The right hand of a man is the symbol of his strength, and the organ by which that strength is most commonly exerted. Hence, in the Scriptures, the special forth-puttings of God's agency on earth are figuratively ascribed to His right hand; and the times in which they occur, are denominated times of His right hand. It is not, however, to be inferred that the sacred writers intend to represent the arm of Omnipotence as idle during all those intervals, in which no startling exhibitions of its energy meet the eyes of men. That arm never rests, is never weary, never intermits its manifold operations in the realms of Providence and of Grace. It rolls round the wheels of the universe, and feeds and upholds all the countless tribes of animated existence. The support of the feeblest insect that lives its brief day and perishes, is as much its work as the deliverance of an empire, or the marshalling of the celestial orbs along their everlasting circuits. Yet, as there are occasions on which the Almighty departs from the ordinary methods of His procedure, and displays His overruling presence under new and more impressive forms, — coming forth to establish right, to defeat wrong, to punish the oppressor in a manner so distinct and emphatic as to arrest the dullest mind, — we may properly regard these occasions as grand eras of Divine power.

Such eras there had been in the experience of the nation over which David reigned. With mighty signs and wonders, God had brought them out of the house of bondage in Egypt, surrounded them during their protracted wanderings in the wilderness by miraculous manifestations of His care, led them into the land of promise, subdued their enemies before them, and settled them in secure and peaceful homes. And often, in later generations, when the environing hosts of the heathen threatened to overwhelm them, and their very existence as a people seemed trembling in the balance, the same succoring Hand was revealed for their rescue. The entire history of the Chosen Tribes was marked by similar features, and formed an almost unbroken series of supernatural interventions. To these instances of marvellous dealing the royal bard alludes; and how deeply they dwelt in his mind, how gratefully he reviewed them, how worthy of commemoration he deemed them, appears from the frequency with which he made them the burden of his inspired song.

The year just closed has been to us and to our country pre-eminently a "year of the right hand of the Most High." In all the vast succession of years that have passed over the earth since time began, no one, save that which hailed the coming of the Saviour, can equal it in the greatness of its events, and in their far-reaching influence on the destinies of our race. Its circling months have been full of stupendous developments — developments not limited to our own land and day, but extending to every land, and to unborn generations. And throughout the advancing centuries, the transactions and results of "the Great Rebellion," and its astounding close, will tower up among the ages as grand peaks in human history, overtopped only by Bethlehem and Calvary. From the high ground of repose and safety on which we now stand, shall we not look back upon these wonders of the Divine Hand, and draw from the review the instruction which it is so fitted to impart? On the memories and the lessons of the year let us fasten our thoughtful ponderings.

One memory of the year, which must ever render it conspicuous among the epochs of Jehovah's power, is the final overthrow of the most atrocious Conspiracy against Freedom and constitutional government, with which the earth's record is stained. At the beginning of the period over which our retrospect extends, that conspiracy, though wounded and staggering, was still unconquered, still defiant. For nearly four years we had been struggling, with changeful fortunes, to subdue it; now saddened by repulses, now jubilant with victory. Treasure, almost fabulous in amount, had been expended. Battles had been fought whose magnitude astonished the nations. Hundreds of thousands of our bravest and noblest were lying in bloody graves. Yet the triumph was not gained. Yet the fight went on. Our sons and brothers were falling still, and still others were going forth to fall. Thus the new year found us still writhing and bleeding in the fell encounter. Huge armies confronted each other. Grant, beleaguering the rebel capital, watched for the favorable moment to hurl a blow at the traitor hordes, which we trusted would be crushing and decisive. But the issue none could certainly foresee. Sherman was on his wonderful march, and though sweeping with the speed and havoc of a tornado through the very heart of the Confederacy, yet he had vanished from our sight amid pathless swamps and wild savannas, and we knew not what disasters might have befallen him. There was progress, there was hope. The ranks of the loyal were growing stronger; the ranks of the disloyal were growing weaker. Yet doubt and gloom still hung in the sky; and no man could assuredly tell when the end would come, or what it would be.

But the time was now ripe for the God of battles to interpose. He had chastened us for our connection with the foul national iniquity that brought on the war. He had purified us by trial, till we were willing to uproot that iniquity, and cast it away. He had humbled our self-confidence. He had taught us dependence on Himself. He had strengthened our love of country by compelling us to venture all in the grapple for its life. The way of His power having been thus prepared, we saw, while the year was yet in its youth, His right hand stretched out from heaven over the rebel host. Sudden as the crash of thunder, the stroke descended, overwhelming, irrecoverable. We looked, and lo! the God-defying Babel which Slavery and Treason had striven to rear, founded on chains, and cemented with fratricidal blood, was shivered into fragments. The House of Bondage was demolished, and all its Upas timbers, State-rights, Secession, Caste, Property in Man, ground to powder. The bloody Despotism of the oligarchs was dead, its citadel taken, its legions disarmed and captive, its officials dispersed, its mock chief flying from the justice of an outraged nation — soon to await that justice in a felon's cell, and soon, we trust, to receive that justice in a felon's death.

That this magnificent result — a result as rapid as it was complete — is to be attributed to the direct agency of the Most High, no believer in His all-disposing providence can hesitate to admit. The crisis was one in which every perfection of His nature, and every principle of His moral administration, demanded His interference. Our cause was His — the cause of law, of order, of human liberty and of human progression; and so, of Truth and Righteousness in the earth. We had not begun the conflict. It had been forced upon us, without provocation, and without the pretence of any, by the ambitious leaders of the South, seeking to set up a sovereignty in which the many should be the thralls of the few, and where those few might riot in the lust and violence of unbridled dominion. We were compelled to decide between the alternatives of putting down the Rebellion by force of arms, or of seeing the Government destroyed, the Union dissolved, and our nationality extinguished. Heaven-led, we chose war — war in its direst form, civil and internecine — war protracted, sanguinary, all-wasting, as we knew such a war must be — yet war better and holier than peace, when peace is bought by the sacrifice of all that patriotism and humanity hold dear. Had we failed in the struggle, what words can paint the evils that would have followed? Or what rewards of inglorious submission could be deemed a recompense for them? This noble Republic, built by the wisdom and prowess of our fathers, — the Home of Liberty — the Refuge of the outcast — the Hope of down-trodden races, — would have been split into antagonistic and ever warring sections, and made the byword of tyrants — the scoff of the privileged orders that have hated and feared it. Amid the roar of intestine anarchy, and the perpetual encroachments of the slave-power, free institutions would have perished from the continent; and while their death-knell rung through the world, civilization and Christianity, the honor of God, and the well-being of man, would have felt the shock, in all lands, and for all time. Shall we not, then, ever hold in vivid remembrance the year, in which the right hand of the All-Merciful warded off from us a catastrophe pregnant with consequences so deplorable, and gave to our principles a new career of development, and to our example a higher plane of influence?

> "Did we dare,
> In our agony of prayer,
> Ask for more than He has done?
> When was ever His right hand
> Over any time or land
> Stretched as now beneath the sun?"

Another event of the year which ought never to be forgotten, is the Restoration of Peace. Who can recall the long and weary months during which the war continued, without a feeling like that which we experience at the recollection of some frightful vision departed, some dread peril escaped, some deadly agony past? How sad were those days! How we rose up, calm and stern indeed, yet full of sorrow, when the tidings came that traitorous guns had dishonored our country's flag; and from city and hamlet, from mountain and valley, from lake and prairie, the cry of a roused nation went forth in its majesty! How our hearts were wrung, what tears we shed, what prayers burst from our lips, as our young heroes left home and loved ones for the gory fields where Freedom summoned them! How we watched and waited for the expected meeting with the foe! How we hoped for victory! How we were startled and appalled by defeat! What trembling and sickness of soul came over us, as the woeful echoes of Bull Run and Ball's Bluff swept through the land! With what harrowing suspense we wore out the dreary winter, in which the ominous words, "All quiet along the Potomac," alone greeted our impatient ears! How our courage drooped at the disasters of the Peninsula, of Fredericksburg and Chancellorsville! With what anxious eyes we scanned the lists of the killed and wounded; and what anguish pierced us, as we read there the name of son, husband, brother, slain in the bloody fray, or, worse still, prisoners in the hells of Libby or of Andersonville! And though better news, reports of battles won, of successes achieved, sometimes came to cheer us, yet, as the contest dragged slowly and painfully on; as army after army was exhausted, and levy after levy went forth to take its place, and still the end seemed no nearer — what ceaseless solicitude hung upon us, banishing sleep from our pillows, and joy from our firesides! Oh, those weary, weary years! Can we ever forget them?

Thank God, they are gone — gone, we trust, never to come back. The conflict is ended, — ended by the triumph of the Right, — and Peace has returned. Oh, what delight swelled all hearts, what gladness shone in all faces, when the glorious fact first stood revealed to our long waiting eyes! It was as when mariners, tossed for many perilous days and nights on the stormy deep, and driven hither and thither by the tempest, reach at last a secure haven, and see the still waters, and the green infolding landscape spread out invitingly before them. It was as when the hurricane has gone by, and the blue skies appear, and the sun looks down from a tranquil heaven, and the earth drinks new life from its beams, and every plant and flower sparkles with fresh loveliness.

> "Oh! those were hours when thrilling joy repaid
> The long, long days of darkness, doubts and fears,
> The heart-sick faintness of the hope delayed,
> The waste, the woe, the bloodshed, and the tears,
> That marked the track of those four frightful years.
> All were forgot in the great jubilee.
> E'en wan affliction raised its downcast eye,
> To sigh a thankful prayer amid the glee
> That pealed the shout of triumph loud and high,
> To hail thy battle won, O Liberty!"

Yes, Peace has returned! From Maine to Oregon, from Canada to the Gulf, a redeemed nation rejoices at her coming. Her glad song rings out from every crag and hilltop, from every ocean-coast and far western river. The ploughman sings it in his furrowed field, the reaper as he gathers the golden harvest. The merchant sings it at his desk, the weaver at his loom, the smith at his anvil. Every centre of business, every walk of occupation, resounds with it; and, at the life-giving music, Industry and Commerce start up like giants refreshed.

No more the land is drained of its productive forces to fill the maw of all-devouring war. No more its fertile plains are converted into deserts by fire and rapine. No more the light of blazing homes flashes on the midnight sky. No more are heard the tread of marching hosts, and the shock of battle. No more the fallen strew the ground like Autumn leaves. No more the mother weeps for her dead boy, lying cold and still when the fight is done, with white face upturned to the silent stars. These are things of the past. They have vanished, like a horrid dream; and, in their place, labor secure of its reward, and revived enterprise, and unfettered material and social improvement, go forth, chanting hymns of deliverance, over the whole expanse of our emancipated country.

To the right hand of the Most High we owe this priceless blessing. He gave to our commanders wisdom, to our soldiers courage and endurance, to our people persistence and fortitude, till His directing agency had brought round that grand conjuncture of widely converging plans and movements, whose mighty folds enveloped and crushed the Rebellion. And then, from out the smoke and turmoil of the terrible arena, from amidst charging squadrons, the roar of strife, and garments rolled in blood, He led the smiling angel, Peace — Peace, not basely born of Concession and Compromise, but the bright Daughter of Victory — Peace, heralded by vindicated Authority and asserted Justice — Peace glorified by the shame of her foes, and rendered immortal by the utterness of their overthrow. "Peace at any price" might have been a fatal boon. But such a peace, a peace so safe, so honorable, so free from submission to disloyal demands, so fraught with securities for its perpetuity, is a gift as ennobling as it is beneficent. And does not the year, in which a propitious Heaven conferred it upon us, deserve an illustrious place in the calendar of the ages?

One more memory of the year, which will make it loom up in regal splendor to all after times, is the Death of Slavery. Human chattelhood has been the chief sin and scourge of our country. Its admission into the organic frame of the Government was a fearful mistake — a political crime — whose consequences have come down to us in a deluge of evils increasing from year to year. The wise and good men who formed the Constitution, were induced to incorporate with it an element so hostile to its great principles, and so abhorrent to the very nature of free institutions, by the hope that it would gradually die out and disappear under the ameliorating tendencies of higher knowledge and advancing civilization. But it was a yielding to expediency that well-nigh destroyed the fabric they toiled so anxiously to erect. They little considered how enduring Wrong is, and how elastic and far-spreading it becomes, when private greed and public tolerance unite to furnish scope for its expansion. Instead of quietly dying, Slavery soon showed itself imbued with a terrible vitality, and a power of extension that defied all attempts to circumscribe and restrain it. It grew, grew rapidly, grew in the number and degradation of its victims, grew in the richness of the prizes which it offered to its patrons, grew in its besotting effects on the national mind, grew in its demands for countenance and support, until it became the dominant interest, overshadowing all others, dictating the policy of every administration, and controlling the entire legislative and executive functions of the country. From being a creeping, ignoble thing, hated by all, confessing its own vileness, and asking only to live till decay should complete the work already begun, it suddenly sprung up into fearful vigor, assumed the port and bearing of a virtue, vaunted itself a blessing, claimed to be God-born and God-descended, and exacted universal homage and obedience.

A few philanthropic thinkers, the prophets of the time, saw the danger, and lifted up the voice of warning. But the nation neither heard nor regarded. Only here and there a moral hero stood forth to swear on the altar of humanity and of God eternal resistance to slavery. As years went on, their numbers increased. The monstrous guilt of making merchandise of the bodies and souls of men became better understood, and more widely acknowledged. Then Conscience woke, and Remonstrance shook the land. There was discussion in Congress, discussion in society — agitation everywhere. Still slavery grew. We knew that the spirit of the age, the world's collected will, the voice of Christianity, and the fiat of Jehovah, omnipotent over all, had decreed the extinction of slavery. Yet it flourished and was strong. We believed that the evil was to be conquered by light and truth; and we poured upon it, without stint or pause, all the artillery which they could supply. Slavery shook our weapons from its brazen hide, and was only made more raging and rampant. We hoped that, after decades and centuries of this moral aggression, the Gospel would finally subdue slavery, and expel it from the land. Slavery laughed at our predictions, and declared itself to be the child of the Gospel, destined to share with it a joint heritage of life and power.

But God, wiser than we, was preparing for this invulnerable foe another kind of logic — "the logic of events." We meant to kill it by argument. God meant to kill it with the sword. We purposed to melt it away by the soft breath of Christian influence. God purposed to blow it out of the universe with Parrott guns. We thought to see it gently decline, and, like other old sinners, repent at the last, ask pardon of the world, and depart in peace. God intended that its exit should be amid the rocking of the earthquake, the commotion and carnage of battle, the fall of cities, and the rout of armies — amid demonstrations of such awful vengeance, as should make its death a warning to ungodly nations forevermore. We expected it to die by the verdict of a jury, with benefit of clergy, and with all the parade and honors of a public execution. God determined that it should die by suicide, and lie unburied at the cross-ways, with a stake thrust through its body, a mockery and a horror to all the ages.

Hence, by that all-governing energy which causes even the wickedness of man to subserve His purposes, He chose the very madness which slavery begets in its votaries, as the instrument of its destruction. In their insane attachment to it, the States of the South rushed into treason and civil war, with the design of extending and perpetuating its supremacy. But this enormous crime, inaugurated for the preservation of their idol, proved to be the signal of its fall. The free North was compelled, by the stern necessities of the crisis, to gather up its might, and repel the assault aimed at the nation's life. We thought only of defending the

Government, and maintaining the Union. But God had other and broader views. He refused to go forth with our armies. He inflicted calamities upon us. He led us deeper and deeper into the conflict. He made the darkness thicker, and the woe heavier. He sent us failure in the work which we sought to do; and all the while pointed, with the finger of His Providence, to the work which He meant us to do. At length, we saw that slavery must die, that the nation might live. Then, high above the tumult and the wailing, rung out the immortal words of our martyred President, proclaiming the emancipation of the bondmen throughout the rebel domain. This was the first step in the right path, and it changed at once the aspect of the strife. Still it was but the beginning. The proclamation of freedom could take effect only so far as the victorious forces of the Union carried with them its fulfilment. It was a dead letter wherever the rebellion continued to hold sway. And even after the rebellion was suppressed, and the banner of the Republic waved once more over all the land, there was yet enough of life in the prostrate form of slavery to compass, by assassin hands, the murder of the Moses who had guided us across the desert of the strife to the border of recovered peace and unity. Slavery was dying. Slavery was in appearance dead. But what seemed death might prove only a fainting fit, out of which it would hereafter rise in renovated vigor. The Supreme Court might bring it back to life by annulling the decree of emancipation. Or the States in which it had ruled, when rehabilitated and clothed anew with their forfeited authority, might themselves restore it, in essence, if not in name. To give the finishing blow to the monster, there was needed that greatest event of the past year, and of all the years of our country's history — the ratification of the Constitutional Amendment. That killed slavery beyond the power of resurrection. It is now forever prohibited, by organic law, in all the States and Territories of the Union, and can never pollute our soil again, until three-fourths of the States shall vote to repeal the glorious interdict — a contingency as unlikely as that the sun should set in the east, or the Mississippi flow toward the frozen zone.

> "Blotted out!
> All within and all about,
> Shall a fresher life begin,
> Freer breathe the universe,
> As it rolls its heavy curse
> On the dead and buried sin."

Yes, slavery is dead — dead — and cannot be resuscitated. In all the broad land which God has given us for our heritage, there is not a slave; and while the heavens are over the earth there never can be again. As I stand here, and say this, and think what a stupendous fact the statement involves, I can hardly believe what my lips declare. When I recall the former greatness of the Slave-Power, its endless ramifications, its all-pervading and all-controlling influence; when I consider how trade and commerce pandered to it, how wealth and fashion worshipped it, how society caressed it, how Literature and Art flattered it, how the Press and the Pulpit obeyed its behests, how statesmen trembled at its frown, how the mightiest fell before it, how the whole nation lay prostrate under its feet; and then look at its huge corpse, rotting in the sight of a rejoicing world, my faith can scarcely grasp what my eyes behold; and I find it difficult to suppress the fear that the demon-curse may start up again, and rule and ravage as before. But, no! thank God, no! Slavery is dead! My heart swells and grows exultant at the thought of all which such a consummation bears in its bosom for us and for our children, for humanity and for Christ. We can now stand up before the nations, and, with honest pride, point to our country as having purged the foul blot from her escutcheon by a baptism such as no other people could undergo and live; as having broken every shackle at a cost such as no other people has ever paid; a country as great in justice as in power, as merciful in victory as invincible in battle; a country that has proved itself the grandest on the face of the earth — grandest in intelligence, grandest in resources, grandest in military strength, grandest in its freedom, grandest in the glory of its present, grandest in the promise of its future. And, what is infinitely more important, we can now "lift up our face without spot unto God," and supplicate His blessing on the land we love, and on the world for whose salvation we labor, unchilled by the thought that the dread guilt of the nation stands between us and the nation's weal — between us and the darkling myriads we would reach and redeem. This fatal barrier broken down, this prolific fountain of corruption dried up, this blaring scandal put away, there lie before the American people a new era and a new career — an era of peace, union, and equal rights for all — a career of material, social, and moral progress at home, of influence and authority abroad, more benign, wide-stretching and majestic than earth's annals have ever recorded.

True, the clouds are not all gone from our sky. The question of reconstruction in the subjugated States is attended with many and great difficulties. Nor does the condition of the millions so suddenly emerging from the ignorance and helplessness of bondage, present a problem less momentous. In the mighty transition through which we are passing, something of disorder and confusion is inevitable.

But there remain no obstacles in our path which Christian statesmanship and Christian benevolence, following the beckonings of the Divine Hand, may not easily overcome. In the case of the States lately in rebellion, we have only to insist that, before they are received back into the Union, they shall so shape their constitutions and domestic policy, as to insure permanent fidelity to the Government, and justice and the rights of citizens to the victims of their former oppression. Thus guarded, their rehabilitation will be safe. With respect to the emancipated slaves, our work, though more arduous, and requiring a longer time for its completion, is equally plain and simple. They are the nation's wards; and it is alike our interest and our obligation to protect them in their freedom, to remove from them all legal disabilities, and to prepare them, by education and the Gospel, for industry, self-help, and usefulness. These conditions fulfilled, our course will be onward and upward. Capital and labor will soon adjust themselves to the new order of things. All friction and disturbance will cease. The South itself, freed from the incubus that has so long paralyzed her energies, will experience, in the increased production of her great staples, a prosperity which she never knew in the palmiest days of the whip and chain. Side by side with her advancement, the whole country will press forward in the march of civilization; and the happy auguries which the vanished year has left us as its memorial, will be realized in a political horizon without a speck to break its clearness, and in a national growth and a national greatness unexampled through all the centuries that have swept over the globe.

The occurrences which we have reviewed are full of important and varied lessons — lessons bearing on all our relations to God, our country, and the world. But we can now only indicate a few of them, which may be regarded as most comprehensive and suggestive.

In the memories of the year there is a lesson of Hope. How fitted are they to inspire us with confidence in the future of our country, under the same sheltering Arm that has so signally defended it in the past! Who can believe that the Almighty, after the wonderful deliverance which He has wrought for this nation, will suffer it to perish? Would He have led us out from the Egypt of Slavery, through the Red Sea of Civil War, if He did not mean to go with us in the journeying beyond, to guide us in the true course, and conduct us to the Canaan of established harmony and repose? He corrected and scourged us while we clung to the sin which He had determined to extirpate; yet His goodness and mercy were over us still. And now, that, taught by His discipline, we have put that sin forever away, will He abandon us to anarchy and ruin? No, no! In all that He has done for us there is the assurance, not of wrath, but of favor, not of decay, but of stability; the indications of a Providence purposing, not to destroy, but to build up and bless. The manifestations of His kindness in the year that is past are a prophecy and a pledge of similar manifestations in the years that are to come; and we gather from them the firmest grounds for trust in God, and trust, through Him, in the destinies of our glorious land.

The events which we have contemplated should invigorate our faith in the strength and permanence of Republican institutions. It has been the favorite dogma of the advocates of monarchy and absolutism, that free commonwealths were deficient in that energy and concentration which result from the supremacy of a single mind; and that when danger assailed them from without or from within, there was no central authority of sufficient force to call out and wield the resources of the nation. And we ourselves were sometimes disposed to admit the truth of this assertion in reference to our own government, and to regard its excellence in peaceful times as hardly compensating for its anticipated weakness in the hour of a great emergency. But the experience of the last four years has shown the falsehood of the despot's prediction, and the groundlessness of our own fears. The facts of our terrible struggle have disappointed and amazed both the friends and the enemies of freedom throughout the world. We have done what no arbitrary government on earth could have ventured to attempt. At the voice of no king or emperor could such armies have been summoned into being, or such boundless means called forth for their support and efficiency. So vast a demand made on its subjects by an absolute Power would be instantly followed by revolution, the fall of dynasties, and the crash of thrones. Or, if this did not happen, the mighty host evoked would be a greater terror to the land than the danger it was created to repel. We have encountered no perils like these. During the war, more than two millions of our citizens have gone forth to defend the government, because it was their own government, the government which they had aided to establish; and the whole nation poured out its wealth after them in a ceaseless tide, whose fulness and amplitude confounded every onlooker. And when these heroic men had finished their work, the million that survived came quietly back to the occupations which they had left, and were reabsorbed in the industries of the country. This magnificent spectacle, the sublimest which history shows, viewed in connection with the spirit of self-sacrifice, the patriotic zeal, the exhaustless forces, which the crisis developed, has settled forever the question of the stability of free institutions, and demonstrated to the world that a representative government is not only the strongest and most effective of all governments, but the most enduring and indestructible.

The memories of the year are richly fraught with occasions for gratitude. Is there among us a mind so grovelling, a heart so dead, as not to feel, at a moment like this, some emotion of thankfulness to the Dispenser of such unparalleled benefits? One glance at the perils and sacrifices in which He has upheld us, one glance at the redemption which He has accomplished for us, one glance at the bright Future which He has opened to us, is enough to inspire our souls with love and our lips with praise. Our soldiers have done nobly. Cherished be the living; sacred the memory of the fallen. Our commanders have been brave, and wise, and skilful. Let the nation reward and honor them. Our murdered Chief piloted the ship of state well and surely amid the storm. Let his name and his deeds be a hallowed legacy to the generations that are to come after us. But our Deliverer was the God of Hosts. He prepared all, superintended all, achieved all. To Him, then, let our worship and our thanks be rendered evermore.

The memories of the year inculcate a lesson of duty. Never were the Christians of this land placed in circumstances so favorable as the present for the extension of true religion, and for bringing its benign influences to bear upon all classes of our population. The impassable wall of slavery, which has hitherto shut in the whole South, and rendered it impervious to a pure Gospel, and to all the humanizing and elevating agencies which that Gospel carries with it, is thrown down and scattered to the winds; and we may now go where we will, bearing the light of knowledge and the message of salvation. There is no hindrance, no obstruction. All places, all conditions, are open to our efforts. The same enlarged scope is given to our philanthropy in its endeavors to uplift the degraded of all climes and peoples. The one dark stain on our national character, which excluded us from the sympathies of the world, and made our benevolence a mockery, and our Christianity a reproach, is removed forever; and we can toil for humanity with all the moral advantage resulting from the fiery ordeal which we have undergone in its cause. The old prejudice against us has passed away; the old barrier between us and our race has been levelled; and a higher path and a wider sphere await our entrance.

Men of the New Era! I greet you. It is your privilege to labor for God and man in a new civilization, under new auspices, and with new facilities. Be true to your grand position. Recognize the obligations which it involves. And study to show yourselves as unselfish and beneficent in peace as you were patriotic in war.

From the memories of the year we may draw a lesson of admonition. We read in them a solemn revelation of God's wrath against iniquity. They proclaim to us, in words of fire, and with tongues of thunder, that great public wrongs cannot be committed without calling down the vengeance of Heaven; and that, in the day of their doom, their supporters and champions will be overthrown with them. The South clung to its fatal sin, defended it, cherished it, adored it; accounted it more sacred than God and His law, more precious than Christ and His Gospel. Jehovah's right hand smote the foul Dagon to the dust, and with it the whole temple which the South had built for its worship. The desolation that has swept over the rebel States, the havoc that has wasted and impoverished them, the blood that has drenched them, the graves that make their sunny plains one vast sepulchre, are all the legitimate consequences of their adherence to slavery. But the same God, who so fearfully punished them, will as surely punish us, if we break His law, and refuse to repent. He is the Sovereign of individuals as well as of communities; and His authority can no more be despised with impunity by the one than by the other. He commands us to love Him, to obey Him, to forsake our transgressions against Him, and to rely for pardon and acceptance on the merits of His only-begotten Son. If we set at nought His behests, then as certainly as His vengeance overtook the South, so certainly will it overtake us. It may not be now — it may not be here — for while nations are judged in this world, individuals are judged in the next. But the punishment will come, inexorable and endless. The South, if faithful to the Government to which she has now submitted, and just to the freedmen whom she so long oppressed, may rise up from her ruins, and be again prosperous and happy. But if once the retributions of eternity become our portion, there will be for us no recovery. In the delusions of sin we may flatter ourselves that the Holy One will never reckon with us for our disobedience; that He will always be to us as forbearing and merciful as He is now. So thought the devotees of slavery. They were sure that God was on their side, and would ultimately crown their cause with triumph. Nevertheless, their destruction came.

Oh! let the memories and the lessons of the year now ended lead us to repentance, lead us to faith in Jesus, lead us to reconciliation with God, and holy activity in His service. So shall our future years on earth be bright with Hope, and our eternal years blessed in its fruition.

CHAPTER X.

GOD'S METHOD OF RECONSTRUCTION.

"TAKE COUNSEL; EXECUTE JUDGMENT; MAKE THY SHADOW AS THE NIGHT IN THE MIDST OF THE NOONDAY; HIDE THE OUTCASTS; BEWRAY NOT HIM THAT WANDERETH. LET MINE OUTCASTS DWELL WITH THEE, MOAB; BE THOU A COVERT TO THEM FROM THE FACE OF THE SPOILER; FOR THE EXTORTIONER IS AT AN END; THE SPOILER CEASETH; THE OPPRESSORS ARE CONSUMED OUT OF THE LAND." — *Isaiah* xvi. 3, 4.

ON the current of the ages great conjunctures often arise, analogous to those which marked its earlier course, and giving fresh significance to the Divine counsels and warnings which were then enunciated. Human wickedness stamps the same characters on all periods of the world, and creates similar moral crises, which require to be met by the application of similar principles. Thus history repeats itself, and renders the inspired teachings of the far Past ever appropriate and timely.

Sacred narrative supplies an instance of civil reconstruction, closely resembling that which now forms, in our own land, the chief interest of the hour. It grew out of the political relations existing between the Hebrew nation and the adjacent kingdom of Moab. The conquest of the latter country by David, and its annexation to his dominions, was one of the many splendid successes that attended his reign. Though permitted to remain nominally under its own rulers, it became, in fact, a dependency of the Jewish crown, paying tribute to it, and acknowledging its supremacy. When, on the accession of Rehoboam, the Hebrew territory was divided, the subject province followed the fortunes of the Ten Tribes, and continued to adhere to them, till the death of Ahab. The connection was then sundered by rebellion. A strong and wicked king having been succeeded by one who was as weak as he was wicked, the people of Moab took advantage of the imbecility and disorder which ensued, to set up an independent government. Through many conflicts, and for nearly two centuries, they maintained their autonomy. But after the destruction of Israel by the invading hosts of Assyria, an effort appears to have been made for the restoration of Moab to the kingdom of Judah. This portion of the chosen race was now prosperous and powerful under the wise rule of Hezekiah; while its neighbor had sunk into decay. It is probable that Moab herself proposed the alliance. Enfeebled as she had become by frequent wars and protracted anarchy, diminished in population and resources, and exposed more and more to the encroachments of Nineveh, whose colossal might was overshadowing the East, she would naturally desire to strengthen her position by uniting with a kindred people, and securing its aid against the common danger.

It was while this measure was in contemplation, that the prophet gave utterance to the message which we have chosen as the theme of our present remarks. He exhorts the inhabitants of Moab to renew their fealty to the House of David, and to evince their sincerity and good faith by sending the ancient tribute to "the mount of the Daughter of Zion." At the same time, he reminds them that much more than this was necessary to establish a safe and firm basis of reunion. During the long and bitter strife which had raged between them and the Hebrews, large numbers of the latter had fallen into their hands, either as captives taken in battle, or as exiles who had been driven by adversity to seek an asylum among them. These homeless ones they had plundered and enslaved, and had aggravated their misfortunes by every cruelty which malice could invent. A wrong so flagrant must be repaired before there could be any solid and lasting peace. Judah could never allow them to return with their feet on the necks of her children; and even were it possible that she should so forget her duty and her honor, the God of Judah would frown on the unholy compact, and bring it to naught.

Hence the servant of Heaven, commissioned to declare its will, admonishes them to abandon at once a course of conduct so productive of present alienation, and so certain to engender hostility and disruption in the future. "Take counsel; execute judgment." Ponder the outrages which you have committed. Atone for them by doing justice to the victims of your tyranny. "Make thy shadow as the night in the midst of the noonday." As the cool screen of darkness shields the traveller from the heat of the blazing sky, so let your equity and kindness shelter the lowly. "Hide the outcasts." Be to them a refuge from oppression. "Bewray not him that wandereth." Break not your pledge to the exile; cheat him not with a hollow performance. Let the robbed and down-trodden dwell with you in the full enjoyment of every immunity which you claim for yourselves. Accord to them equal rights; guard them from spoliation and violence. Sully not with your old infamies the new national life to which you aspire. In that life, "the extortioner is at an end, the spoiler ceaseth," the tramplers of the weak have no place. Disasters have befallen you; ruin threatens you. In the imminence of your peril, you ask to come back under the protection which you renounced. This can be granted only on the condition that you henceforth forbear to prey upon the helpless. In justice, and in justice alone, can you find deliverance. This accomplished, your reinstatement will be, to both lands, a permanent security. "And in mercy shall the throne be established; and" Judah's ruler — your ruler once more — " shall sit upon it in truth, in the tabernacle of David, judging and seeking judgment, and hasting righteousness."

How suggestive is this fact, which Scripture has brought to us from the dim centuries! What a striking parallel does it bear to events which are occurring in our own time and country! And how clear the light it sheds on the way in which God would have us deal with those events!

The war of the Great Rebellion is ended. Strong hands and bold hearts have upheld the unity of the nation, vindicated its majesty, and swept from its domain the fell Despotism, which shot up, like some Stygian exhalation, to pollute and scare the world. The States which threw off their allegiance, and, in their mad purpose of overturning the Government, drenched the whole land with blood, discomfited and subjugated, are now suppliantly waiting at the doors of Congress, to be invested anew with their forfeited franchises. What answer shall be given them? On what conditions shall they be permitted to resume the rights which they have so enormously misused, and to stand again in the places which they have so frightfully desecrated?

This question should be approached in no revengeful spirit. To measure out to the South the full penalty of its treason, and repay it for all the loss and woe which that treason has cost us, would consign to a felon's death well-nigh its entire population, already decimated by want and carnage. This we cannot do; this we ought not to do, even if we could. Invincible, victorious, honored before the world, raised to the highest point of national greatness by the stupendous energies which the struggle has developed, we can afford to lay aside vindictiveness, and leave retribution to Him who is sovereign alike over communities and individuals, and from whose sentence none can escape. Vengeance is His; and in His own time and way He will dispense to the guilty the appointed punishment. It is ours to manifest forbearance, clemency, magnanimity.

Yet, along with the exercise of these qualities, it is of the utmost importance that impregnable barriers should be erected against the dangers which remain. While we demand not retaliation, we must demand security. The method of the Divine government indicates to us our true line of action. The All-Ruler pardons transgressors, and restores them to the favor which they have lost. But He does it only on grounds that sustain the sacredness of His law, and the happiness of His moral empire. The principles on which He acts should be our guide. In dealing with the conquered rebels, we must so blend mercy with firmness, as not to ignore their criminality, and encourage its repetition. The process of rehabilitation must be accompanied and guarded by every precaution requisite to insure the public faith and the public safety. And it must be put forever out of their power to plunge the nation again into civil war, or to embarrass it in the noble career of freedom and equality on which it has entered.

How, then, can this be done? In what circumstances, under what safeguards, may the insurgent Commonwealths, that tore themselves away from the Union with intent to destroy it, be installed in their former position, without imperilling the welfare of the country, and sapping the foundations of liberty and justice? Here is the great problem which the people of this land have to solve; a problem so intricate, so complex, so many-sided, that the profoundest statesmanship stands baffled before it; and yet a problem so grave and momentous as to involve the very life of the Republic, and the destinies of unborn generations.

We cannot hope to bring to this vexed subject

any elucidation that will fully remove the doubt and uncertainty which have gathered round it. Where senators long versed in political affairs are at fault, and men, equal in wisdom and in patriotism, entertain views widely divergent, we may well hesitate to propound our conclusions. Nevertheless, we are thoroughly persuaded that, vast as the difficulty is, and environed as it is with manifold antagonisms, it may be met and overcome, by withdrawing it from the realm of theory and prepossession, and applying to it the simple test of common sense and experience. Putting aside, therefore, the various conflicting hypotheses in reference to the status of the communities lately in rebellion — pausing not to inquire whether secession took them out of the Union, or whether they were still held in it by a bond which they could not break — we come to the real, actual fact that, with regard to all the practical workings of government, they were and are out of the Union. Thus, by a single step, we reach the naked, vital question, In what manner, and by what provisions, can they be safely brought back into the Union? And the same plain, straightforward course of reasoning will give the answer.

Every thoughtful mind must perceive that the wound which treason has inflicted on the nation, is too deep to be healed by any superficial treatment. The remedy must be radical and fundamental. To pardon and restore the traitors, while they profess no repentance, while their disloyalty is, as pronounced as ever, and while they accept the proffered amnesty only because their means of resistance are exhausted, is an expedient as vain as it is dangerous. Nothing can be gained, everything is hazarded, by concession and compromise. The disease, checked for a time, will break out afresh, in a new-form it may be, but with all its old virulence. No bridge of half measures can span the gulf between the free North and the oligarchic South. That gulf must be filled up. The only reconstruction that will be sound and permanent, must rest on the grand basis of Equal Rights for all. If we would not have our work crumble into fragments, we must build here — here, on the broad platform of the Constitution — here, on the Rock of Eternal Justice. But, on such a foundation, the subjugated States are no more prepared to build with us now, than they were in the palmiest days of their pride and power. Even the dread schooling of defeat and humiliation has failed to teach them the first lesson in the lore of freedom. It is, therefore, indispensable that they should be kept in a state of abeyance and probation, till, by the logic of events, and the discipline of delay, they are educated into harmony with the spirit of republican institutions, and the great ideas of humanity, civilization and progress. If we would eradicate Disunion so utterly that it shall never show a sprout or leaf again, we must expel from the soil the poison seeds from which it sprung, and the poison roots which ministered to its growth.

One of the principal causes of the unrest and repulsion which finally culminated in civil war, was the doctrine of State Rights. It was a ground principle in the political creed of the South, that the States were complete sovereignties within themselves; that to them supreme allegiance was due; that the Union was a mere League of independent Commonwealths; and that the General Government was but the Deputy of the States, having no authority beyond the limits which they prescribed. This fatal heresy, long a prolific source of discord and strife, obstructing every national measure, and crippling every national interest, occupied a conspicuous place in the Dance of Devils that ushered in the Rebellion. And when the Rebellion was put down, we thought it dead, crushed, with Slavery and the whole sisterhood of Furies, under the trampling feet of our triumphant armies. But recent indications have undeceived us. It is not dead. Though weakened and shattered, it still lives, and lives for mischief. A demon's spell has recalled breath into its nostrils, and vigor into its limbs. It is struggling up from its fall, and shaking itself for fresh combats. It swaggers in the haughty port of impenitent rebels. It blares in Executive Vetoes. It is arrogant, defiant. No other relic of the Southern past is so full of danger. Its malign influence is at this moment a chief obstacle to any just and comprehensive settlement of our difficulties. It taints the fountain-head of the Federal Administration, and thus prevents the consummation of laws for the succor of the oppressed, on the plea that such laws are an interference with the prerogatives of the States. It is a centrifugal force, pregnant with the elements of disintegration; and so long as it exists, it will continue to be the foe of order, and a standing menace to the perpetuity of the Union. While the South clings to this destructive dogma, no confidence can be reposed in her loyalty. However she may accept for the time what she cannot resist, her submission will be insincere, her homage false; and whenever opportunity shall be ripe, she will again abjure her allegiance, and renew the horrors of fratricidal war. How evident, then, is it that every dictate of prudence, every law of safety, all the lessons of the past, all the omens of the present, combine to forbid her return, till the firebrand of State Supremacy be hurled into the abyss of forgetfulness, and quenched forever in its unrestoring waters!

The Right of Secession is another evil root that must be extirpated. As the branches of the banyan tree, drooping to the ground, throw out radicles, and become themselves trees; so from the assumed sovereignty of the States grew the belief, that to each state belonged the power of lawfully separating itself from the Union, and breaking up the glorious fabric cemented with the blood of heroes. And if once the premise is admitted, the inference logically follows. Let it be conceded, as the South even now asserts, that the authority of a State is paramount, and that her people owe obedience to the Union only at her command, and the conclusion is impregnable that rebellion, sanctioned by her behest, is no treason. The noxious sucker springs naturally from the noxious stem. True it is that the trunk and limbs of this deadly offshoot have been shivered and laid prostrate by the levin-bolts of battle. But its stock remains in the earth, and will be sure to reproduce the same baleful growth, unless it be dug up, even to its minutest fibres, committed to the flames, and its very ashes scattered to the winds of heaven. Ought we not, then, to insist that the people of the South, before resuming their share in the Government, should proclaim secession, past or future, a nullity and a lie, and renounce it for all time?

A perilous influence exists, also, in the spirit of

Caste by which Southern society is pervaded. This is the child of Slavery. The mother, having crowned a long career of crimes and ignominies by the attempted murder of a nation, has perished under the curse of God, and the vengeance of man. But its vile progeny survives, in pride of race, color-exclusiveness, and the self-assertion of the dominant few. Southern communities have been bred up in the idea, that both Nature and Providence intended one class to enjoy a monopoly of political and social power, and to live in ease and luxury; while all other classes were designed to obey their will and serve their pleasure. And it was with the view of more fully realizing this idea, of reducing it more completely to practice, and of guarding it more securely from the invasion of whatever might be in conflict with it, that they undertook to dissolve the Union, and to found an Oligarchy, in which the lordly race were to rule over an empire of serfs. They failed; but the tone of thought and feeling which begot the infamous endeavor, is as potent now as in the days of the Confederacy. In some respects, it appears to have been even intensified by the disappointment it has suffered. The impoverished planter, clothed in rags, and dependent for bread on the bounty of the Government he sought to overthrow, still regards himself as belonging to a privileged order, and looks with as haughty a scorn on all whom he deems beneath him, as when he feasted in marble halls, and rolled in wealth coined from the tears and blood of his slaves. He looks upon labor as a degradation, and despises the working man, whether white or black. And to these aristocratic prejudices is now added a bitter hatred of the class lately in bondage, and of the power which has freed them. Such a state of public sentiment — with few exceptions, universal wherever slavery existed — not only tends to discourage industry and enterprise, and thus to hinder the material renovation of the South, but impedes also its political and moral recovery, by disqualifying its people for the new issues and the new relations which the result of the war has necessitated. Their whole history is alien to the principles on which alone the Union can be securely re-established. The Constitution guarantees a republican form of government to all the States; and this vital provision, imperfectly carried out in the past, must henceforth be rigidly maintained. But not one of the Southern States ever had a republican form of government, and not one is prepared to adopt such a government now. In all the movements which those States have inaugurated for re-organizing their civil institutions, the same narrow policy is everywhere apparent. Class distinctions and class interests govern throughout. Predominance of race is the beginning and the end. There is no recognition of the equality of all men before the law; of their common brotherhood as the children of one Father; nor of the sameness of rights with which that brotherhood invests them. And, until the South receives and comprehends these great truths, her presence in the councils of the nation cannot but be incongruous and belligerent.

The most formidable difficulty, however, in the way of reconstruction, arises from its bearing on the present and future condition of the millions just emerged from slavery. Of a similar nature was the obstacle to which Isaiah referred, as opposing the alliance of Moab with Judah; and the command of the Almighty respecting it is not less pertinent to our own circumstances. We are in like peril of setting aside the claims of justice; of neglecting to "hide the outcasts"; and of so consummating national unity as to "bewray", with broken or deceitfully kept promises, the fugitives from oppression.

The organic law of the land now inhibits forever the ownership of man by man. Slavery, therefore, can never be restored in name and in form. But conditions may exist, under which it will be possible to revive many of its most odious features, and to render emancipation comparatively a worthless boon. When once the States which seceded, have been recognized as full members of the Union by the admission of their representatives to Congress, military supervision must be withdrawn, and the internal affairs of each left to its own management. They will then have it in their power to pass such laws, and to impose on the freedmen such disabilities, as to take from them nearly all that is valuable in their liberty, and subject them to a state of serfdom and civil inferiority little less cruel than the chattelhood from which they have escaped. And who believes that they will not use this power? Already, in many of the States, "Black Codes" have been enacted, based on the same principles, and instinct with the same spirit, that pervaded the old Slave-Laws. And the general feeling of hostility, which has given birth to this legislation, shows itself in acts of personal violence and outrage, often more shocking and barbarous than any with which the darkest annals of slavery were stained. For the slave as property, there was some love, and some care. For the slave transformed into a free man, there is neither. We say not that all thus dislike and abuse him. Doubtless, many of the old masters honestly "accept the situation", and are disposed to deal fairly with their former vassals. But the number of such, not small perhaps in itself, is small in comparison with the multitudes whose temper and conduct are widely different. It is to be feared, that equity and forbearance are the exception; wrong and cruelty the rule. And if this is so, while the Federal Government still holds them under military control, and the pressure of its authority checks and restrains them, what will it be when that control is relinquished, and they are lords again in their own domain? What is there in their past history, what in their present attitude, which will warrant the confidence that they will treat with kindness, or even justice, the helpless ones whom they once enslaved? The abolition of bondage was not effected by their co-operation, nor with their consent. They look upon it as an evil, wantonly inflicted on them by their conquerors — an evil to which they submit on compulsion, and under protest. They regard the negroes as property of which they have been unrighteously despoiled; believe that capital should own labor; that God meant the blacks to work without compensation, and created the whites for the express purpose of making them do it; and that any other relation between the races must be injurious to both. Can we expect them to bring forward any measures, or to put forth any efforts, the success of which will prove the falseness of their own theories? No, they have no faith in the freedom of the negro; they deem it a bane and a delusion; and will do all they can to render it so. They will surround him with oppressive restrictions, hedge up his path with special statutes and prohibitions and penalties, and strive, in all possible ways, to prevent his raising himself to a higher social and intellectual level. If they cannot fasten the chain on him again, they will keep him in a state of ignorance, helplessness and debasement.

Humanity and justice, therefore, alike require that men, entertaining such views, and cherishing such malign intentions, should not be restored to their place in the Union, until they have given the most satisfactory evidence of their readiness to fulfil to the freedmen all the pledges of the nation. This should be, in every case, an indispensable prerequisite to their return. And for this Congress should provide by adequate legislation. Such a course is demanded of us by all the claims of public faith and honor, and by all the sanctions of everlasting Righteousness. We have abrogated slavery, and proclaimed its death to the world. We have invited the emancipated slaves to aid us in putting down the Rebellion, under a promise, expressed or implied, that their liberty should be assured, and their race elevated to citizenship in the redeemed Republic. Two hundred thousand of them have fought valiantly by the side of our sons and brothers, and eighty thousand have died for a country, which yet treats them as outcasts. On many a bloody field, in many a desperate charge, they have proved their courage, their manhood, their loyalty, their fitness for civil enfranchisement. And if we now abandon them to the power of their old oppressors, and give them, in place of solid, real freedom, a base counterfeit — shadow for substance, stones for bread — of what shameful ingratitude and treachery shall we be guilty? This is the very sin which the prophet denounced. "Bewray not him that wandereth." Left to the mercy of reconstructed rebels, the poor freedmen will be indeed "bewrayed" — exposed naked and defenceless to their adversaries — defrauded, by an empty semblance, of the reward for which they have toiled and suffered. What a stigma will rest on the American name! And how will the friends of Humanity mourn, and despots exult, over our perfidy!

But this is not all. In proving false to the men who have trusted us and bled for us, we prove false to ourselves. We cannot sacrifice their liberties without sacrificing our own. A brief experience of the true nature and scope of the Rebellion, revealed to us the fact, that its animus, its impulse, its strength was Slavery; and that, to save the nation, we must destroy Slavery. But we killed only its body. Its soul migrated — underwent a sort of metempsychosis — took another form. Nor has it yet gone to its own place. It is still "marching on." It is still among us, like the cast-out demon of whom Christ spoke, "walking through dry places, seeking rest, and finding none." If we deny the claims of the freedmen, we give it rest. It will return to its old place of power, in a new shape, and with a new name. It will go back to the Chamber of Southern Brass and Northern Copper, whence it came out, but will not find it "swept and garnished." We shall have the same meanness, the same truckling to wrong, the same betrayal of the right, the same insolence and domination, the same corruption, and time-serving, and falsehood; which, before the war, made the land a Babel, and our institutions a by-word. All the substantial fruits of victory will be wrested from us. The great prize for which we strove — a recovered, purified Union — will turn to ashes in our hands; and those glorious children of Freedom's Battle — Equal Rights, Equal Justice, National Righteousness — will be strangled in the hour of their birth. With the South, not with the North, will be the final triumph. And shall this be? Shall the struggle, and the woe, and the agony have been in vain? Shall those terrible years leave us no harvest? Have our billions of treasure been cast into the sea? Is the precious blood, poured out like water all over the Southern soil, only seed sown upon a desert? Forbid it, shades of the noble dead that fell on a thousand gory fields! Forbid it, ye myriad martyrs, immolated in rebel prisons! Forbid it, ye countless homes, whose loved ones will return no more! Forbid it, Truth, Honor, Patriotism! Forbid it, Mercy! Forbid it, Christianity! Forbid it, all-ruling Heaven!

There is more than this. No people can afford to be unjust. In the Divine administration, nations are regarded as entities, having moral existence and responsibility. Their judgment-hour, however, is in time. And retribution follows their sins in this world as certainly as it follows the sins of individuals in the next. Can we doubt this? After the dread outstretchings of Jehovah's arm which we have witnessed, is it any longer a question with us whether He visits collective bodies for their collective guilt? From cotton-field and rice-swamp, from the auction block and the slave-pen, from under the whip and the branding-iron, the cry of our fettered brother long went up into the ear of the all-avenging One. The skies gave no response. Generations, centuries, rolled away, and still the earth was green, and heaven was silent. But when the iniquity was ripe, and wrath was full, down thundered the answer, and shook the globe. Oh! yes — we have seen, we have felt that the Almighty can punish. The battle's shock, the cannon's roar, the ensanguined land, the million graves, the mourners in every street, have attested that the Almighty can punish. And dare we again brave His displeasure? If we repeat the wrong, will He not repeat the punishment? And will not that punishment be more severe, because of the greater hardihood that could venture to provoke it? Sure may we be that if judgments so awful fail to instruct us, the lesson will be voiced in judgments yet more awful.

Let none imagine that the Sovereign of the universe is too high, or too remote in His majesty, to concern Himself about the uplifting of a trampled race. The very thought is impiety. It is the glory of our God that He cares for the lowly. No perfection of His nature has been more clearly revealed in His word, or more impressively illustrated in His providence. "He shall deliver the poor that crieth, and him that hath no helper." "He giveth power to the faint, and to them that have no might He increaseth strength." What characters are more explicitly denounced in Scripture than the down-treaders of the weak? All along the pages of Inspiration threatenings flame out against oppressors, and against those who countenance and abet them; and all along the track of History those threatenings loom up in terrible fulfilment. And can we hope to escape, if, from want of sympathy with the wronged, or indifference to their needs, we fail in the exigency that is now before us?

"We see dimly, in the present, what is small and what is
  great;
Slow of faith how weak an arm may turn the iron helm of
  Fate;
But the soul is still oracular; — amid the market's din,
List to the ominous stern whisper from the Delphic cave
  within;
They enslave their children's children who make compromise
  with Sin."

What, then, ought to be done? More, doubtless, much more than it is in our present power to accomplish. The surest and readiest way of defending the freedmen, is to confer on them the elective franchise. The ballot is the most effectual safeguard. Give them that, and they can protect themselves. But, in the existing state of public opinion, not only at the South, but in the North as well, it were vain to expect this, and idle to insist upon it. Until the national mind is more broadly educated, and rises to a higher conception of the natural rights of all men, it would be putting ourselves on impracticable ground, to demand the immediate bestowment of political immunities. These will come with the growth of freedom, and the progress of events. In the mean time, we shall find ample occasion for all our energies in securing to the emancipated the enjoyment of those civil rights — the rights of person, the rights of labor, and the rights of property — without which their freedom will be but a shadow. Here let us take our stand. Here all who hate vassalage can unite. And here we can begin and prosecute the work which shall end in perfect enfranchisement.

Some there may be, avowed friends of emancipation, and of the elevation of the colored race, who will refuse to come up to this point. However true to the Union, however loyal in intention to Liberty, they cannot so far shake themselves from the influence of old prejudices and old affiliations, as to take the part of the negro against the tyranny of the white man. When such are invested with vast power, their scruples are the more to be regretted, inasmuch as they may seriously retard the righteous adjustment of the questions now agitating the country. It is not in the school of slavery that Freedom's champions are trained. Pharaoh may bear the rod of Moses, and profess to guide the people to the Promised Land; but, in such hands, the rod, instead of pointing across the sea, and straight on to Canaan, will whirl round, and point directly back to Egypt. Nevertheless, whether the rod beckon falsely or truly, we must obey, not the rod, but the Shekinah. That never misleads. As the Pillar of Cloud and of Fire went before the Tribes, shaping all their movements, so the Word of the living God appoints and marshals our way. And the course which it prescribes is onward, ever onward, farther and farther from the house of bondage, nearer and nearer to the goal of full deliverance and rest.

God's Moses, after conducting his charge through the returnless waters that separated them forever from their former thraldom, watched and taught them during the long delay of the wilderness; and it was not till the period of probation had passed, and discipline and culture had prepared them for the ordained inheritance, that they entered upon its fruition. Let us follow in his steps. We are already over the sea, and the reign of chattelhood is behind us. Protection, guidance, preparation, constitute the work which we have now to do. While we guard the freedmen from wrong and violence, we must endeavor, at the same time, to improve their condition, by bringing to bear upon it all the ameliorating appliances of education and Christianity. In this direction lies their way to Canaan; and by such a process must they be fitted for its responsibilities. Redeemed by intelligence and religion from the darkness and debasement which ages of servitude have induced, they cannot long be debarred from political privileges. In a country like ours, men so qualified must sooner or later acquire the right of suffrage, whatever antipathies and repulsions may array themselves against it. And when this is gained, the machinery of their elevation will be complete. A race, acted on by the three mighty levers, Education, the Gospel, and the Ballot, must rise. No force of prejudice, no power of custom, no ban of exclusiveness can keep it down. As well might an eagle lie grovelling in the dust, with three pairs of wings beating the air, as a people remain in a low social status, when schools, Bibles, and the right to vote, combine to lift them up. Advancement is the necessary result of the influences operating upon them. They will rise — rise in spite of every clog and of every attempt at repression — rise in manliness, in civilization, in knowledge, in skill, in industry — rise in all that imparts dignity to the citizen, in all that insures repose and prosperity to the state.

> "I held it truth, with him who sings
> To one clear harp in divers tones,
> That men may rise on stepping-stones
> Of their dead selves to higher things."

So simple and yet so thorough is the method of reconstruction, which the supreme Governor sets before us. If we "hide the outcasts" under the shelter of equal laws, make the justice of the nation "a covert to them from the face of the spoiler," and do not "bewray" them by any device of compromise or any yielding to expediency, the great problem will be solved. On such a basis, the Union may be rebuilt with a firmness and solidity that will defy all the shocks of change, and all the assaults of time. And to this consummation we believe the providence of God is leading us. We believe that the same unerring Wisdom that directed our steps in all the critical hours of the Rebellion, will continue to guide us in the perplexities and perils by which we are now surrounded. The All-Ruler has too grand a purpose to work out in the future of this country, to permit our folly to frustrate or endanger it. If we disregard His teachings, and set His commands at defiance, He may humble us by failure, and visit us with rebuke, till, in despair of our own counsels, we consent to execute His; but He will not surrender us to anarchy and ruin. What He has done for us is a pledge of what He will do. The past foreshadows the future. His agency will so mould opinion, and so shape events, that, however dying treason may toss and struggle, the calm, strong heart of the nation will remain steadfast to the right; loyalty and humanity will triumph; and this mighty Federation of States be perfect once more, with every breach repaired, every element of discord eliminated. And thus will our political system, founded on the Civil Equality of all men, rest-ing on the firm arches of Free Schools and Universal Suffrage, pillared by Justice, and buttressed by Christianity, tower up in **MATCHLESS STRENGTH AND GRANDEUR, THE MARVEL OF THE AGES, AND THE HOPE OF THE WORLD.**

> "No floundering more, for mind or heart,
>   Among the lower levels;
> No welcome more for moods that sort
>   With satyrs and with devils;
> But over all our fruitful slopes,
>   On all our plains of beauty,
> Fair temples for fair human hopes
>   And altar-thrones for duty.
>
> "Wherefore, O ransomed people, shout!
>   O banners, wave in glory!
> O bugles, blow the triumph out!
>   O drums, strike up the story!
> Clang, broken fetters, idle swords!
>   Clap hands, O States together!
> And let all praises be the Lord's,
>   Our Saviour and our Father."

CHAPTER XI.

OUR DAY AND ITS WORK.

"A WISE MAN'S HEART DISCERNETH BOTH TIME AND JUDGMENT."
Ecclesiastes viii. 5.

NOTHING is more essential to success in the work of life, than an intelligent comprehension of the period in which that work is to be done. Whoever would achieve aught of moment for the welfare of his race, must ponder well the salient features of his own time, and know the channels along which the current of the world's thought is moving. From a defect here, many noble men, gifted with great powers, and stirred by lofty aims, have lived in vain. They understood not their age; and their age neither understood nor heeded them. Striving to draw back the live, progressive Present into the dead, still Past; or laboring, with equal folly, to hurry forward the immature Present into the ripe Future, they won only scorn, neglect, and failure; and, after all their efforts, all their enthusiasm, all their sacrifices, their whole history may be written in the one brief sentence, "Born out of due time." He who would influence men in politics, in social reforms, in the industrial arts, must not hope to do it by shaking over them the dry bones of by-gone ideas; but must take his stand on those living questions of the day, in which humanity feels a warm and active interest.

> "New occasions teach new duties. Time makes ancient good uncouth;
> They must upward still, and onward, who would keep abreast of Truth;
> Lo, before us gleam her camp-fires! we ourselves must Pilgrims be,
> Launch our Mayflower, and steer boldly through the desperate winter sea,
> Nor attempt the Future's portal with the Past's blood-rusted key."

This knowledge of the Present, however indispensable it may be to the right conduct of secular affairs, is far more so to the progress of religion. The Christian, of all men, most needs to understand the time in which the claims of his high calling are to be met. The truths of the Gospel, and the obligations which grow out of them, are the same at all periods; but the manner in which the one is to be applied and the other fulfilled, varies with the shifting scenes of the world's history. And he who, in our versatile and rapid age, thinks to push on the victories of the Cross, and combat the thousand new forms which error and sin are every moment assuming, with precisely the same weapons, and the same methods of attack, that were used in slower and less eventful generations, is as unwise as the soldier who should bring the cumbrous mail, the battle-axes and battering rams of the old crusaders, to contend against minnie muskets and rifled cannon; or as the naval commander who should oppose the wooden walls of a lumbering seventy-four to steel-pointed rams and iron-clad Monitors.

This is the thought enunciated by the Sacred Writer, when he says, " A wise man's heart discerneth both time and judgment." In other words, he comprehends his epoch, and forms a just estimate of its character and of its demands. The subject, therefore, to which I invite your attention, is — Our Day, and its Work.

That the features of our day are diverse and many-hued, no thoughtful observer can doubt. They accord strikingly with the sublime description of prophecy, that "the light shall not be clear nor dark; a day, not day nor night " — that is, neither shining in full splendor, nor overshadowed by unbroken gloom. How accurate a portrait is this of the time in which our lot is cast! Some of its aspects apparently indicate the triumph of evil; others the triumph of good. Some are dark with prognostics of the gathering tempest; others bright with the precursors of coming peace and joy. It is, however, my firm conviction that, in any comprehensive view that may be taken of the social and moral movements of the present day, hope must greatly preponderate over fear; and that these movements furnish far more cause for encouragement than for despondency. This will be evident if, beginning with those characteristics that are most unfavorable, we pass on to the more cheering ones by which they are overbalanced and counteracted.

Our day is marked by flagrant wickedness. I am not about to commit the folly which Solomon so pointedly rebukes in the complainers of his age. "Say not thou, What is the cause that the former times were better than these? for thou dost not inquire wisely concerning this." It is not my design, therefore, to institute any comparison between the amount of sin in our own and in other periods of the world's dark annals. Man has always been vile; and man always will be vile, till the Gospel has pervaded and purified the race. Yet while the inward corruption of our nature remains ever the same, the degree of outbreaking iniquity may be greater in one generation than in another. It is according to the course of human depravity, that the farther it proceeds, and the longer its base impulses continue to act, the more daring and shameless it should become. But however this may be, the most careless onlooker must acknowledge that ungodliness is now fearfully rampant. When were the claims of Jehovah more disregarded; the authority of His law more contemned; the sanctities of His Sabbath, His Word, and His House more dishonored? When was irreligion more dominant among the masses — the power of earthliness more intense — neglect of the great salvation more determined and universal? If we pass from the domain of things spiritual to that of morals, there too we find a downward tendency equally decided. Does any one doubt this? Let him examine the statistics of crime, furnished by the records of police and the proceedings of criminal courts, and he cannot but be appalled both at the number and the enormity of the offenses which they proclaim. Who has not shuddered at the frightful increase of murder and suicide? Who does not stand aghast at the growing frequency of crimes against property — the defalcations in office — the dishonesty in business — the adulterations and robberies that permeate all departments of trade? With respect also to those sins of which human laws take little or no cognizance, we perceive the same startling and abnormal development. Even Intemperance, for whose suppression so much has been done, is at this moment rapidly spreading; while the enormous sin of Licentiousness has attained a prevalence in all classes of society, and shows itself with an unblushing boldness, that must cause every friend of his species to shrink back in dismay and horror.

Along with this growth of atrocious immoralities, there have sprung up also an effrontery in guilt, a disregard of decency, and a contempt for the very name and appearance of goodness, which indicate a most polluted state of public sentiment and feeling. Formerly, men reverenced Virtue, if they did not follow her. But now they throw dust on her sacred head, and trample down her altars in scorn; while Vice, caressed and honored, decked in gaudy trappings, with multitudes shouting in her train, is paraded forth in the light of the sun, and beneath the gaze of astonished Heaven.

In like manner, the temptations to evil are more numerous and open now than in other days. No longer hidden under the veil of darkness, nor confined in their influence to the loathsome purlieus of profligacy, they stand out before all eyes, spreading their snares in every walk of life, and in every path of human pursuit. So insidious, so all-reaching are they, that no asylum is sacred, no retreat secure from their presence.

Connected with this increase of vice and of the incitements to it, there has been, as alike its precedent and its consequent, a most deplorable extension of skeptical and infidel opinions. In every age, there have been men of minds so distorted and depraved as to reject the authority of Revelation. But hitherto these have been mostly retired scholars and idle speculatists who, dwelling apart from the intercourse and sympathy of the masses, have muttered their doubts in the seclusion of the study, without doing much harm to any except themselves. It is a peculiar feature of our day, that Infidelity has gone forth from the closets of philosophers and theorizers into the walks of common life, and claims its votaries among merchants and tradesmen, mechanics and artisans, the tillers of the land, and the wanderers of the sea; thus infecting that practical class which gives character and tone to the community. No longer elaborating its destructive dogmas in learned disquisitions and ponderous folios, destined to be safely entombed in the dust and silence of some vast library, it gives them lighter and more winged forms; and in the shape of small books, magazines, and newspapers, scatters them through the dwellings of the poor, the cottage of the laborer, the bar-rooms of taverns, the cabins of steamboats and ships, in the solitude of the rural hamlet, and in the bustle of the thronged city. By this change in the mode of its operations, it not only manifests a hostility to revealed truth unusually active and bitter, but employs a species of attack most of all to be dreaded.

From these few and brief references, it seems evident that glaring impiety is a prominent characteristic of the present day. Whether this constitutes one of those alarming portents, which, as prophecy informs us, shall appear in the closing age of the world, when Satan shall come down in great wrath, knowing that his time is short, we venture not to decide; but certainly some of the marks of that predicted period are now clearly and strongly developed. And we cannot avoid the conviction that wickedness will become more and more outrageous, until it shall be at last overthrown and annihilated by the final victories of the Cross.

Our day is pre-eminently a day of change. The human mind roused from the torpor of centuries, seems determined to make amends for its past apathy by tearing everything in pieces. Like a blind giant, it deals forth its blows of power in all directions, eager only to destroy, and little heeding what it assails. Confounding together worthless abuses, and institutions whose value has been proved by the experience of ages, it attacks all without discrimination, bent only on making a clean sweep. In political affairs this spirit of innovation is strikingly apparent. The whole continent of Europe is at this moment one vast bed of fire, smouldering and seething under the thin crust of external quiet; and though suppressed for a time by the strong hand of military rule, yet all the while collecting its forces for a grand, terrific explosion, which shall scatter kings and thrones and all existing governments, like the dust of the summer's threshing-floor. Nor are other quarters of the globe exempt from similar commotion. Over our own land the hurricane has already swept. Justice and Oppression, Freedom and Slavery have here met and grappled in the mightiest and bloodiest struggle which the earth has ever seen; and the signal triumph which Liberty has won is a sign of hope for all the down-trodden races of suffering humanity. And everywhere among those races we see the stir and tumult of preparation for a similar conflict of antagonistic principles. In the sphere of morals and religion the same tokens of the coming strife are manifest; while, through all the departments of civil and social life, there is a restlessness, a discontent, a yearning after some dimly apprehended good, which cannot but be deemed ominous of mighty convulsions in the near future. The whole face of the world, like the ocean before the tempest breaks upon it, is agitated and upheaved as by some unseen power. Everywhere there is disturbance, tumult, revolution. All things betoken the approach of the great Battle of Armageddon, where, in the last final encounter of truth with error, holiness with sin, every principle and every institution, not emanating from Heaven, and rendered immortal by righteousness, shall be destroyed by the breath of Jehovah.

> "Not in vain the distance beacons. Forward, forward let us range.
> Let the great world spin forever down the ringing grooves of change,
> Through the shadow of the globe we sweep into the younger day."

Viewing thus the gathering of the thunder-cloud ere it burst, and listening to the deep mutterings of the volcano ere it sends forth the desolating eruption, where is our confidence, where our comfort, except in Him to whom the thunder and the volcano are but ministers, and who wields all the movements both of physical and of intellectual nature for the promotion of His own sovereign purposes? On the simple, but all-comprehending truth, "The Lord reigneth," the Christian may plant his feet, and stand secure, while worlds are crashing around him.

The present is a day of unwonted activity. Numerous causes now combine to call out the energies of men, and stimulate them to intense endeavor. The opening of new fields of enterprise and of new sources of wealth; the inventions and improvements in science and the arts, which render them available; the facility with which, by the present rapid means of communication, the most distant points may be reached, and the almost instantaneous transmission of intelligence, have supplied fresh objects of human desire, and given fresh vigor to human effort. Every sphere, every occupation, feels the awakening impulse. The sea swarms with ships exchanging the products of all climes. The land echoes with the bustle of trade, the din of manufactures, the noise of multitudes hurrying to and fro; and even the far wilderness rings with the tramp of eager adventurers, seeking homes or treasure in its hitherto silent wastes. Over all the secular pursuits and employments of man there has come the breath of a new life. The whole earth quivers with the excitement. Its pulsations have reached even the insulated Chinese, and he longs to leap the wall of the Celestial Empire, and mingle in the rush of "the outside barbarians." The sleep of the world is over — its long dream is broken. A spirit is now abroad that is destined to move onward from continent to continent, rousing up the slumbering nations in its course, until it shall convert the globe into one wide theatre of stirring life.

This increased activity, which is now animating all ranks, is capable, if rightly directed, of working out the most beneficent results in the physical, intellectual, and moral condition of men. But there is also great danger that by fixing their regards too exclusively on earthly things, it may become a snare to their souls, and contribute to their everlasting ruin. How urgently does this call for corresponding activity on the part of Christians, in order to counteract the overflowing tide of worldliness that is now setting in upon society!

Our day is distinguished by the wide diffusion of knowledge. In point of intelligence, we stand on an eminence far above any of the ages that have preceded us. This distinction lies not in the fact that the scholars of our day are more learned than those of other periods; although in the most recondite departments of science advances have been made, the possibility of which our fathers would not have believed—advances which are producing great practical effects on the whole circle of social existence. But the true glory of modern knowledge is its dissemination. For the first time in the history of the world, the subject of general education is enlisting the sympathies of governments, of statesmen, and of philanthropists. The change which has thus been wrought is as wonderful as it is cheering. By means of public and Sabbath schools, the multiplication of books in a cheap form, and the teeming issues of the Periodical Press, there is now educed, from myriads of minds hitherto neglected, an amount of intellectual and moral energy, that must be fraught with vast influence on the destinies of coming ages. We rejoice in this diffusion of intelligence, and long for the day when its light shall reach every darkling inhabitant of our earth. At the same time, it must be remembered that knowledge, divorced from religion, may become only an engine of mischief and destruction. How important, then, is it that we should cast into these growing streams of secular learning that element of Wisdom from above, which alone can render them healthful and salutary!

Our day is characterized by an ardent spirit of reform. Christianity, acting in concert with expanding knowledge, and giving impulse and direction to it, is now developing its benign influence on human welfare with unprecedented power. The wrongs of centuries have been redressed. Abuses, hoary with age, and fenced round by interest and prejudice, have been partially or wholly swept away. Without pausing to mention other specific instances, let me refer you to the progress which has been made in the cause of human freedom. By freedom, we mean not that wild anarchy which has sometimes been invested with its sacred name, but that well organized, rational liberty, which is the friend of order and of law, and which, while it teaches men to respect the rights of others, impels them to assert and maintain their own. And this — a blessing of inestimable price — is growing apace with the spread of intelligence and religion. Indeed, wherever true Christianity and Knowledge combine, Freedom must always spring from the union. They are allied to each other by the indissoluble relation of cause and effect; and any attempt to sunder them would be as futile as that of the ancient despot to still the winds with his breath, and bind the Hellespont in his chains.

In the administration of civil governments, a great advance has been made on the theory and the practice of former times. The truth has been demonstrated, and is rapidly extending, that governments were ordained, not for the aggrandizement of the few, but for the good of the many; that the subject is not a mere machine, to serve the caprice or ambition of irresponsible lords, and bound to obey their arbitrary will, but a being endued with the sacred attributes of humanity, possessing inalienable rights, entitled to share in the enactment of the laws and in the choice of the rulers under which he shall live, and claiming to stand forth in the unshackled dignity of his nature, beneath the broad protection of universal Equality and Justice. This is, of itself, a noble triumph, and is fraught with the promise of triumphs yet more noble. Such a principle, once fixed in the minds of men, cannot remain inert and unproductive. Like a buried seed, it will swell and expand, till it bursts through all impediments, and flowers forth into a new and better civilization. On the progress and development of this social revolution the example of our own country has exerted a most powerful influence. The success of free institutions here has kindled in the oppressed masses of other climes an intense longing for similar immunities — a longing which has been immensely deepened and emphasized by the recent terrible ordeal through which those institutions have passed. In conquering the rebellion of the oligarchs — a rebellion inaugurated for the overthrow of liberty — a rebellion so vast in its proportions that to all but ourselves its subjugation appeared impossible — we have demonstrated the strength and stability of popular government; and have shown, in the sight of the nations, that such a form of government is not only the most beneficent, but the most invulnerable and deathless. The nations will not forget the lesson. Henceforth Freedom will walk the earth with a bolder step and a loftier brow. And we cannot but believe that she has now reached a position, where her uplifted banner shall no longer stream against the wind, or hang downward in a sluggish and leaden atmosphere, but float gladly and victoriously before the favoring breeze, till its starry folds shall wave over an emancipated world.

While so much has been done to ameliorate the civil condition of men at large, the case of one isolated class, peculiar in its degradation and misery, has not been forgotten. Christian benevolence is putting forth a great and glorious effort in behalf of the bondmen of all races and in all lands. Nearly all civilized nations have united to brand as piracy the accursed traffic in human flesh on the shores of Africa. England has abolished slavery throughout her dominions. France and Holland have done the same. Even Russia, despotic, autocratic Russia, has proclaimed that over all her broad steppes serfdom shall cease. And now redeemed America stands by their side, purified like them from the stain of bondage. By a wondrous intervention of Divine Providence, she, too, rejoices in the removal of the fearful scourge which has so long blighted her prosperity. Here, however, the emancipation, though equally benign in its results, has been widely different in its method. Not by slow and silent changes — not by the calm force of moral opinion — has the chain of servitude been broken. The hand of an avenging God has rent it suddenly and violently asunder. From the shock of battle, from the crash and din of internecine strife, has sprung the deliverance of the slave. The devotees of barbarism, the buyers and sellers of men, madly opposed themselves to the power of the advancing age. Luxurious taskmasters, fattening on the sweat and blood of their thralls, vented their rage against the

Jubilee that was drawing nigh, and lifted their puny hands to push it back. Venal rhetoricians defamed as mere "glittering generalities" the great words which Liberty had graven on her charter; and political aspirants, and mercenary placemen, and Traffic's minions, and scared conservatives, peeping out from holes and corners, cried, "Halt," to the millions rushing on with the shout of "Free Soil for Free Men." The propagandists of slavery, in their insane struggles to uphold it, "played such fantastic tricks," as to make them the scorn of earth, and the abomination of Heaven. But their resistance was vain. The decree of the Omnipotent had gone forth, that slavery must die. The voice of Christianity, the voice of the world, the voice of the world's Ruler proclaimed that slavery must die. Then came the death-grapple. To perpetuate and extend the institution, the South rushed into treason and civil war, and marshalled all its resources and all its hate for the destruction of the Government and the Union. Long and fierce was the conflict. The land was convulsed by the uproar of encountering legions, desolated by their fury, and red with slaughter. And when victory crowned the right at last, and the smoke of battle rolled away, lo! slavery lay dead amid the hecatombs of the slain, smitten down in the gory combat which its champions had provoked.

In the work of general enfranchisement thus begun — a work which is destined never to cease, until men shall recognize in their fellow-man of every race and complexion a brother and an equal — we behold a movement to whose moral grandeur history affords no parallel. Whether we contemplate the stupendous agencies which energize and guide it, or the magnificent issues to which it leads, we are alike impressed by its greatness and its beneficence. If this be the spirit of the time — and can any one doubt it? — who must not long for its continuance and increase, and for the going out of its redeeming influence to all the nations of the earth? May He, whose sovereign purposes have called it forth, so consecrate and direct it, that it shall wander into no wild excess, but move on, steady, uniform, unsullied, till Humanity shall everywhere be disenthralled, and the world present one glorious scene of Freedom and Peace.

But the grandest feature of our day yet remains to be considered. It is pre-eminently the Era of Evangelism. All its aspects, all its tendencies, denote that such is its place in history. It is distinguished beyond all former times for the opportunities which it affords for the spread of the Gospel, and for the success which the Gospel is achieving. The proclamation, in all lands, of the Sacrifice offered on Calvary, is the great agency which God has ordained for the spiritual improvement and salvation of men. To this all the ages have looked forward as their chief scope and end. Whatever their position along the stream of Time — whether in the gray mists that veil its earlier course, or amid the light of its later scenes — each has gazed ever with steadfast face toward that shining point in the flowing centuries, when the Angel of the Apocalyptic Vision should "fly through the midst of heaven, having the everlasting Gospel to preach to all that dwell on the earth."

The whole world now teems with tokens that this glorious epoch is close at hand. The facilities for the universal diffusion of Divine Truth are such as no other days have seen. Until recently, restrictions arising from hostile governments, prohibitory laws, and various other causes, have, like mountain barriers, shut out the Word of Life from a large proportion of the human family. These restrictions are now in all instances greatly diminished; in most entirely removed. In our own country, the curse of bondage, which sealed up the Bible to four millions of immortal souls, and barred from them all means of instruction, has been extirpated forever; and a free path opened for the light of education and of a pure Gospel to reach and penetrate this mass of darkened humanity. In the far climes of Heathenism a similar preparation is in progress.

Everywhere obstructions are disappearing; everywhere hills of difficulty are falling; everywhere the strong bulwarks of caste and prejudice are giving way. The Church of the Redeemer enjoys rest from external conflict. No longer is she required to expend all her resources in merely providing refuge for her harassed and scattered flocks; nor are her Apostles and Evangelists condemned to the silence of prison walls, or the deeper silence of the martyr's grave. With no hindrances but such as spring from her own want of faith and zeal, she may go forth wherever she will on her sublime mission of subduing the world to Christ. And for this work all the modern discoveries and improvements in science and the arts contribute to equip her. Geography, Navigation, Commerce — not limited as of old to the narrow waters and shores of the Mediterranean or the Euxine, but embracing every ocean and every continent — the Printing Press, Steam, the Telegraph — all these are her ministers and auxiliaries, enabling her to multiply her points of attack and her means of victory almost to an indefinite extent. The modes of communication between nation and nation are easy and rapid. From the mercantile and other relations which connect the different parts of the globe, ready avenues are provided for conveying the message of salvation to the most distant abodes of the human race. There is no spot on earth so remote or secluded, no island so hidden amid the wastes of unexplored seas, that Christian intelligence has not heard of it, that Christian sympathy does not go out to it, that Christian effort cannot reach it.

The whole world is accessible to the Gospel. Aye, more — the whole world is waiting for the Gospel. A spirit of inquiry, of hope, is abroad among the nations, pointing them to the Star of Bethlehem, to the Sun of Righteousness, just rising on their awakened vision. Myriads have renounced their superstitions, and welcomed the truth as it is in Jesus; and myriads more need only to be taught that truth, to receive it with joy. And while Christianity is thus growing stronger, and is making constant inroads upon false religions, those false religions themselves, through all their motley systems, show marks of decrepitude, paralyzation, decay. Nor are the people of God altogether insensible to the obligations which these facts involve. Though but half awake to their duty, they are awake to it as never were the people of God before. Never before were the wants of the world so fully understood and felt. Never before was labor for the world so thoroughly recognized as the rule of Christian life. Never before were offerings for the world so large and free. Never before was prayer for the world so universal and so fervent. Never before was the conversion of the world, the entire world, so deliberately, solemnly, unblenchingly proposed as the one great purpose of the Church of Christ. The harvest of the earth is ripe. The harvest of the earth is begun. Go where you will on the face of the peopled globe — the reapers are there before you. And already, in places not few — God increase them a thousand-fold! — the golden sheaves stand thick over all the field.

Such are some of the bright indications of the day in which we live. And do they not more than compensate for those that are dark and ominous? Can we study them without perceiving that they are rich with auguries of the approaching triumphs of the Gospel? We should do violence to Reason and Religion alike, did we not recognize in them the Voice of Providence, crying in the Wilderness of this outcast world, "prepare ye the way of the Lord; make straight in the desert a highway for our God." And as that way is now being prepared, we seem to hear, mingling with the sounds of the pioneer's axe, the trencher's spade, and the builder's hammer, the distant roll of His chariot wheels, as He comes onward, onward, "conquering and to conquer."

We mean not indeed to say that all things are now ready for the ushering in of Messiah's final reign. Many and great changes must take place before that glad consummation can arrive. There are mountains to be levelled, valleys to be raised, gulfs to be bridged, ere the word of the Lord can have free course, and be glorified over all the earth. Even in the character and position of the Church itself there is much that needs to be reformed. But what then? Shall we do nothing because we cannot at once do everything? Shall we abandon the work, because our coadjutors in it are not all that they ought to be, and all that they yet shall be? Oh! no, no. Let us rather wait on, pray on, toil on, till a mightier effusion of the Spirit from above shall so renovate the Church, that the Church shall renovate the world. The Host of God's Elect, though but imperfectly organized, ill disciplined, and broken into separate and often belligerent bands, is nevertheless passing through a course of training that shall fit it for glorious deeds. And soon, marshalled in one vast phalanx under the great central Banner of "One Lord, One Faith, one Baptism," marching shoulder to shoulder, and keeping step to the music of the angel's Hymn, "Glory to God in the Highest, on earth Peace, Good will toward men," it shall be led forth by its Omnipotent Captain to the conquest of the world.

We have thus finished our promised review of the time in which we live. It is emphatically a time of transition, important and exciting, not only for the grand events which are taking place in it, but for the still grander ones of which they are the forerunners. Regarded thus as a season of preparation for the world's enfranchisement, — the Saturday evening that heralds the world's Sabbath, — it manifestly brings with it peculiar obligations, and inculcates momentous lessons. With a distinctness that cannot be mistaken, and an emphasis that should thrill every heart, it summons the people of God to be not merely indolent observers, but earnest actors in the great scenes which are opening before them.

We are called upon to survey our work. To understand precisely what we have to do, is as necessary as it is to discern the fitting season for its performance. In the development of human affairs, each generation of men has a specific part assigned it, which, from the prominence it holds in the movements of the period, may be denominated the work of that generation. In physical progress this law may be observed. The province of one age is Discovery. Public enterprise is strongly bent in that direction; and wealth and talent and ambition find their chief outlets in traversing unknown seas, and giving new continents to the world. Another is the age of Colonization, in which realms hitherto uninhabited or barbarous are peopled with civilized races. Then follows the age of Material Improvement, clearing the forests, constructing highways, founding cities, developing industry, creating commerce. The growth of Science is marked by the same successive stages. One century thinks out the philosophies on which it rests. Another invents the instruments for giving practical effect to those philosophies. Another perfects the instruments, sets them at work, moves the wheel, plies the spindle, drives the car along the track, speeds the steamship over the deep, sends the harnessed lightning round the globe.

There has been a similar order in the establishment and spread of the Gospel. Since its first promulgation by Christ and His Apostles, it has passed through various conditions, and stood in different attitudes to society and the world, requiring of its votaries corresponding lines of conduct. It has had its eras of persecution, when suffering was the testimony of the Church, and calm endurance her highest duty. It has had its eras of doctrinal discussion, in which the course of events summoned its adherents to examine its foundations, and strengthen its defences. But these eras are not ours. The call on believers now is not to die for the Truth, but to live for it; not to discover the Truth, but to publish it; not to surround the Truth with intrenchments, but to carry it out into open combat with the powers of darkness and sin. The army of the Lord is not now in garrison, and, therefore, cannot meet the claims of its Divine Leader by merely fortifying its position, and repulsing the attacks of the foe. Not alone the parade, the drill, but the onward march, the battle array, the charge, are demanded of us. The great business of Christians in our day is to hold forth the Word of Life; to confront with it every public and every private vice, every system of wrong, every form of falsehood and imposture; to illumine with it every home of ignorance, every den of crime, every dwelling of sorrow; to overthrow the empire of Satan; to liberate his captives; to enlighten, reclaim and save the whole family of man. This is the work which the voice of Jehovah, emphasized by the time, commands — the work of the entire Church — of each individual member — your work, and mine. Survey it; measure its extent; weigh its importance; mark the authority which prescribes it; look out over the field which it covers; listen to the cry of the darkling nations — and you cannot but feel that the end of your calling, your life-mission, is to bear the message of redemption to a perishing world.

To prepare for our work, is another behest of the time. No great undertaking can be accomplished without adequate preparation. It is the law of all human affairs, that a neglect to provide the means requisite for success is sure to be followed by defeat. In secular enterprises this law is universally recognized and acted on. How strikingly has its operation been witnessed in the gigantic war which has just closed! What vast and manifold arrangements were necessary to its prosecution; what wisdom in the choice of commanders; what labor in raising, disciplining, replenishing the armies; what forethought and system in supplying the material and apparatus of effective service. In the earlier periods of the struggle, what terrible reverses we suffered from deficiency in some or all of these particulars. And when, taught by disaster, we brought to the conflict the most perfect equipment which the resources of the country could furnish, how speedily its aspect changed, and how magnificently it went on to its triumphant end. In the mighty warfare which "the sacramental host" is waging against the powers of wickedness, there is need of the same completeness in the appliances essential to its vigorous ongoing. The instrumentalities which God has ordained for carrying forward His designs of mercy in the earth, are the preaching of the Gospel by the lips of living ministers whom He calls and sets apart to this service; and the bringing its truths into personal contact with the minds of men through the example and efforts of private Christians. Both of these departments require to be greatly enlarged and energized.

The work before us calls for more and for better qualified ministers. To proclaim the tidings of salvation in all lands, and to all the diversified tribes of our outcast race; to meet the endlessly varying phases of character which human nature presents; to lead on the armies of Zion in their assault upon the strongholds of ungodliness, that bristle defiance against Christ in every community and in every clime — men are wanted in vast numbers, and of more ample endowments than the Church has seen since her primitive confessors left the earth. In this day of popular excitements, when society is borne hither and thither in ceaseless agitation, and greed and worldliness reign supreme, the messengers of Heaven can make little impression, if they lack the power to grapple with the crisis. None can do this but men of ardent piety, thorough culture, ready skill, and earnest purpose. The Apostle Paul exhorts his disciple Timothy to "make full proof of his ministry;" or, according to the literal meaning of the Greek word, to "give it full measure" — make it round and complete in all its functions and capabilities. Such rounded ministers are needed now. Of flat ministers there are enough. Of square ministers, angular ministers, one-sided ministers, there are enough, more than enough.

The demand of the time is for round ministers — ministers symmetrically developed in all the qualities that pertain to their office — robust in body, vigorous in mind, mighty in faith and love. If in any of these particulars defect exist, there will be proportional weakness. Our age is a strong one — strong in impulse, strong in action — and only strong hands can guide it. Physical strength alone cannot do it. Intellectual strength alone cannot do it. Moral strength alone cannot do it. These must unite, and form a ministry muscular, educated, holy — a ministry elastic with health, full of courage and zeal, in sympathy with God and humanity. Such are the men to "endure hardness," scale mountains, cross oceans, traverse continents, laugh at fatigue, brave cold and heat, "quench the violence of fire, stop the mouths of lions, turn to flight the armies of the aliens," and carry the banner of salvation in triumph round the world. And such are the men whom the Church must raise up in hosts, if she would be found ready for the solemn emergencies that await her. Glancing over the fields ripe for the sickle, and at the reapers few and feeble, she must pray the Lord of the Harvest to send forth more laborers; to touch by His Spirit the hearts of her most gifted young men, separate them from their secular callings, and devote them to the ministry of reconciliation. And she must feel herself sacredly bound to supply whatever may be necessary to train and furnish them for their work in the most effective manner, sustaining them in their course of education, sympathizing with them in their struggles, bearing them ever on her heart — animated by the conviction that in thus aiming to provide a more numerous and a more able ministry, she is meeting a most imperative want in the kingdom of the Saviour.

In the Christian Body at large increased activity and power are still more urgently demanded. It is a fact as strange as it is mournful that the vast majority of those who profess allegiance to the Redeemer, do nothing directly to advance His cause. They regard their connection with the church solely in its bearing on their own comfort and salvation, ignoring the grave truth that they have been brought into the family of God, not only that they may taste the sweetness of Christian hope, but proffer that hope to others; not only that they may reach heaven themselves, but draw after them the perishing multitudes of their fellow-men. Having thus little sense of religious obligation, they are content to enjoy the privileges of the Gospel, and resign to others the richer privilege of extending it. They are always receiving, never imparting. Like the sands of the desert, like the salt waves of the sea, they drink in the sweet rain of heaven, but give back no products to feed a starving world.

In Ezekiel's vision of the emblematic waters which, issuing from under the threshold of the Temple, flowed into the surrounding country, increasing in volume as they flowed, till they grew to a broad and deep river — certain marshy places are described, that received the waters, but instead of sending them out again to fertilize the regions beyond, absorbed them, and became, in consequence, stagnant pools, breeding disease and death. The traveller in Italy may often see this imagery illustrated in those districts where, from a scarcity of rain, irrigation is extensively practised, and reduced to a system. A mountain stream, gushing from its parent lake high up among the Alps is conducted, by a series of embankments and sluices, from terrace to terrace, along the face of the hills, and down through the valleys, wherever its refreshing tribute is needed. The distribution and use of the water are regulated by strict laws. While all have the right to turn it in upon their fields, none are permitted to confine it there; but each one, as soon as his thirsty crops are satisfied, must lift the gate and let the stream pass to the terrace below; the owner of which must, in turn, send it down to the next; and so on in succession, till the last terrace is reached. It sometimes happens, however, that the sluiceways get stopped up by earthy deposits; or that some selfish cultivator, caring only for his own supply, heedless of his neighbor's needs, neglects to open them. In this case a double mischief is done. The fields from which the water is kept back are parched and withered; and those in which it is shut up are converted into swamps, where nothing can grow but reptiles and malaria. Alas! how many of these swamps are there in the church of Christ—spots flooded with privileges, drowned in mercies—spots on which the waters of the sanctuary fall in a constant stream, and are seen no more,—swallowed up by spongy consciences and souls of mud! God's farm lacks drainage. This mass of dead material, lying cold, sluggish, inert, in the mire of sloth and worldliness, must be broken by the ploughshare of the Spirit, stirred, pulverized, thrown up to the sun, warmed by love, quickened into activity, before that grand Harvest can come, which is to strew the earth with salvation, and fill full the garners of heaven. Too long has the relation of members to the church been practically that of the parasite to the tree—living on its juices, but yielding it no support. Too long and too largely have the troops of Zion been composed of non-combatants—silken soldiers, whose highest idea of warfare is going once a week to the commissary's tent for rations, dressing for parade, and mustering at reviews and anniversaries, to show their feathers, and do the sham fighting; while the real fighting is left to a few pastors, Sunday-school teachers and missionaries.

From the stern conflict of principles that is now going on — from the stupendous issues that are soon to be decided — from the high vantage ground which we have already reached — there comes a summons louder than the blast of a thousand trumpets, invoking every soldier of the King of kings to take part in the struggle, and battle for the right. There is room and work for all. None can do so little, that they may be excused for not doing that little. None can do so much, that they may be excused from putting forth their whole strength. There are vices to be extirpated, miseries to be relieved, wrongs to be redressed, chains to be riven, darkness to be dispelled, sinners to be saved, humanity to be reclaimed to God and happiness. To these noble ends every redeemed man and woman may contribute. One can seek out a neglected child, and place it under Chrstian teaching. Another can scatter Bibles and tracts along the highways of traffic, and in the abodes of Want and Guilt. One can consecrate his fresh, young powers to a course of study for the Gospel ministry. Another can give him the needed aid. One can speak of Jesus in the private circle, and in the social gathering. Another can proclaim him in the great congregation.

One can go with the message of Life to heathen climes. Another can furnish the means to sustain and cheer him in his exile. One can devote his personal labor to the uplifting of the millions from whose limbs the war has rent the fetters of servitude, but whose minds are still shrouded in ignorance and debasement. Another can help on the god-like work by his contributions and his prayers.

All can do something, and that something, be it little, be it much, is equally necessary to the final result. The rain-drops are necessary to fill the brooks, the brooks to fill the rivers, the rivers to fill the ocean, the ocean to bear wealth and gladness to its farthest shores. So, in the chain of agencies by which our race is to be lifted out of its ruin, there is the same system of connections and dependencies. And it is only when every link of this chain is in its place, prepared for its portion of the strain, and the Church along the whole line of her membership, cries "All ready!" that God will put his hand to the spokes, and the great wheel of His power go round, and this sunk planet be drawn up from the abyss, and hung to its Redeemer's throne.

The great interests of the hour give special emphasis to the duty of following Providence in our work. As the Shekinah led the Chosen Tribes in the wilderness, so "God in History" guides the march of His Church. His agency pervades all the movements of men and nations, and makes them the exponents of His will. Events are our teachers. They are the beckonings of an all-ruling Hand, showing us what to do, and where to do it. And this, which has everywhere and always been true, is peculiarly true in our own land and day. The present posture of public affairs indicates, with unmistakable clearness and authority, the direction which our efforts should take. The Rebellion of the Southern oligarchs has been conquered by the military strength of the Government; and in its fall Slavery, the foul mother that gave it birth, has perished. War's dread mission is ended. To other weapons the task that remains must now be committed. Moral influences alone are competent to effect the social regeneration of the lately insurgent States, remove the evils entailed on them by centuries of bondage, and spread over their wasted domains the blessings of order, industry and peace. Free labor, education, Christianity must take up and perfect the transformation which the sword has begun.

Here, then, is a broad field distinctively marked out by Providence as the scene of our most energetic endeavors. In this field there are four millions of emancipated slaves, who have been rendered helpless and abject by long years of vassalage, and who have hitherto been purposely excluded from the light of knowledge, and the inspirations of hope. By a display of His power as unexpected as it was awful, Jehovah has struck the fetters from their limbs; and has thus opened the way for us to strike from their souls the heavier fetters of darkness and degradation. And has not this in itself all the force and significance of a command? Can we fail to read in it the purpose of Heaven? Does it not speak to us in tones imperative and solemn as if uttered from the eternal Throne, calling us to go to the help of these spoiled and trampled ones, raise them up from the barbarism in which they have been held, and educate them for the new life to which the Divine hand is conducting them? They are struggling to lift themselves out of their depression — struggling to stand forth, free and self-reliant, on the high ground of equal rights for all. Their past wrongs and their present privations appeal to us for sympathy and succor, and urge us, trumpet-tongued, to put forth our utmost exertions to aid them in this momentous crisis of their destiny. And as we listen to their prayer, there comes mingling with it the cry of eight millions of white men, like them, sufferers from slavery; but not, like them, guiltless sufferers. They have upheld and cherished the institution which has been their ruin. They have sinned for it — fought for it — for its sake have committed treason, rebellion, murder, and drenched the land with their own and their brothers' blood. By that law of righteous compensation, which arms the injustice of the oppressor with a rod for his own punishment, the wrong which they have done to others has recoiled upon themselves. In robbing the slave of freedom, they have lost their own. In chattelizing him, they have imbruted their own nature. The fell curse for whose continuance they have striven so fiercely, has debased their civilization, corrupted their morals, defiled their Christianity — has eaten out patriotism, paralyzed enterprize and thrift, and nourished indolence and pride into an abnormal and monstrous growth. The blight of slavery, and the destructive war for slavery, have covered the whole region in which they dwell with anarchy and desolation. To reorganize the South, bring order out of the confusion that now distracts it, recast its society, and breathe into its dead form the new life of intelligence, of compensated industry, of a religion which inculcates justice to the lowly — is the stupendous undertaking to which the benevolence of our time and country should be directed. We say not that this is our only work; nor that, in order to effect it, we should withdraw from all other departments of Christian labor. But we do say that here lies the chief duty of the hour — the grand arena of toil and conflict to which the finger of God points the moral heroism of the nation. And in all that we attempt for His glory and the well-being of our race, the more closely we follow the intimations of His Providence, the more signally will the Pillar of His Presence go before us, and herald us on to victory.

The nature of our work requires us to make the Word of God the great instrument in its prosecution. This admonition derives peculiar fitness and importance from the attitude which many, while professing to seek earnestly the good of men, have assumed toward the Revelation that has come down from heaven as the sole restorer of an outcast world. In instances not few, those who stand prominent in the philanthropic movements of the day, manifest a hatred of Divine Truth, and a contempt of its authority, as criminal in themselves as they are fatal to the cause with which they are allied. Setting aside the Gospel as an effete superstition—rejecting its inspired verities as dogmas that have lost their power—they think to banish evil from the earth by the mere force of unsanctified enlightenment and culture. Such schemes can have no result but to show the blindness and folly of their authors. They always have failed, and they ever must fail, while the moral character of our race remains what it is. They are as impotent against the outgoings of human depravity, against the surges of passion, against the encroachments of selfishness and violence, as an embankment of reeds would be against the overflowing of the ocean. The wisdom of the All-Merciful has set forth the only agency that can subdue the wickedness of men, and extinguish the woes which it engenders. That agency is to be found in the redemptive work of Christ. In the sublime facts of His mission, in the propitiation which He made, in the doctrines which He taught, in the renewing energies of the Spirit which He procured, there resides a power, and the only power, that can raise the fallen, and recover the lost. All the ills which humanity suffers have been inflicted on it by its alienation from God. The sinfulness of man's heart is the poisoned fountain whose waters have spread contagion and death over the world. Thence flow the manifold disorders, the vice and irreligion, the crimes and outrages, the injustice, the wrong-doing, the domination of the strong, the down-treading of the weak, the darkness, pollution, misery, that deluge the globe; and thence they will continue to flow with undiminished volume, till their source is dried up. There is no hope for man, here or hereafter, but in the purification of his spiritual nature. And this the Gospel only can achieve. The Gospel, and the Gospel alone, has a remedy adequate to his necessities. In its provisions and influences are contained all the elements of social and moral amelioration in this life, and of perfection and blessedness in the life which is to come. Let us, then, while devoting ourselves heart and soul to the noble work of vindicating the oppressed, and elevating the degraded, stand fast by the Bible. Let us carry it with us into whatever field of reformatory labor we enter, and refuse to go where we cannot carry it. While we welcome its teachings as the rule of our own life, and the balm of our own sorrows, let them be also the guide, the measure and the means of our endeavors to do good to others. So shall our plans and our efforts be in harmony with the moral administration of God, and the highest interests of mankind.

The magnitude and arduousness of the work before us call for special dependence on the aid of the Holy Spirit. Without Him, all else is vain. Without Him, the preaching of the Gospel, the dissemination of truth, and every attempt to succor the distressed, to gather in the wanderers, to purify and save the world, will be ineffectual and powerless. Without Him, the words of mercy which we speak to the wretched around us, will be like music floating over graves, unheard by the sleepers below. Without Him, whatever improvement may be wrought in the material and intellectual aspects of society will be but as the flowers which affection strews over a putrefying corpse, veiling its ghastliness, yet leaving it a corpse still. "Not by might, nor by power, but by my Spirit, saith the Lord." The voice of the Redeemer in His Word and in His Providence is now saying to each one of us, "Arise and pray!" Arise and pray for the promised coming of the Paraclete, the second Pentecost, which is to baptize the Church anew, and regenerate the nations. "Awake, awake, O arm of the Lord, and put on strength!" Let this be our cry, and the cry of God's people in all lands, and soon a redeeming power will go forth over the whole face of this apostate earth, expelling from it all unrighteousness, and filling it with light, holiness and salvation.

Having thus seen what our work is and what it demands, nothing remains but to do it. This is the crown and consummation of all. To survey our work is well. To prepare for our work is well. To watch the bearings of Providence on our work is well. To shape our work by the Bible is well. To rely on the Spirit in our work is well — aye, more than well. But the real matter, the vital matter, is to do our work. To this point we have now come. And as in the time of Ezra, when the Temple was rebuilt, let one say to another, "Arise, and work; the Lord God of our fathers is with us; Arise, and do it."

Wait not for great opportunities and a conspicuous theatre. If you love Jesus and the souls for which He died, you will quickly discover an appropriate sphere, and good in it that you can accomplish. Begin with the first thing your hand finds, the doing of which will honor God, and make a fellow-creature better and happier. Begin with that drunkard whom you saw to-day reeling by your door. Begin with that den of infamy in the next street. Begin with that pale widow who so often passes your dwelling, gazing — Oh, so sadly — at its cheerful home joys. This morning, as you took your happy little ones for a walk, you met a ragged orphan, dragging his bare feet wearily over the rough stones, and looking into your face with hopeless, beseeching eyes. Begin with that orphan. Begin with that freedman, just risen from the mire of slavery, who, with his body scarred by the lash, and his mind shrouded in the night of ignorance, implores you to give to him and to his children the rights of manhood, and the uplifting power of knowledge. Begin with your unconverted family, with your servants, your operatives, your neighbors, your acquaintance. If you cannot influence masses, influence individuals. If you cannot save man in the lump, save him piecemeal. If you cannot rear in the house of the Lord the ponderous column or the lofty entablature, carry up a single pebble, and with it fill some unsightly hole in a corner.

> "How speaks the present hour? Act!
>   Walk, upward glancing;
> So shall thy footsteps in glory be traced,
>   Slow, but advancing.
> Scorn not the smallness of daily endeavor,
> Let the great meaning ennoble it ever;
> Droop not o'er efforts expended in vain;
> Work, as believing that labor is gain."

The claims of Christ and of the world are before you. Would you not place one stone in the Living Temple? Would you not pluck one brand from the burning? Would you not emancipate one captive from the prison house? Would you not set one gem in the glittering crown which the Saviour shall wear through eternal ages? The Hour — the Cause — Time and Eternity — God waiting to be glorified — Jesus waiting to see of the travail of His soul — the groaning earth waiting to be delivered, invoke you to action. Do your work — do it lovingly, do it earnestly, do it now, do it to the end. And when that end shall come — when the Angel, with one foot on the land, and the other on the sea, shall lift up his hand to heaven, and swear by Him that liveth forever and ever, that time shall be no longer — when the last trumpet shall unlock the sepulchres, and the Throne shall be set, and the Books of Doom opened — then your Master and Judge, unfolding the record of your Time and its Obligations — your Day and its Work — shall say — DONE — WELL DONE!

> "Work away!
> For the Father's eye is on us,
> Never off us, still upon us,
> Night and day!
> Work and pray!
> Pray, — and work will be completer;
> Work, — and prayer will be the sweeter;
> Love, — and prayer and work the fleeter
> Will ascend upon their way."

THE END.

Valuable Works,

PUBLISHED BY

GOULD AND LINCOLN,

59 Washington Street, Boston.

GOD REVEALED IN NATURE AND IN CHRIST; including a Refutation of the Development Theory contained in the "Vestiges of the Natural History of Creation." By Rev. JAMES B. WALKER, author of "THE PHILOSOPHY OF THE PLAN OF SALVATION." 12mo, cloth, 1.50.

THE SUFFERING SAVIOUR; or, Meditations on the Last Days of Christ. By FRED. W. KRUMMACHER, D.D., author of "Elijah the Tishbite." 12mo, cloth, 1.75; cloth, gilt, 2.75; half calf, 3.50.

"The narrative is given with thrilling vividness and pathos and beauty. Marking, as we proceeded, several passages for quotation, we found them, in the end, so numerous that we must refer the reader to the work itself." — *News of the Churches (Scottish).*

THE TESTIMONY OF CHRIST TO CHRISTIANITY. By PETER BAYNE, M. A., author of "Christian Life," etc. 16mo, cloth, 90 cts.

☞ A work of great interest and power.

THE BENEFIT OF CHRIST'S DEATH; or, The Glorious Riches of God's Free Grace, which every True Believer receives by Jesus Christ and Him Crucified. Originally written in Italian by Aonio Paleario, and now Reprinted from an Ancient English Translation. With an Introduction by Rev. JOHN AYER, M. A. 16mo, cloth, 75 cts.

WREATH AROUND THE CROSS; or, Scripture Truths Illustrated. By the Rev. A. MORTON BROWN, D. D. Recommendatory Preface, by JOHN ANGELL JAMES. With a beautiful Frontispiece. 16mo, cloth, 1.00.

EXTENT OF THE ATONEMENT IN ITS RELATION TO GOD AND THE UNIVERSE. By Rev. THOMAS W. JENKYN, D. D., late President of Coward College, London. 12mo, cloth, 1.50.

"We consider this volume as setting the long and fiercely agitated question, as to the extent of the Atonement, completely at rest. Posterity will thank the author, till the latest ages, for his illustrious argument."— *N. Y. Evangelist.*

CHRIST IN HISTORY. By ROBERT TURNBULL, D. D. A New and Enlarged Edition. 12mo, cloth, 1.75.

THE SCHOOL OF CHRIST; or, Christianity Viewed in its Leading Aspects. By the Rev. A. R. L. FOOTE, author of "Incidents in the Life of our Saviour," etc. 16mo, cloth, 75 cts.

Gould and Lincoln's Publications.

PHILOSOPHY OF THE PLAN OF SALVATION; a book for the Times. By an AMERICAN CITIZEN. With an Introductory Essay by CALVIN E. STOWE, D. D. ☞ New improved and enlarged edition. 12mo, cloth, 1.25.

THE PERSON AND WORK OF CHRIST. By ERNEST SARTORIUS, D. D., Konigsberg, Prussia. Translated by Rev. OAKMAN S. STEARNS, D. D. 18mo, cloth, 60 cts.

THE GREAT DAY OF ATONEMENT; or, Meditations and Prayers on the Last Twenty-four Hours of the Sufferings and Death of our Lord and Saviour Jesus Christ. Translated from the German of CHARLOTTE ELIZABETH NEBELIN. Edited by Mrs. COLIN MACKENZIE. Elegantly printed and bound. 16mo, cloth, 1.25; cloth, gilt, 2.00; Turkey mor., gilt, 3.50.

THE HEADSHIP OF CHRIST, and the Rights of the Christian People; A Collection of Personal Portraitures, Historical and Descriptive Sketches and Essays, with the Author's celebrated Letter to Lord Brougham. By HUGH MILLER. Edited, with a Preface, by PETER BAYNE, A. M. 12mo, cloth, 1.75.

THE MISSION OF THE COMFORTER; with copious Notes. By JULIUS CHARLES HARE. With the NOTES translated for the AMERICAN EDITION. 12mo, cloth, 1.75.

THE IMITATION OF CHRIST. By THOMAS A KEMPIS. With an Introductory Essay by THOMAS CHALMERS, D. D. Edited by HOWARD MALCOM, D D. A new edition, with a LIFE OF THOMAS A KEMPIS, by Dr. C. ULLMANN, author of "Reformers before the Reformation." 12mo, cloth, 1.25.

FINE EDITION, TINTED PAPER. Square 8vo, cloth, red edges, 2.25; cloth, gilt, 3.00; half calf, 4.00; full Turkey mor., 6.00.

The above may safely be pronounced the best Protestant editions extant of this celebrated work.

LESSONS AT THE CROSS; or, Spiritual Truths Familiarly Exhibited in their Relations to Christ. By SAMUEL HOPKINS, author of "The Puritans." With an Introduction by REV. GEORGE W. BLAGDEN, D. D. New edition. 16mo, cloth, 1.00.

THE BETTER LAND; or, The Believer's Journey and Future Home. By the Rev. A. C. THOMPSON. 12mo, cloth, 1.25; cloth, gilt, 1.75.

A most charming and instructive book for all now journeying to the "better land."

HEAVEN. By JAMES WILLIAM KIMBALL. With an elegant vignette title-page. 12mo, cloth, 1.25; cloth, gilt, 2.00; Turkey morocco, gilt, 3.25.

"The book is full of beautiful ideas, consoling hopes, and brilliant representations of human destiny, all presented in a chaste, pleasing, and very readable style." — *N. Y. Chronicle.*

THE STATE OF THE IMPENITENT DEAD. By ALVAH HOVEY, D. D., Prof. of Christian Theology in Newton Theol. Inst. 16mo, cloth, 75 cts.

SAINTS' EVERLASTING REST. By RICHARD BAXTER. 16mo, cloth, 75 cts.

HARVEST AND THE REAPERS. Home Work for All, and how to do it. By Rev. HARVEY NEWCOMB. 16mo, cloth, 90 cts.

Gould and Lincoln's Publications.

THE CHRISTIAN LIFE, SOCIAL AND INDIVIDUAL. By PETER BAYNE, M. A. 12mo, cloth, 1.75; half calf, 3.50.

> There is but one voice respecting this extraordinary book,— men of all denominations, in all quarters, agree in pronouncing it one of the most admirable works of the age.

THE CHRISTIAN'S DAILY TREASURY; a Religious Exercise for every Day in the Year. By Rev. E. TEMPLE. A new and improved edition. 12mo, cloth, 1.50.

> ☞ A work for every Christian. It is, indeed, a "Treasury" of good things.

THE CHURCH MEMBER'S GUIDE. By the Rev. JOHN A. JAMES. Edited by J. O. CHOULES, D. D. New Edition. With Introductory Essay, by Rev. HUBBARD WINSLOW. Cloth, 60 cts.

THE CHURCH IN EARNEST. By Rev. JOHN A. JAMES. 18mo, cloth, 75 cts.

CHRISTIAN PROGRESS. A Sequel to the Anxious Inquirer. By JOHN ANGELL JAMES. 18mo, cloth, 65 cts.

THE MEMORIAL HOUR; or, The Lord's Supper in its relation to Doctrine and Life. By JEREMIAH CHAPLIN, D. D., author of "Evening of Life," etc. 16mo, 1.25.

> This is a precious volume, strictly devotional in its character, exhibiting the Lord's Supper in many aspects, presses home the lessons which it teaches, shows the feelings with which it should be regarded, and by its suggestions and admirable selections of hymns assists the communicant to prepare for this solemn service.

THE MEMORIAL NAME. Reply to Bishop COLENSO. By ALEXANDER MACWHORTER. With an Introductory Letter by NATHANIEL W. TAYLOR, D. D., late Dwight Professor in Yale Theological Seminary. 16mo, 1.25.

THE MERCY SEAT; or, Thoughts on Prayer. By A. C. THOMPSON, D.D., Author of "Better Land," etc. 12mo, cloth, 1.50.

Fine Edition, Tinted Paper. 8vo, cloth, red edges, 2.50; cloth, gilt edges, 3.50.

THE STILL HOUR; or, Communion with God. By Prof. AUSTIN PHELPS, D. D., of Andover Theological Seminary. 16mo, cloth, 60 cts.

CHRISTIANITY AND STATESMANSHIP; with Kindred Topics. By WILLIAM HAGUE, D. D. A new, revised, enlarged, and much improved edition. 12mo, cloth, 1.75.

THE EVIDENCES OF CHRISTIANITY, as exhibited in the writings of its apologists, down to Augustine. By W. J. BOLTON, of Gonville and Caius College, Cambridge. 12mo, cloth, 1.50.

CHRISTIAN BROTHERHOOD. By BARON STOW, D. D., Pastor of Rowe-street Church, Boston. 16mo, cloth, 75 cts.

THE CHRISTIAN WORLD UNMASKED. By JOHN BERRIDGE, M., Vicar of Everton, Bedfordshire. With a Life of the Author, by Rev. THOMAS GUTHRIE, D. D., Minister of Free St. John's, Edinburgh. 16mo, cloth, 75 cts.

Gould and Lincoln's Publications.

LYRA CŒLESTIS. HYMNS ON HEAVEN. Selected by A. C. THOMPSON, D. D., author of the "BETTER LAND." 12mo, cloth, red edges, 1.75.

FINE EDITION, TINTED PAPER. Square 8vo, cloth, red edges, 2.50; cloth, gilt, 3.50; half calf, 6.00; full Turkey mor., 8.00.

☞ A charming work, containing a collection of gems of poetry on Heaven.

GOTTHOLD'S EMBLEMS; or, Invisible Things Understood by Things that are Made. By CHRISTIAN SCRIVER, Minister of Magdeburg in 1671. Translated from the Twenty-eighth German Edition, by the Rev. ROBERT MENZIES. 8vo, cloth, 1.50.

FINE EDITION, TINTED PAPER. Square 8vo, cloth, 2.50; cloth, gilt, 3.50; half Turkey mor., 5.50; Turkey mor., 7.00.

THE EXCELLENT WOMAN, as Described in the Book of Proverbs. With an Introduction by Rev. W. B. SPRAGUE, D. D. Containing *twenty-four splendid Illustrations*. 12mo, cloth, 1.50.

FINE EDITION, TINTED PAPER. Square 8vo. New and greatly improved edition, cloth, red edges, 2.50; cloth, gilt, 3.50; half calf, 4.50; full Turkey mor., 7.00.

MOTHERS OF THE WISE AND GOOD. By JABEZ BURNS, D. D. 16mo, cloth, 1.25.

MY MOTHER; or, Recollections of Maternal Influence. By a New England Clergyman. With a beautiful Frontispiece. 12mo, cloth, 1.25; cloth, gilt, 1.50.

OUR LITTLE ONES IN HEAVEN. Edited by the Author of the "Aimwell Stories," etc. 18mo, cloth, 90 cts.; cloth, gilt, 1.25.

This little volume contains a choice collection of pieces, in verse and prose, on the death and future happiness of young children.

LITTLE MARY. An Illustration of the Power of Jesus to Save even the Youngest. With an Introduction by BARON STOW, D. D. 18mo, cloth, 40 cts.

GATHERED LILIES; or, Little Children in Heaven. By Rev. A. C. THOMPSON, Author of "The Better Land." 18mo, flexible cloth, 40 cts.; flexible cloth, gilt, 45 cts.; boards, full gilt, 60 cts.

SAFE HOME; or, the Last Days and Happy Death of Fanny Kenyon. With an Introduction by Prof. J. L. LINCOLN, of Brown University. 18mo, flexible cloth cover, gilt, 42 cts.

HEALTH; ITS FRIENDS AND ITS FOES. By R. D. MUSSEY, M. D., LL. D., &c., late Professor of Anatomy and Surgery at Dartmouth College, and of Surgery at the Medical College of Ohio. With Illustrations and a Portrait of the Author. 12mo, cloth, 1.50.

THE EVENING OF LIFE; or, Light and Comfort amidst the Shadows of Declining Years. By Rev. JEREMIAH CHAPLIN, D.D. A new, revised, and much enlarged edition. With elegant Frontispiece on Steel. 12mo, cloth, 1.50.

FINE EDITION, TINTED PAPER. Square 8vo, cloth, red edges, 2.50; cloth, gilt, 3.50.

RUTH: A SONG IN THE DESERT. 16mo, cloth, flexible covers, gilt, 60 cts.; cloth, boards, gilt, 65 cts. ☞ A neat and most charming little work.

Gould and Lincoln's Publications.

WILLIAMS'S LECTURES ON THE LORD'S PRAYER. By WILLIAM R. WILLIAMS, D. D. Third edition, 12mo, cloth, 1.25.

"We are constantly reminded, in reading his eloquent pages, of the old English writers, whose vigorous thought, and gorgeous imagery, and varied learning, have made their writings an inexhaustible mine for the scholars of the present day." — *Ch. Observer.*

WILLIAMS'S MISCELLANIES. By WILLIAM R. WILLIAMS, D. D. New and improved edition. 12mo, cloth, 1.75.

"Dr. Williams is a profound scholar and a brilliant writer." — *N. Y. Evangelist.*

WILLIAMS'S RELIGIOUS PROGRESS; Discourses on the Development of the Christian Character. By WILLIAM R. WILLIAMS, D. D. Third edition, 12mo, cloth, 1.25.

"His power of apt and forcible illustration is without a parallel among modern writers. The mute pages spring into life beneath the magic of his radiant imagination. But this is never at the expense of solidity of thought, or strength of argument. It is seldom, indeed, that a mind of so much poetical invention yields such a willing homage to the logical element." — *Harper's Monthly Miscellany.*

HARRIS'S GREAT TEACHER; or, Characteristics of our Lord's Ministry. By JOHN HARRIS, D. D. With an Introductory Essay by H. HUMPHREY, D. D. Sixteenth thousand. 12mo, cloth, 1.50.

"Dr. HARRIS is one of the best writers of the age; and this volume will not in the least detract from his well-merited reputation." — *American Pulpit.*

HARRIS'S GREAT COMMISSION; or, The Christian Church constituted and charged to convey the Gospel to the World. A Prize Essay. With an Introductory Essay by W. R. WILLIAMS, D. D. Eighth thousand. 12mo, cloth, 1.75.

"This volume will afford the reader an intellectual and spiritual banquet of the highest order." — *Philadelphia Ch. Observer.*

HARRIS'S MAN PRIMEVAL; or, The Constitution and Primitive Condition of the Human Being. With a finely-engraved Portrait of the Author. 12mo, cloth, 1.50.

"His copious and beautiful illustrations of the successive laws of the Divine Manifestation have yielded us inexpressible delight." — *London Eclectic Review.*

HARRIS'S PRE-ADAMITE EARTH. Contributions to Theological Science. By JOHN HARRIS, D. D. New and revised edition. 12mo, cloth, 1.50.

"We have never seen the natural sciences, particularly geology, made to give so decided and unimpeachable testimony to revealed truth." — *Christian Mirror.*

HARRIS'S PATRIARCHY; or, The Family, its Constitution and Probation. 12mo, cloth, 1.75.

This is the last of Dr. Harris's valuable series entitled "Contributions to Theological Science."

HARRIS'S SERMONS, CHARGES, ADDRESSES, etc., delivered by Dr. HARRIS in various parts of the country, during the height of his reputation as a preacher. Two elegant volumes, octavo, cloth, each 1.50.

The immense sale of all this author's works attests their intrinsic worth and great popularity.

Gould and Lincoln's Publications.

WAYLAND'S LETTERS ON THE MINISTRY OF THE GOSPEL. By FRANCIS WAYLAND, D. D. 16mo, cloth, 90 cts.

WAYLAND'S SALVATION BY CHRIST. A Series of Discourses on some of the most Important Doctrines of the Gospel. By FRANCIS WAYLAND, D. D. 12mo, cloth, 1.50; cloth, gilt, 2.25.

THE LIFE OF TRUST; being a Narrative of the Dealings of God with the REV. GEORGE MÜLLER. Edited and condensed by Rev. H. LINCOLN WAYLAND. With an Introduction by FRANCIS WAYLAND, D. D. Cloth, 1.75.

This work has a peculiar charm, as an unadorned story of the experience of a Christian man who believed in the mighty power of prayer, who gave a literal interpretation to the precept, "Take no thought for the morrow," and lived by daily faith in God's providence and grace.

THE YEAR OF GRACE: a History of the Great Revival in Ireland in 1859. By Rev. WILLIAM GIBSON, Professor of Christian Ethics in the Presbyterian College, Belfast. 12mo, cloth, 1.75.

A remarkable book on a remarkable subject. Next to a visit to the scenes of the Revival, nothing can give so adequate an idea of the wonderful work as the thrilling narrative of Prof. Gibson.

MEMORIALS OF EARLY CHRISTIANITY; Presenting, in a graphic, compact, and popular form, Memorable Events of Early Ecclesiastical History, etc. By Rev. J. G. MIALL, author of "Footsteps of our Forefathers." With numerous Illustrations. 12mo, cloth, 1.50.

FOOTSTEPS OF OUR FOREFATHERS; What they Suffered and what they Sought. Describing Localities, and Portraying Personages and Events, conspicuous in the Struggles for Religious Liberty. By JAMES G. MIALL. Containing thirty-six Illustrations. 12mo, cloth, 1.50.

MODERN ATHEISM; Under its forms of Pantheism, Materialism, Secularism, Development, and Natural Laws. By JAMES BUCHANAN, D. D., LL. D. 12mo, cloth, 1.75.

"The work is one of the most readable and solid which we have ever perused." — *Hugh Miller.*

MORNING HOURS IN PATMOS. The Opening Vision of the Apocalypse, and Christ's Epistle to the Seven Churches of Asia. By Rev. A. C. THOMPSON, D. D., author of "The Better Land," "Gathered Lilies," etc. With beautiful Frontispiece. 12mo, cloth, 1.50.

FIRST THINGS; or, the Development of Church Life. By BARON STOW, D. D. 16mo, cloth, 90 cts.

THE GREAT CONCERN; or, Man's Relation to God and a Future State. By NEHEMIAH ADAMS, D. D. 12mo, cloth, 1.25.

"Pungent and affectionate, reaching the intellect, conscience, and feelings; admirably fitted to awaken, guide, and instruct. Just the thing for distribution in our congregations." — *N. Y. Observer.*

EVENINGS WITH THE DOCTRINES. By Rev. NEHEMIAH ADAMS, D. D. Royal 12mo, cloth, 1.75.

TRUTHS FOR THE TIMES. By NEHEMIAH ADAMS, D. D., Pastor of Essex-street Church, Boston. 12mo, paper covers, 15 and 30 cts.

Gould and Lincoln's Publications.

THE PURITANS; or, The Court, Church, and Parliament of England, during the reigns of Edward VI. and Elizabeth. By SAMUEL HOPKINS, author of Lessons at the Cross," etc. In 3 vols. Octavo, cloth, per vol., 3.00; sheep, 4.00; half calf, 6.00.

It will be found the most interesting and reliable History of the Puritans yet published, narrating, in a dramatic style, many facts hitherto unknown.

THE PREACHER AND THE KING; or, Bourdaloue in the Court of Louis XIV.; being an Account of the Pulpit Eloquence of that distinguished era. Translated from the French of L. F. BUNGENER, Paris. Introduction by the Rev. GEORGE POTTS, D. D. *A new, improved edition*, with a fine Likeness and a BIOGRAPHICAL SKETCH OF THE AUTHOR. 12mo, cloth, 1.50.

THE PRIEST AND THE HUGUENOT; or, Persecution in the Age of Louis XV. From the French of L. F. BUNGENER. Two vols. 12mo, cloth, 3.00.

☞ This is not only a work of thrilling interest, — no fiction could exceed it, — but, as a Protestant work, it is a masterly production.

THE PULPIT OF THE AMERICAN REVOLUTION; or, The Political Sermons of the Period of 1776. With an Historical Introduction, Notes, Illustrations, etc. By JOHN WINGATE THORNTON, A. M. 12mo, cloth, 1.75.

THE LEADERS OF THE REFORMATION. LUTHER, CALVIN, LATIMER, and KNOX, the representative men of Germany, France, England, and Scotland. By J. TULLOCH, D. D., Author of "Theism," etc. 12mo, cloth, 1.50.

A portrait gallery of sturdy reformers, drawn by a keen eye and a strong hand. Dr. Tulloch discriminates clearly the personal qualities of each Reformer, and commends and criticises with equal frankness.

THE HAWAIIAN ISLANDS; their Progress and Condition under Missionary Labors. By RUFUS ANDERSON, D. D., Foreign Secretary of the American Board of Commissioners for Foreign Missions. With Maps, Illustrations, etc. Royal 12mo, cloth, 2.25.

WOMAN AND HER SAVIOUR in Persia. By a RETURNED MISSIONARY. With beautiful Illustrations and a Map of the Nestorian Country. 12mo, cloth, 1.25.

LIGHT IN DARKNESS; or, Christ Discerned in his True Character by a Unitarian. 16mo, cloth, 90 cts.

LIMITS OF RELIGIOUS THOUGHT EXAMINED, in Eight Lectures, delivered in the Oxford University Pulpit, in the year 1858, on the "Bampton Foundation." By Rev. H. LONGUEVILLE MANSEL, B. D., Reader in Moral and Metaphysical Philosophy at Magdalen College, Oxford, and Editor of Sir William Hamilton's Lectures. With Copious NOTES TRANSLATED for the American edition. 12mo, cloth, 1.50.

THE CRUCIBLE; or, Tests of a Regenerate State; designed to bring to light suppressed hopes, expose false ones, and confirm the true. By Rev. J. A. GOODHUE, A. M. With an introduction by Rev. E. N. KIRK, D. D. 12mo, cloth, 1.50.

SATAN'S DEVICES AND THE BELIEVER'S VICTORY. By Rev. WILLIAM L. PARSONS, D.D. 12mo, cloth, 1.50.

Gould and Lincoln's Publications.

CRUDEN'S CONDENSED CONCORDANCE. A Complete Concordance to the Holy Scriptures. By ALEXANDER CRUDEN. Revised and re-edited by the Rev. DAVID KING, LL. D. Octavo, cloth arabesque, 1.75; sheep, 2.00.

The condensation of the quotations of Scripture, arranged under the most obvious heads, while it diminishes the bulk of the work, greatly facilitates the finding of any required passage.
"We have in this edition of Cruden the *best made better*." — *Puritan Recorder.*

EADIE'S ANALYTICAL CONCORDANCE OF THE HOLY SCRIPTURES; or, the Bible presented under Distinct and Classified Heads or Topics. By JOHN EADIE, D. D., LL. D., Author of "Biblical Cyclopædia," "Ecclesiastical Cyclopædia," "Dictionary of the Bible," etc. One volume, octavo, 840 pp., cloth, 4.00; sheep, 5.00; cloth, gilt, 5.50; half calf, 6.50.

The object of this Concordance is to present the SCRIPTURES ENTIRE, under certain classified and exhaustive heads. It differs from an ordinary Concordance, in that its arrangement depends not on WORDS, but on SUBJECTS, and the verses *are printed in full.*

KITTO'S POPULAR CYCLOPÆDIA OF BIBLICAL LITERATURE. Condensed from the larger work. By the Author, JOHN KITTO, D. D. Assisted by JAMES TAYLOR, D. D., of Glasgow. With over five hundred Illustrations. One volume, octavo, 812 pp., cloth, 4.00; sheep, 5.00; half calf, 7.00.

A DICTIONARY OF THE BIBLE. Serving also as a COMMENTARY, embodying the products of the best and most recent researches in biblical literature in which the scholars of Europe and America have been engaged.

KITTO'S HISTORY OF PALESTINE, from the Patriarchal Age to the Present Time; with Chapters on the Geography and Natural History of the Country, the Customs and Institutions of the Hebrews. By JOHN KITTO, D. D. With upwards of two hundred Illustrations. 12mo, cloth, 1.75.

☞ A work admirably adapted to the Family, the Sabbath School, and the week-day School Library.

WESTCOTT'S INTRODUCTION TO THE STUDY OF THE GOSPELS. With HISTORICAL AND EXPLANATORY NOTES. By BROOKE FOSS WESTCOTT, M. A., late Fellow of Trinity College, Cambridge. With an Introduction by Prof. H. B. HACKETT, D. D. Royal 12mo, cloth, 2.00.

☞ A masterly work by a master mind.

ELLICOTT'S LIFE OF CHRIST HISTORICALLY CONSIDERED. The Hulsean Lectures for 1859, with Notes Critical, Historical, and Explanatory. By C. J. ELLICOTT, B. D. Royal 12mo, cloth, 1.75.

☞ Admirable in spirit, and profound in argument.

RAWLINSON'S HISTORICAL EVIDENCES OF THE TRUTH OF THE SCRIPTURE RECORDS, STATED ANEW, with Special reference to the Doubts and Discoveries of Modern Times. In Eight Lectures, delivered in the Oxford University pulpit, at the Bampton Lecture for 1859. By GEO. RAWLINSON, M. A., Editor of the Histories of Herodotus. With the Copious NOTES TRANSLATED for the *American edition* by an accomplished scholar. 12mo, cloth, 1.75.

"The consummate learning, judgment, and general ability, displayed by Mr. Rawlinson in his edition of Herodotus, are exhibited in this work also." — *North-American.*

Gould and Lincoln's Publications.

HACKETT'S COMMENTARY ON THE ORIGINAL TEXT OF THE ACTS OF THE APOSTLES. By HORATIO B. HACKETT, D. D., Prof. of Biblical Literature and Interpretation in the Newton Theol. Institute. ☞ A new, revised, and enlarged edition. Royal octavo, cloth, 3.00.

☞ This most important and very popular work has been thoroughly revised; large portions entirely re-written, with the addition of *more than one hundred pages of new matter;* the result of the author's continued investigations and travels since the publication of the first edition.

HACKETT'S ILLUSTRATIONS OF SCRIPTURE. Suggested by a Tour through the Holy Land. With numerous Illustrations. A new, Improved, and Enlarged edition. By H. B. HACKETT, D. D., Prof. of Biblical Literature in the Newton Theol. Institution. 12mo, cloth, 1.50.

FINE EDITION, TINTED PAPER. Square 8vo, cloth, red edges, 2.50; cloth, gilt, 3.50; half calf, 5.00; full Turkey mor., 7.50.

Prof. Hackett's accuracy is proverbial. We can rely on his statements with confidence, which is in itself a pleasure. He knows and appreciates the wants of readers; explains the texts which need explanation; gives life-like pictures, and charms while he instructs. — *N. Y. Observer.*

MUSIC OF THE BIBLE; or, Explanatory Notes upon all the passages of the Sacred Scriptures relating to Music. With a brief Essay on Hebrew Poetry. By ENOCH HUTCHINSON. With numerous Illustrations. Royal octavo, 3.25.

This book is altogether a unique production, and will be found of interest not only to Biblical scholars and clergymen generally, but also to Sabbath-school teachers, musicians, and the family circle. It is illustrated with numerous engravings.

MALCOM'S NEW BIBLE DICTIONARY of the most important Names, Objects, and Terms found in the Holy Scriptures; intended principally for Sabbath-School Teachers and Bible Classes. By HOWARD MALCOM, D. D., late President of Lewisburg University, Pa. 16mo, cloth, 1.00.

☞ The former Dictionary, of which more than *one hundred thousand copies* were sold, is made the basis of the present work.

PATTISON'S COMMENTARY ON THE EPISTLE TO THE EPHESIANS, Explanatory, Doctrinal, and Practical. With a Series of Questions. By ROBERT E. PATTISON, D. D., late President of Waterville College. 12mo, cloth, 1.25.

RIPLEY'S NOTES ON THE GOSPELS. Designed for Teachers in Sabbath Schools and Bible Classes, and as an Aid to Family Instruction. By HENRY J. RIPLEY, Prof. in Newton Theol. Inst. With Map of Canaan. Cloth, embossed, 1.75.

RIPLEY'S NOTES ON THE ACTS OF THE APOSTLES. With a beautiful Map, illustrating the Travels of the APOSTLE PAUL, with a track of his Voyage from Cesarea to Rome. By Prof. HENRY J. RIPLEY, D. D. 12mo. cloth, embossed, 1.25

RIPLEY'S NOTES ON THE EPISTLE OF PAUL TO THE ROMANS. Designed for Teachers in Sabbath Schools and Bible Classes, and as an Aid to Family Instruction. By HENRY J. RIPLEY. 12mo, cloth, embossed, 90 cts.

The above works by Prof. Ripley should be in the hands of every student of the Bible, especially every Sabbath-school and Bible-class teacher. They contain just the kind of information wanted.

Gould and Lincoln's Publications.

***LIFE, TIMES, AND CORRESPONDENCE OF JAMES MAN-
NING,*** AND THE EARLY HISTORY OF BROWN UNIVERSITY. By REUBEN
ALDRIDGE GUILD. With Likenesses of President Manning and Nicholas
Brown, Views of Brown University, The First Baptist Church, Providence, etc.
Royal 12mo, cloth, 3.00.

A most important and interesting historical work.

MEMOIR OF GEORGE N. BRIGGS, LL. D., late Governor of Massachusetts. By JOHN TODD, D D. With Illustrations. Royal 12mo. *In preparation.*

THE LIFE OF JOHN MILTON, narrated in connection with the POLITICAL, ECCLESIASTICAL, AND LITERARY HISTORY OF HIS TIME. By DAVID
MASSON, M. A., Professor of English Literature, University College, London.
Vol. I., embracing the period from 1608 to 1639. With Portraits and specimens
of his handwriting at different periods. Royal octavo, cloth, 3.50.

***LIFE AND CORRESPONDENCE OF REV. DANIEL WILSON,
D. D.***, late Bishop of Calcutta. By Rev. JOSIAH BATEMAN, M. A., Rector
of North Cray, Kent. With Portraits, Map, and numerous Illustrations. One
volume royal octavo, cloth, 3.50.

☞ An interesting life of a great and good man.

THE LIFE AND TIMES OF JOHN HUSS; or, The Bohemian Reformation of the Fifteenth Century. By Rev. E. H. GILLETT. Two vols. royal
octavo, 7.00.

"The author," says the *New York Observer*, "has achieved a great work, performed a valuable service for Protestantism and the world, made a name for himself among religious historians, and produced a book that will hold a prominent place in the esteem of every religious scholar."

The *New York Evangelist* speaks of it as "one of the most valuable contributions to ecclesiastical history yet made in this country."

MEMOIR OF THE CHRISTIAN LABORS, Pastoral and Philanthropic, of THOMAS CHALMERS, D. D. L.L. D. By FRANCIS WAYLAND. 16mo, cloth, 1.00.

The moral and intellectual greatness of Chalmers is, we might say, overwhelming to the mind of the ordinary reader. Dr. Wayland draws the portraiture with a master hand. — Method. Quart. Rev.

LIFE OF JAMES MONTGOMERY. By Mrs. H. C. KNIGHT, author of
"Lady Huntington and her Friends," etc. Likeness, and elegant Illustrated
Title-Page on steel. 12mo, cloth, 1.50.

DIARY AND CORRESPONDENCE OF AMOS LAWRENCE. With
a brief account of some Incidents in his Life. Edited by his son, WM. R. LAWRENCE, M. D. With elegant Portraits of Amos and Abbott Lawrence, an Engraving of their Birthplace, an Autograph page of Handwriting, and a copious
Index. One large octavo volume, cloth, 2.50.

THE SAME WORK. Royal 12mo, cloth, 1.75.

DR. GRANT AND THE MOUNTAIN NESTORIANS. By Rev. THOMAS LAURIE, his surviving associate in that Mission. With a Likeness, Map of
the Country, and numerous Illustrations. Third edition Revised and Improved.
12mo, cloth, 1.75. ☞ A most valuable memoir of a *remarkable man.*

www.ingramcontent.com/pod-product-compliance
Lightning Source LLC
Chambersburg PA
CBHW021154230426
43667CB00006B/394